Royal Aircraft Factory
S.E.5

1916 onwards (S.E.5, S.E.5a, S.E.5b & SE-5E)

COVER IMAGE: Royal Aircraft Factory S.E.5.
(Mike Badrocke)

© Nick Garton 2017

All rights reserved. No part of this publication may be reproduced or stored in a retrieval system or transmitted, in any form or by any means, electronic, mechanical, photocopying, recording or otherwise, without prior permission in writing from Haynes Publishing.

First published in March 2017

A catalogue record for this book is available from the British Library.

ISBN 978 0 85733 846 4

Library of Congress control no. 2016959353

Published by Haynes Publishing,
Sparkford, Yeovil,
Somerset BA22 7JJ, UK.
Tel: 01963 440635
Int. tel: +44 1963 440635
Website: www.haynes.com

Haynes North America Inc.,
859 Lawrence Drive, Newbury Park,
California 91320, USA.

Whilst the publisher has made every effort to trace the copyright ownership of photographs, this has not proved possible in every case. If a copyright holder has inadvertently been offended, please contact the Editorial Director at Haynes Publishing.

Printed in Malaysia.

Royal Aircraft Factory **S.E.5**

1916 onwards (S.E.5, S.E.5a, S.E.5b & SE-5E)

Owners' Workshop Manual

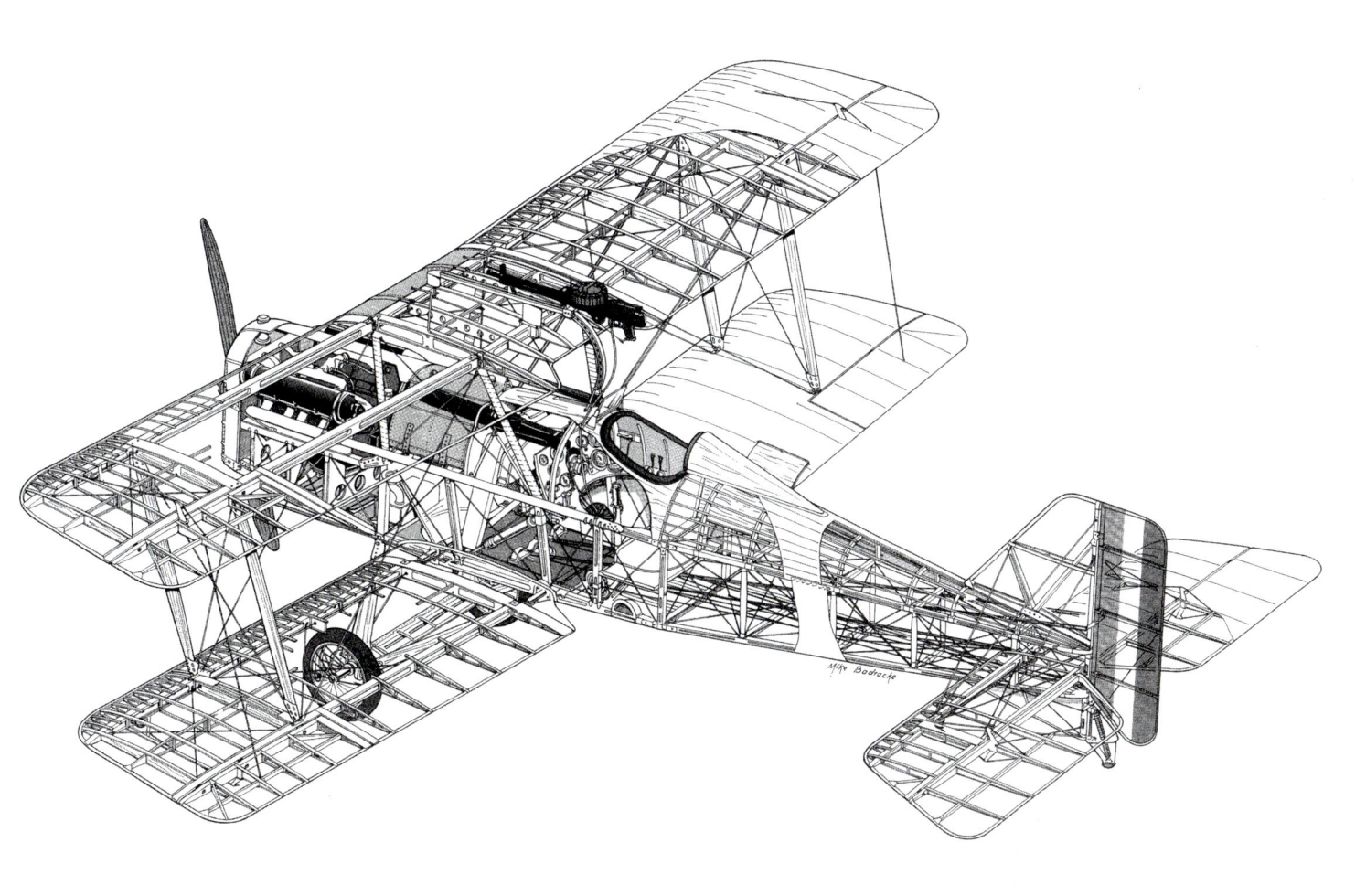

An insight into the design, engineering, restoration, maintenance and operation of Britain's First World War 'mount of aces'

Nick Garton

Contents

6	Author's note

8	Introduction

14	The S.E.5 story

The mighty monobloc	16
The S.E.series 1911–15	20
Designing the S.E.5	23
Albert Ball and the S.E.5	26
Tested to destruction	28
To war with 56 Squadron	31
Mass production	40
S.E.5/S.E.5a production batches	48
Home Defence and the Royal Air Force	48
Service in foreign fields	51

52	Restore to flight

Shuttleworth's original masterpiece	56
The return of an original	59
An Imperial Gift	61
Brand new S.E.5s from New Zealand	62

68	Anatomy of the S.E.5

Construction of the S.E.5	70
Finishing touches	78
Jimmy McCudden's high-flying bird	80
The Hispano-Suiza V8 and Wolseley derivatives	82

86	The pilot's view

Pilot training in 1917–18	88
The S.E.5a in action	90
Life on the airfield	93
Laddie's war	99
'Mick' Mannock: Ace of Aces	100
Flying the S.E.5a today	104

112	The owner's view

Post-war and civilian aircraft	114
Major Savage's skywriting aeroplanes	116
Wingnuts take flight: Sir Peter Jackson	119
Other surviving S.E.5s	122
Operating the S.E.5 today	124

128	The engineer's view

Fuelling victory	131
How to build an S.E.5	132
Variants and experiments	137
German report on the Hispano-Suiza V8	139

146	Appendices

1: Star performers: the S.E.5 in fiction	146
2: Interview with Derek Robinson	148
3: Albert Ball's ripping cake	150
4: Surviving S.E.5 aircraft and places of interest	151
5: Scale models of the S.E.5a	154
6: Glossary of airmen's slang	156

161	Postscript

Requiem, Robert Louis Stevenson	161

162	Index

OPPOSITE Air-to-air with the Shuttleworth Collection's S.E.5a F904, the last airworthy example of a genuine First World War aeroplane. *(Darren Harbar)*

Author's note

In the late 1980s and early 1990s, Pattishall village hall was the focal point of a unique social whirl. Kids from nearby villages would gather dressed in their finery: rented tuxedos and idiotic grins for the boys; bare shoulders, big hair and taffeta for the girls.

These were heady, dream-like nights when hands were held, dances were danced and chaste kisses were shared. By midnight most of these mayfly romances were over and the youngsters would un-tug themselves from one other and return home. Few if any would have known that this little corner of Northamptonshire had many other stories to tell beyond the joys and sorrows of the local teens.

Nearly 75 years earlier, during the Great War, the surrounding fields and the buildings that stood in them had played host to the biggest British prisoner-of-war camp of World War One. The first village hall had been the camp's guardhouse.

At first, Pattishall housed German nationals who were living and working in Britain when war was declared. Before long, the camp grew in size to accommodate captured sailors, soldiers and airmen until it held close to 10,000 people.

Records of exactly who was interned in the camp were destroyed during a bombing raid on London in 1941. Yet we can be fairly confident that a number of those interned at Pattishall in 1917–18 would have been airmen who arrived after encountering the greatest all-round fighter aeroplane to be built in Britain: the Royal Aircraft Factory S.E.5.

This is just one example of the myriad of ways in which World War One still touches us, even after a century, if only we choose to look. Today, Pattishall village hall goes about the business of hosting toddler groups, parish events and parties. Every week, more memories are being built upon those century-old foundations. Long may they be good ones.

A quarter of a century ago, your author was one of those young romantics who congregated in Pattishall. My other passion was discovering the stories of aeroplanes and airmen in World War One: devouring endless letters, diaries and official documents; delighting in the novels of Derek Robinson; badgering my father into outings to the Shuttleworth Collection and interviewing surviving pilots such as Leslie Sanderson, Tim Hervey and Edward Gillingham.

Writing this book has therefore been an incredible pleasure, and I must start by thanking Steve, Jonathan and all at Haynes Publishing for entrusting me with it and Ian Heath for editing the manuscript.

RIGHT **The fields around Pattishall were once home to the biggest prisoner-of-war camp in Britain.** *(Author)*

LEFT Nearly 10,000 German prisoners of war were held in Pattishall, including airmen. *(Imperial War Museum)*

Many pages would be bare without the generous support of the Farnborough Air Sciences Trust, the Brooklands Museum, Rob Millinship, Richard Grace, Henry Labouchere and Gene de Marco. I am also grateful for the time and knowledge of the Shuttleworth Collection, the Vintage Aviator Ltd, Hawker Restorations, Sarah Hanna and the Old Flying Machine Company, the RAF Museum, the South African Air Force Museum, the Australian War Memorial, the Canadian Air Force Museum, the National Museum of the US Air Force, the Imperial War Museum, Stow Maries Great War Aerodrome, Wingnut Wings, Nottingham Castle and the National Archive.

Further thanks must go to the regulars at Britmodeller.com and The Scarf & Goggles for their knowledge and encouragement and in particular to Andrew Eaton for the pictures of his beautiful Wingnut Wings S.E.5a 'Hisso'. Thanks also to Darren Harbar, Brian Harmer, Clive Boyce, Phil Makanna and Matt Howell for their flawless photography, to all of the agencies who took time to find the amazing archive shots, my mother-in-law Judy Southwell for the use of her camera, to 'Rew Tucker, Frances Anderson, Richard Southwell, Steve Sperring, Paul Brozynski and John Exley for their companionship on the road, and to my wonderful wife and our five beautiful children for waiting patiently for me to finish.

Finally thank you to Derek Robinson, without whom I never would have wanted to write anything. Meeting your heroes is never a disappointment if you pick wisely.

This book is dedicated to the 'unknown' airman who has lain in Grave 12, Row F, Plot 3 of Laventie Military Cemetery since 1920. Now that science can identify the bones of a Plantagenet king it must be hoped that experts can soon be encouraged to give you back your name.

BELOW Postcard of an S.E.5a signed by Leslie Sanderson, who went to war in the type. *(Author)*

AUTHOR'S NOTE

Introduction

At the dawn of the 20th century, Great Britain was not a nation that was given to flights of fancy. The advent of internal combustion had sparked a wildfire of innovation across Continental Europe and the United States of America, but amongst the patrician classes in London anyone who trifled with the motor car or the aeroplane was generally written off as a crackpot.

Britain was a nation that had forged an Empire upon which the sun never set – and it had done so using iron, steam and above all good breeding. Such faddish foreign diversions as Grand Prix racing or looping the loop could not hope to compete with the rock solid certainty of a Dreadnought or the magnificent railways that had tamed the Raj.

Then, in 1908, Imperial Germany proudly showed off the Zeppelin airship *LZ 4* as she covered a distance of 240 miles. It just so happened that, almost simultaneously, H.G. Wells published his sensational novel *The War in the Air*, imagining a voraciously imperialistic German air fleet crossing the Atlantic to bomb the USA and thereby spark an aerial battle in which London, Paris, New York and Berlin were razed.

Wells' vision was among many concerns that prompted the Chancellor of the Exchequer, David Lloyd George, to enquire of experts such as the Secretary of State for War, the First Lord of the Admiralty, engineer Charles Rolls (of Rolls-Royce renown), and Hiram Maxim (creator of the automatic machine gun), if airships could conceivably bomb foreign cities in the way that Wells had described. Maxim's response was that a fleet of bomb-carrying airships would leave London 'looking like last year's buzzard's nest'.

Suddenly the case for Britain to take an interest in powered flight gained a new and

RIGHT Zeppelin *LZ 4* floats over Lake Constance in 1908. *(Getty/Library of Congress)*

RIGHT A full-size replica of Samuel Cody and his groundbreaking aeroplane stands in pride of place at the Farnborough Air Sciences Trust. *(Author)*

ardent supporter. While Lloyd George sought to encourage governmental interest it fell to an American showman and adventurer, Samuel Franklin Cody, to build a cathedral of wires and spruce in his shed at Farnborough – the Army Aeroplane No.1. This unlikely contraption flew for a total distance of 420 metres in October 1908, making Cody the first man to make a powered flight from British soil.

Cody's achievement, while spectacular, was put into sobering perspective only nine months later when his French counterpart, Louis Blériot, flew his highly advanced Type XI monoplane for 23 miles across the English Channel. Lobby groups such as the Royal Aero Club, National Defence Association and Aerial League of the British Empire added their weight to the push for aviation to become a governmental priority.

Meanwhile, inspired by Cody and Blériot, a whole generation of ambitious young engineers was being drawn into the new world of aeroplane design. Among the leading lights were the Short brothers on the Isle of Sheppey, Alliott Verdon-Roe at the Brooklands racetrack in Surrey, Claude Grahame-White at Hendon aerodrome in Colindale and Thomas Sopwith, who built seaplanes in Kingston-upon-Thames.

By 1911 the government had finally taken notice. The Royal Balloon Factory at Farnborough, under the management of superintendent Mervyn O'Gorman, would soon be renamed the Royal Aircraft Factory and equipped with the lavish resources, brilliant minds and scientific processes with which to explore the unknown.

The Royal Aircraft Factory was intended to be a centre of excellence for the British aviation industry in the private sector – a resource for all the nation's aeroplane designers and manufacturers to call upon. There was

RIGHT The vast wind tunnels built at Farnborough were vital for taking British aircraft design forward. *(Author)*

RIGHT Mervyn O'Gorman was superintendent of the Royal Aircraft Factory from 1911 to 1916, taking a measured and science-based approach to aircraft design.
(Imperial War Museum)

BELOW As First Lord of the Admiralty, Winston Churchill set a different tempo for aviation to that of the War Office and Army.
(Getty/Hulton Archive)

considerable grumbling among these same manufacturers, therefore, when the Factory wheeled out the first aeroplane to be designed and built in-house.

This 'new' machine was in fact rebuilt from the wreck of a crashed Blériot monoplane, reconfigured as a tail-first biplane. It had been penned by the Royal Aircraft Factory's chief designer, Geoffrey de Havilland, and was given the name of S.E.1, short for Santos Experimental 1 in deference to Brazilian designer Alberto Santos-Dumont, who had pioneered the use of forward-mounted control surfaces.

O'Gorman and de Havilland continued to develop new aeroplane designs in-house at Farnborough. In theory these were simply experiments in wood and canvas, resulting in O'Gorman's insistence upon naming the Factory's aircraft designs as B.E. (short for Blériot Experimental and attached to front-engined 'tractor' aeroplanes), or F.E. (short for Farman Experimental and attached to rear-engined 'pusher' aeroplanes). In practice, however, they were fully functioning designs that were wholly endorsed by the government.

In 1912 a series of open trials was held on Salisbury Plain to identify a suitable design for widespread military use. At stake was the biggest contract ever seen in British aviation to supply the Royal Flying Corps with its primary reconnaissance and observation platform. The aircraft that performed best was the Royal Aircraft Factory B.E.2 – but the repercussions from awarding the contract to Farnborough would carry on for years.

From the outset, the War Office was heavily censured for its decision. The independent aircraft manufacturers cried foul and Charles G. Grey, in his editorial for *The Aeroplane* magazine, lambasted the Farnborough establishment as being 'the most scandalously mismanaged civilian department that has ever existed'.

At this moment the Royal Navy gained a new, youthful and hawkish First Lord of the Admiralty in the form of 37-year-old Winston Churchill – a vigorous advocate for aviation as a potential weapon of war. Before Churchill, the Admiralty had been content to let the War Office and the Army dictate the pace of development in aviation. Now there was a clear intent to push Britain to the forefront of the technological arms race.

Doubtless the Admiralty was infuriated when Brigadier-General David Henderson, commander of the Military Wing, ordered in 1913 that no Royal Aircraft Factory products should be powered by an engine of more than 100hp because he believed that 'no useful flying' could be done if the speed of the aeroplane was too high.

Henderson was a great believer in the value of aviation to the military and had learnt to pilot an aeroplane at the age of 49, making him the oldest qualified pilot in the country. He had persisted in fighting the cause of aviation while the Army remained rooted in the primacy of its cavalry, yet even Henderson's vision was limited: it would take the onset of trench warfare to prove y the true value of flying to the military.

In the field, the Royal Naval Air Service was led by Commander Charles Rumney Samson, who believed that if one were heading over enemy territory in an aeroplane it would be as well to do some damage before departing. So it was that he and his men spent the early months of the Great War launching raids of great daring to bomb the Zeppelins in their home bases and attacking facilities deep behind enemy lines. When his supplies of aircraft ran short, Samson fixed machine guns to his staff cars and sent them out to wreak havoc behind the lines!

All of this led to the same question on both sides of the lines: how to stop the enemy's aircraft spying from the sky or dropping explosives on your prized assets. Anti-aircraft artillery was one measure but the real solution came first to the French, who fitted metal plates to the propeller of a Morane monoplane to deflect bullets from a machine gun that could fire straight ahead.

This crude solution led the Germans to commission a more advanced design from Dutchman Anthony Fokker: a mechanical interrupter gear that allowed more regulated fire to be brought to bear. British airmen in their docile B.E.2s were as good as a sitting target for these new German machines and fingers were pointed at the War Office and, more specifically, at the Royal Aircraft Factory, for the carnage that followed.

This anti-Farnborough sentiment gained a dynamic mouthpiece in the divisive form of Noel Pemberton Billing. An imposing and flamboyant man, 'PB' had founded the Supermarine flying boat works in Southampton and then sold it without one machine having flown. He was a Navy reservist who went and spied on the Zeppelin base at Friedrichshafen as a prelude

LEFT Sir David Henderson, described as the 'true father of the Royal Air Force'. *(RAF Museum)*

BELOW The Royal Aircraft Factory B.E.2 was blamed for the heavy losses among British airmen in 1915–16. *(Author)*

to the spectacular bombing carried out by Rumney's RNAS. Then in 1915 he became an elected Member of Parliament and immediately set about undermining confidence in the Royal Aircraft Factory.

It was PB who coined the phrase 'Fokker Scourge' in his opening speech to Parliament in which he described the intolerable air supremacy enjoyed by Germany in 1915–16. He blamed poor design at the Royal Aircraft Factory and an unwillingness to support other manufacturers, resulting in a virtual monopoly. Support came for PB both politically and in the press, as Charles G. Grey and Lord Northcliffe's *Daily Mail* newspaper accused the Royal Aircraft Factory of receiving preferential treatment from the War Office.

All the ill-feeling towards Mervyn O'Gorman and the Farnborough establishment that had built up since the appearance of the S.E.1 and the awarding of the B.E.2 contract was suddenly unleashed. The final straw came when PB stood up in the House of Commons and quoted the accusation of Lieutenant-Colonel Walter Faber that airmen were being 'murdered rather than killed' thanks to the poor quality of their aeroplanes. Accusations of such magnitude could not pass the democratic system and an independent governmental committee was immediately set up to investigate them.

The committee was chaired by Sir Richard Burbidge, the managing director of Harrods department store. The Burbidge Committee report was made swiftly and, while it held nobody at individual fault, contained damning evidence of inefficiencies within British aircraft production as a whole. In 1915 a total of 34 companies received orders for aeroplanes, with nearly 1,700 being delivered. In 1916 this figure increased to 76 different types on order, totalling 9,400 airframes, with supporting orders of 20,000 engines of 60 different types with which to power them!

By highlighting the true cost in both financial and logistical terms caused by mismanagement of this scale, the reputation of the Royal Aircraft Factory was saved from the complete ruin that Pemberton Billing had no doubt envisaged.

BELOW The Burbidge Committee looked into the role of the Royal Aircraft Factory and its effect upon British aircraft development and construction. *(Farnborough Air Sciences Trust)*

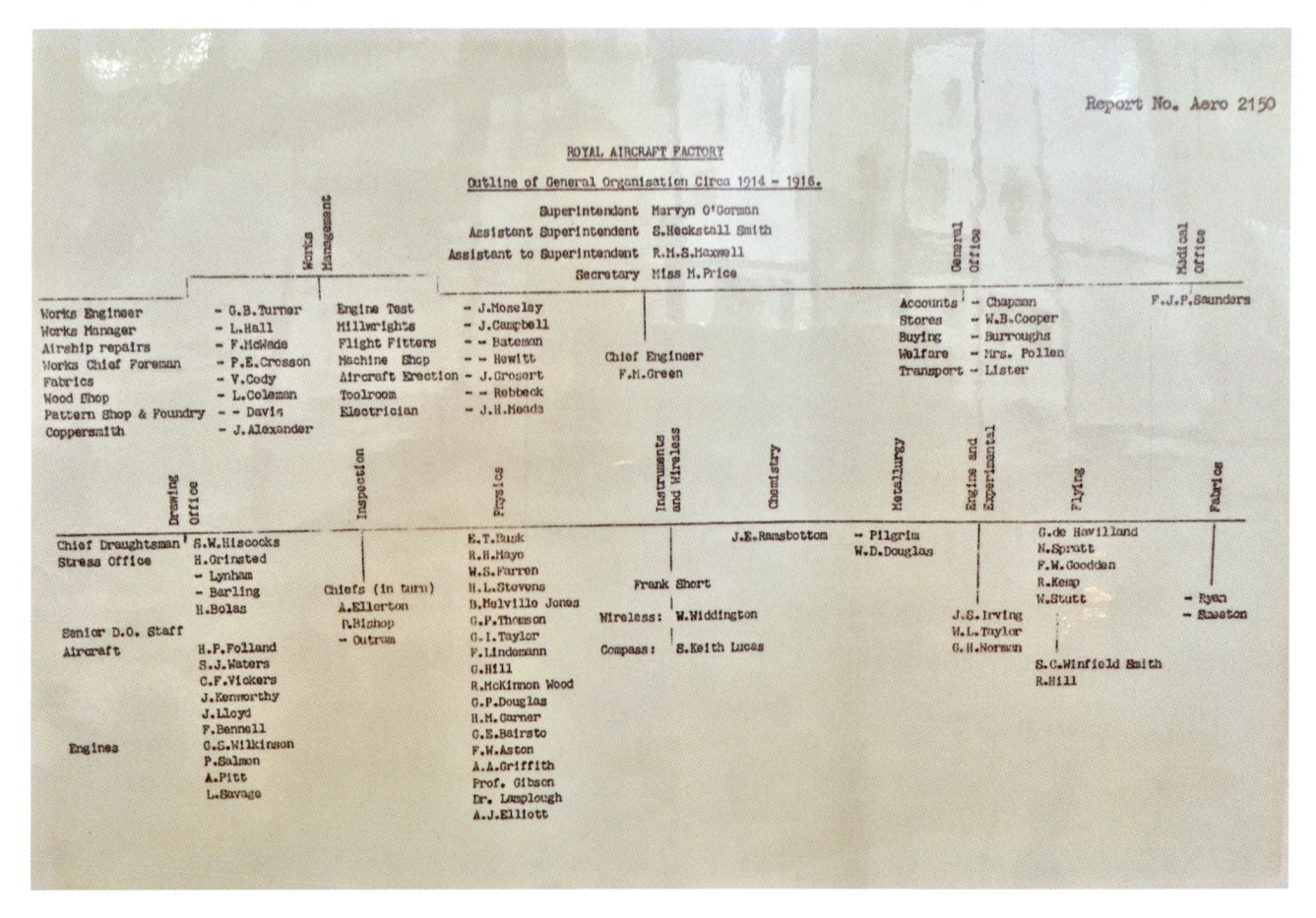

Mervyn O'Gorman and Brigadier-General Sir David Henderson worked tirelessly to prove that more than half of the work undertaken at Farnborough consisted of problem-solving and finding remedies for inadequate designs produced in the private sector.

There was also the much bigger picture of disorganisation in the supply of materials to consider, from engine components to wood and linen. As a final consideration there was an increasing amount of industrial action being taken by workers, both among the women who were now filling the majority of manufacturing jobs and among the men keen to wrest them back once the conflict was over. All of these factors had a far greater effect in provoking delays in the production and delivery of new types than did any shortcomings of the Royal Aircraft Factory.

The fallout from Burbidge ensured that while O'Gorman stepped aside from his stewardship at Farnborough, soon to be followed by other key members of the Royal Aircraft Factory, it was achieved discreetly and without rancour. Yet even before his departure, O'Gorman's team had already laid the foundations for its finest product of all: the S.E.5.

In February 1916 Brigadier-General Hugh Trenchard, commander of the Royal Flying Corps in France, laid out the specification to which a new fighting scout should be built by the end of the year. Although he would prefer a two-seat design, single-seat scouts would be considered provided that their fully laden performance met the following criteria:

- Ability to climb to 10,000ft within 15 minutes.
- Capacity to reach no less than 100mph at 10,000ft.
- Have a ceiling of no less than 18,000ft.
- Have an endurance of three hours – ideally four.
- Be able to fire straight ahead.

This specification is what led to the design and deployment of the three aircraft that would come to define British air power over the Western Front: the S.E.5, the Bristol F2 Fighter and the Sopwith F.1 Camel.

BELOW Brigadier-General Trenchard's specification of February 1916 set the template for the S.E.5. *(Author)*

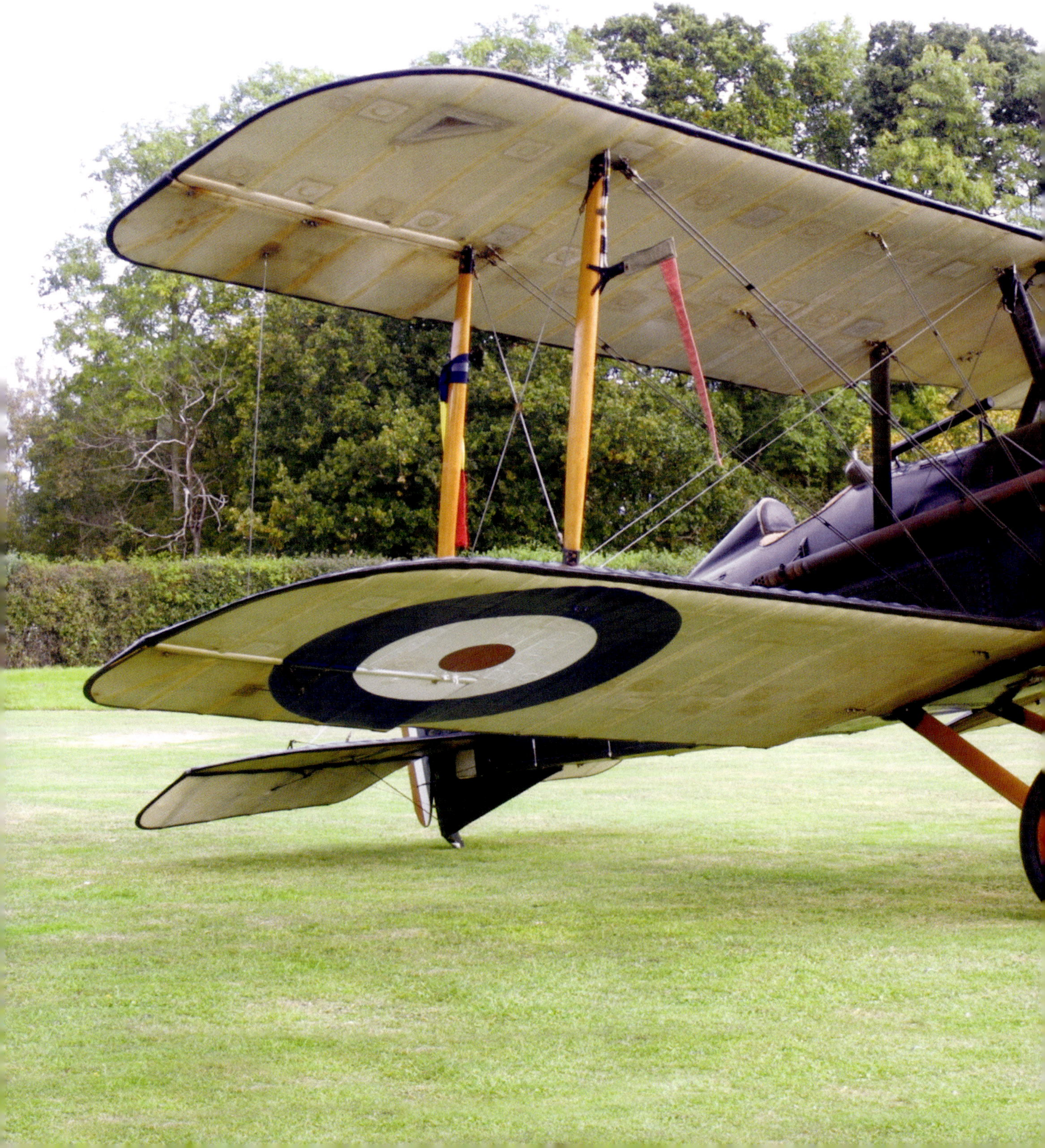

Chapter One

The S.E.5 story

Motor racing technology merged with aircraft design to produce a winning combination in the S.E.5 – although fulfilling its potential would be a long and winding road. Political intrigue, the newly discovered cult of celebrity and personal ambition would all play a part alongside the sometimes tragic process of developing an aeroplane through trial and error.

OPPOSITE The S.E.5a in its definitive form, which emerged almost a year after the prototype first flew. *(Doolittle Media)*

ABOVE King Alfonso of Spain takes the wheel of his first Hispano-Suiza XIII in 1907. *(Getty/Heritage Images)*

BELOW An example of the original Hispano-Suiza 8a V8 with direct drive. *(RAF Museum)*

The mighty monobloc

The origins of the S.E.5 can be traced to Barcelona where, in February 1915, the Hispano-Suiza automobile company revealed its contribution to the war effort: its Type 8A 'monobloc' V8.

Hispano-Suiza was already famous for its innovative motor racing technology. In the 1890s, a Spanish artillery captain named Emilio de la Cuadra had founded a company to develop practical electric cars. In this he failed, so he joined forces with Marc Birkigt – a Swiss watchmaker becoming known for elegant and precise internal combustion engines – and together they became known as Hispano-Suiza.

Birkigt developed smooth and powerful four-cylinder engines that punched well above their weight in performance terms. Among the first customers was the young King Alfonso XIII of Spain, in whose honour the most celebrated Hispano-Suiza cars were henceforth named.

Motor racing was the best way to win international acclaim, and to this end Birkigt designed a lightweight 'Voiturette' called the 45CR, which featured a 2.4-litre engine developing 45hp from what was then the standard configuration of a 'T-head' sidevalve, with intake valves on one side of the engine block and the exhaust valves on the other. The 45CR won the prestigious Coupe de l'Auto and cemented the marque's renown – although Birkigt's racing team and technology was immediately spirited away by Peugeot for its Grand Prix racing programme.

With his passion for developing power through efficient design, Birkigt naturally looked at aeroplane engines as an outlet for his talents. At the outbreak of the war the favoured layout was the rotary engine, which was manufactured by machining separate steel cylinders and then bolting these assemblies directly to the crankcase, the engine rotating around the crank and carrying the propeller with it.

Birkigt believed that it would be much more effective to make a stationary engine block from a single piece of cast aluminium, within which the routing for water and gas was pre-formed and into which thin steel liners would be screwed and secured. To make it compact, the new design would feature two cylinder blocks arranged in a 90° 'V' form, operating a single crankshaft.

Through the extensive use of alloys, Birkigt very effectively minimised the engine's weight. The pistons and cylinder heads were made of aluminium, into which a rotary driveshaft tower gear was connected to service the final drive. Although the weight and power of the engine were of paramount importance reliability was no less vital, and Birkigt ensured that the aluminium parts were coated in vitreous enamel to ensure their integrity and extend their working life, while

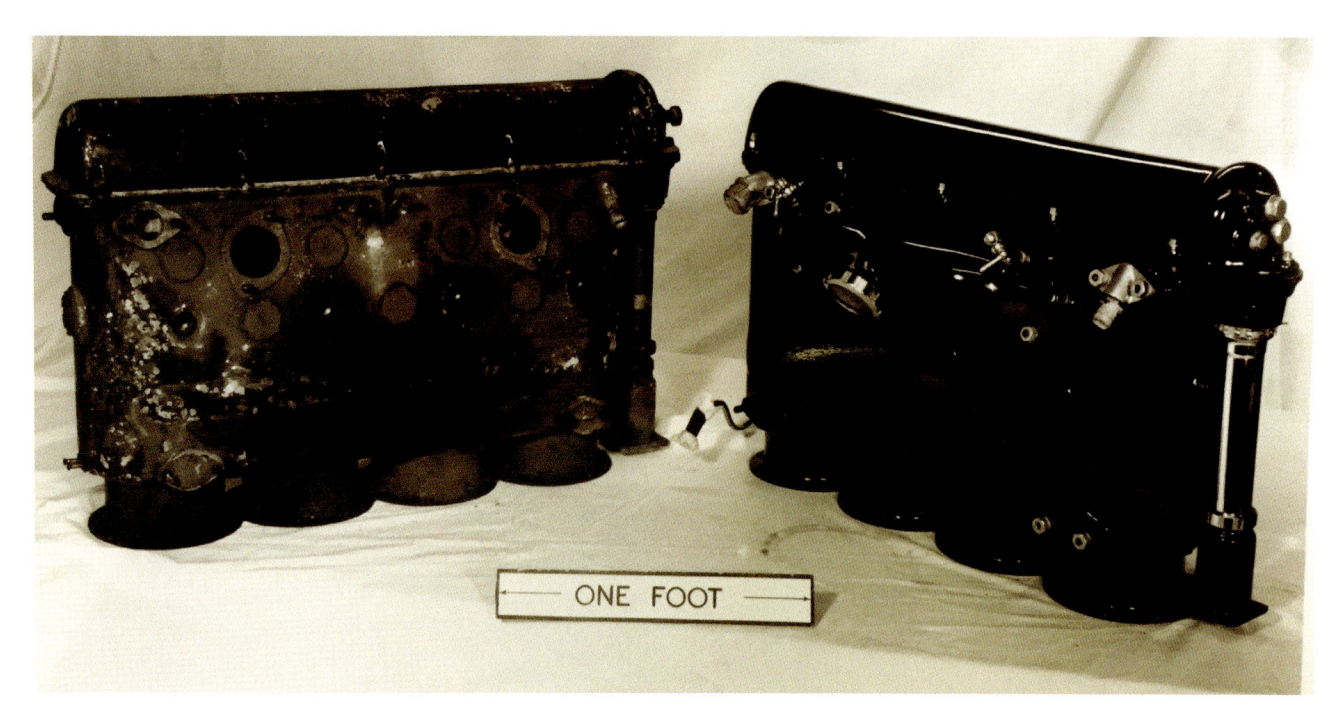

ABOVE **The Hispano-Suiza cylinder block was compact and contained the routing for water and oil within its structure.** *(Farnborough Air Sciences Trust)*

all high-wear and consumable items, such as spark plugs and valve springs, were duplicated.

In its initial form, the Hispano-Suiza 8A had a displacement of 11.76 litres (717.8in^3), generating 140hp at 1,900rpm. In total the engine weighed just 185kg, less than two-thirds the weight of a rotary engine of equivalent power, which it could deliver with greater fuel efficiency and ease of handling. In effect, Birkigt had combined the light weight of a rotary engine with the improved reliability and enormous development potential that came with a stationary design.

This was extremely bad news for the incumbent French engine suppliers such as Gnome and le Rhône, who lobbied hard against this Spanish usurper. As a result, the Hispano-Suiza was subjected to the harshest possible series of bench tests, including 50 hours' solid running at full throttle. The engine didn't break, and the remarkable performance that it displayed in these tests was witnessed by Lieutenant-Colonel Robert Brooke-Popham, the Chief Staff Officer of the Royal Flying Corps, who immediately called the War Office with a recommendation to obtain Birkigt's amazing new power plant.

By this stage the previous insistence of General Sir David Henderson that aeroplanes of more than 100hp were too fast to be useful for military flying had thankfully been forgotten. In August 1915 the War Office completed its negotiations. As part of an agreement to trade much-needed raw materials from across the British Empire, the French were obliged to provide 150 le Rhône rotary engines, 50 new Hispano-Suiza V8 engines and a licence for the Hispano to be built by the Wolseley Tool and Motor Car Company of Adderley Park in Birmingham.

The true value of the Hispano-Suiza engine was nevertheless masked by the quality of the aeroplanes into which it was first fitted. In France, the equivalent of the Royal Aircraft Factory was the Société Pour d'Aviation et ses Dérivées (SPAD), which had at first played only a minor role in aeroplane production behind the independent French manufacturers like Nieuport and Morane-Saulnier.

The first SPAD to really make headlines was the Hispano-powered SA series, which was also known as the 'pulpit fighter'. The reason for this nickname was that SPAD designer Louis Béchereau's idea was to marry the performance advantages of a front-engined aeroplane to the need for a forward-facing machine gun. The pilot therefore sat behind the engine while the gunner sat in a plywood box – the pulpit – mounted in front of the engine and propeller by struts that attached it to the top wing and the undercarriage.

The drawbacks of the design were many

RIGHT After a false start with his 'pulpit fighter', SPAD designer Louis Béchereau struck gold with the S.VII, seen here in the hands of Georges Guynemer. *(Alamy)*

and varied, foremost of which (among the aircrew at least!) was doubtless the certainty of death for the gunner in even the most minor landing accident. Among the more mundane problems caused by the 'pulpit' layout were the obscuring of the pilot's view, the atrocious aerodynamics and the total inability of the crew to communicate with one another. Despite these very obvious flaws the SPAD S.A. was built and sent into action.

Meanwhile, in August 1916 the first Hispano-Suiza engine to arrive in Britain went to the Royal Aircraft Factory where, remarkably (in the light of Pemberton Billing and the ongoing Burbidge inquiry), the decision was taken to build a 'pulpit' design based upon the dreaded B.E.2. The resulting B.E.9 prototypes lived for a mercifully brief period and inflicted no undue casualties, during which time the true measure of the Hispano-Suiza's abilities was being shown in another new machine.

Back in France, Louis Béchereau removed the 'pulpit' from his S.A. model, pushing the wings forward and the pilot's cockpit back to make arguably the most elegant single-seat scout of the war: the SPAD S.VII. A mechanical interrupter gear, based upon that which had given the Fokkers such an advantage, was added to the propeller, allowing a machine gun to fire through the arc of the spinning blades.

The gun – a single Hotchkiss or Vickers – sat on top of the engine cowling and allowed the pilot to aim using the whole aeroplane.

These sleek new machines began to reach the Front in August 1916. The first victory recorded by a SPAD S.VII was scored by its greatest exponent, the brilliant *Sous-Lieutenant* Georges Guynemer, who shot down an Aviatik C.II on 2 September and began to pile up a huge tally – including the destruction of five aeroplanes in the space of five minutes on 23 September.

Guynemer's successes began to be replicated as more SPADs made their way into service, which clearly showed that the Hispano-Suiza was essential to meet Trenchard's specification for fast, high-flying fighting aeroplanes with front-mounted machine guns. It was at this stage that the Admiralty stepped in, pushing for an order of 8,000 Hispano-Suiza engines to be built using British-sourced materials. The engines and the cost would be distributed between Britain (receiving 3,500 engines), France (receiving 3,000 engines), and Russia (receiving 1,500 engines). To bolster the production of these engines within the UK, Wolseley's factory in Birmingham would be supported by a new facility operated by the French manufacturer Emile Mayen. After some delays, funding of £2 million (equivalent to perhaps £210 million today) was approved, and the Admiralty's plan was put into effect.

As yet there was no British design worthy of the engine, however. The Admiralty had never shown any qualms about buying in technology from overseas and it duly placed an order for sufficient SPAD S.VIIs to equip two complete squadrons (although it later passed these on to the Royal Flying Corps, in exchange for an equivalent order of Sopwith Triplanes). Among the home manufacturers, meanwhile, there was a two-seat multi-role fighter called the Bristol F2 under development at the British and Colonial Aeroplane Company that would be powered by the Rolls-Royce Eagle, while Sopwith was putting the finishing touches to its new two-gun rotary-engined F.1 scout, which was fast becoming known as the Camel.

Although beset by the fallout resulting from the Burbidge Committee, this meant that the Royal Aircraft Factory alone was working on a potential Hispano-powered scout. Brigadier-General Sefton Brancker, assistant director of Military Aeronautics, was dispatched to Farnborough to discuss how the Factory planned to meet Trenchard's specification. Brancker was doubtless dismayed when he was shown senior design engineer John Kenworthy's plan for a single-seat 'pulpit' machine, the F.E.10.

Brancker insisted that a front-engined scout like the SPAD would be better, whereupon a sketch was put forward by the Royal Aircraft Factory's chief test pilot, Major Frank Goodden. This was much closer to the SPAD S.VII in concept, and it was from this foundation that Henry Folland set to work in drawing up data. The S.E.5 project was under way.

BELOW John Kenworthy designed the stillborn F.E.10 as a single-seat 'pulpit' fighter. It bequeathed its tail to the S.E.5. *(Farnborough Air Sciences Trust)*

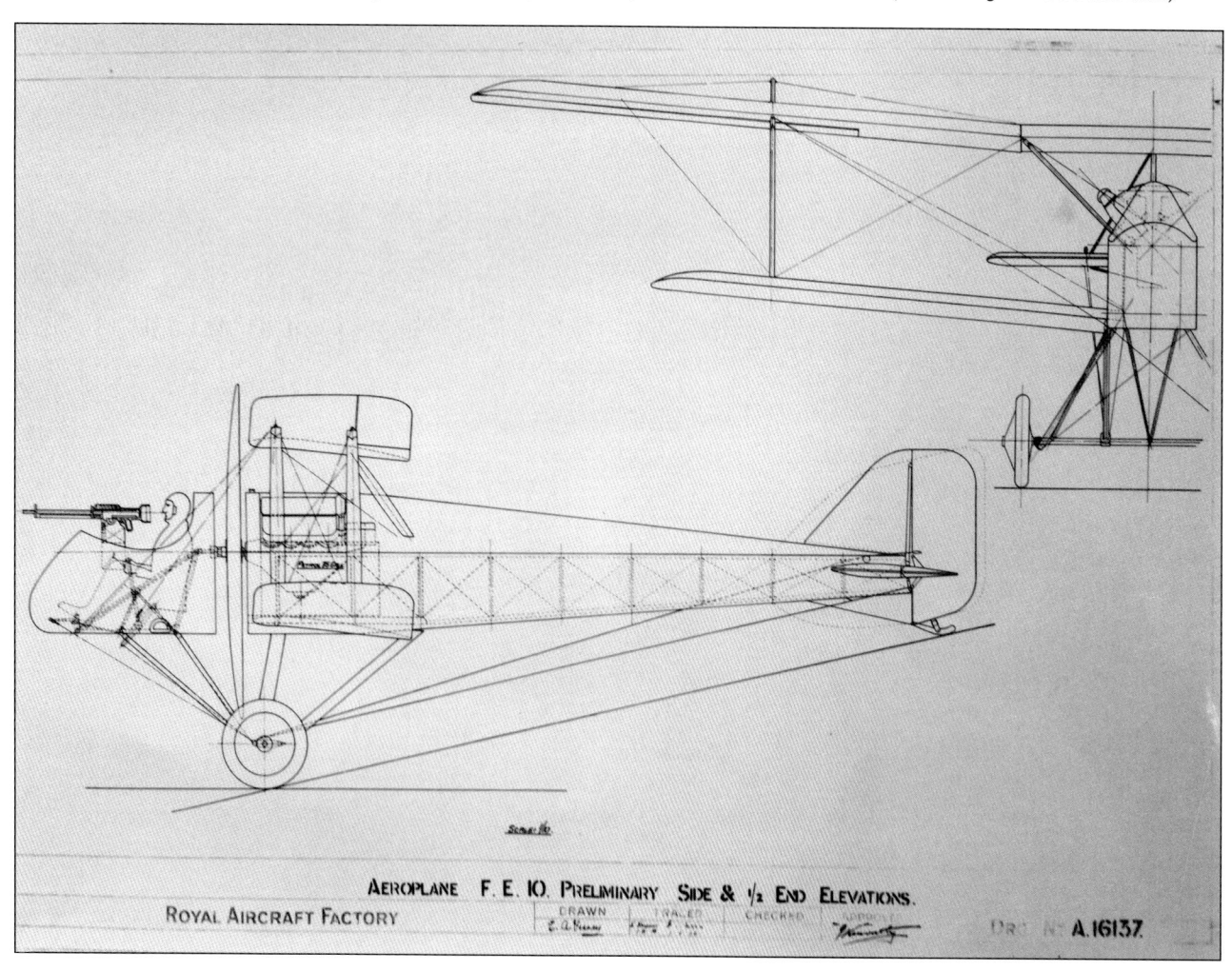

ABOVE **The Royal Aircraft Factory Santos Experimental 1.** *(Farnborough Air Sciences Trust)*

THE S.E. SERIES 1911–15

The S.E.1 can really be discounted from the ancestry of the S.E.5 as a quirk of history. The 'Santos Experimental 1' had a short and unhappy career, making its first flight in the hands of its creator, Geoffrey de Havilland, in April 1912.

De Havilland found the design unstable in flight and the project was shelved, but on 18 August the assistant superintendent of the Royal Aircraft Factory, Theodore Ridge, took the machine up – against de Havilland's advice. Ridge lost control while attempting to make a turn and spun into the ground, suffering fatal injuries.

In January 1912, O'Gorman put forward a list

RIGHT **The Factory produced its first scout – the B.S.1/S.E.2 – in 1912.** *(Farnborough Air Sciences Trust)*

of new types for approval, including a small, fast and lightweight single-seat 'scout' design. This was duly designed by Geoffrey de Havilland and named the B.S.1, for 'Blériot Scout 1', to reflect its front-mounted engine. Before it made its first flight on 13 March 1912, however, the design was renamed S.E.2 – the initials now short for 'Scouting Experimental'.

The S.E.2 was a really forward-looking machine. The fuselage as a whole was rounded and streamlined behind its 100hp Gnome rotary engine, with the section from the cockpit to the tail being of stress-bearing monocoque construction. Equal-span biplane wings were attached, and the new machine proved sleek enough to achieve 92mph in level flight and an 800ft per minute rate of climb.

Where de Havilland felt that his design fell short was in rudder authority, and a new, larger unit was being designed when he took the machine up again on 27 March. At 100ft he lost control in a turn and spun into the ground, breaking his jaw, smashing his teeth and dislocating his ankles – although surviving the encounter.

The crash marked the end of de Havilland's time with the Royal Aircraft Factory, however, and into his role as chief designer came H.P. Folland. Unlike the well-heeled de Havilland, Henry Folland was born in Cambridge to a relatively humble family. He apprenticed in engineering with the Lanchester Motor Company in Birmingham and then became a draughtsman for Daimler in 1908. Through Daimler he came into contact with aeroplanes and his interest in aviation blossomed, resulting in him joining the Royal Aircraft Factory in 1912.

Folland took the remnants of the S.E.2 and rebuilt it throughout the summer of 1912 with a smaller 80hp Gnome engine and a much larger rudder and tail section, which featured a sprung tail skid that could be steered using the rudder pedals. Although considerably slower than de Havilland's original, it proved to be a worthwhile 'hack' that was then commandeered by the War Office and sent to 5 Squadron in January 1914, returning three months later suffering severely from the rough handling it had received.

The S.E.2 was rebuilt again with a traditional tail section replacing the monocoque, further enlargement to the tail surfaces and the abandonment of Folland's steerable tail skid. Its engine cowling was more streamlined and a rounded propeller boss was added, together with the new 'Rafwires' (aerodynamically shaped wires produced by the Royal Aircraft

BELOW Henry Folland rebuilt the S.E.2 along more conventional lines. *(Farnborough Air Sciences Trust)*

ABOVE The S.E.4a went to war in 1914–15 but was not put into production. *(Farnborough Air Sciences Trust)*

Factory) for the rigging, which further reduced drag. In this guise the S.E.2 was sent on active duty with 3 Squadron in France during October 1914, surviving until March 1915 before it was withdrawn.

The development of fast scouts was for a long time stymied by the War Office's insistence that a limit of 100hp be placed on aeroplane engines. This was because it was felt that extra power and speed would be redundant and actively hinder the practical work to be done by an airborne observation platform.

A planned S.E.3 was laid out to meet these stipulations but was abandoned when the opportunity was taken to try the new 160hp Gnome 'Lambda Lambda' engine – effectively two standard rotary engines bolted together. The object was to build the fastest aeroplane in the world – and Folland set about the task with gusto when devising the S.E.4.

Weight reduction and aerodynamic efficiency were paramount – with less emphasis on stability or pilot safety than had ever been seen at the Royal Aircraft Factory. Folland's design used enhanced streamlining around the nose, single 'I'-shaped struts between the wings, ailerons that could act as flaps, a plywood-skinned fuselage with enclosed cockpit and an undercarriage formed of just three struts. Lightweight Ramie fabric replaced Irish linen on the skin, all control horns and turnbuckles were mounted internally and fine plastic mesh smoothed over the gaps between control surfaces and the main structures.

No pilot could be found who was willing to use the cockpit cover, but on 27 July 1914 chief test pilot Norman Spratt recorded 134.5mph in level flight and a rate of climb of 1,600ft per minute. In the clamour that followed the outbreak of war the S.E.4 was commandeered for military duty but crashed before it went on active service.

A revised airframe, the S.E.4a, was hastily designed, and three examples were built in early 1915 with a flat-sided fuselage, more conventional controls and a conventional 80hp Gnome engine. Two of these went on to Home Defence assignments, while the third became development airframe at Farnborough.

By the time that the S.E.4a was flying the rules of air combat were already being written by the first 'aces' of the war – German huntsmen Oswald Bölcke and Max Immelmann – in their Fokker monoplanes. Soon the role of the scout would be to attack enemy observation and reconnaissance machines, defend their own two-seaters and fend off attacks from enemy scouts. The S.E.5 would need to be a very different beast to its forebears.

Specification	S.E.1	S.E.2	S.E.2A	S.E.4	S.E.4	S.E.4a
Layout	Pusher biplane	Tractor biplane	Tractor biplane	Tractor biplane	Tractor biplane	Tractor biplane
Engine	E.N.V. 90° V8 water-cooled	Gnome Lambda 80hp rotary	Gnome Lambda 80hp rotary	160hp Gnome Lambda Lambda double rotary	100hp Gnome Lambda rotary	80hp Le Rhône rotary
Wingspan	38ft	27ft 6¼in	27ft 5in	27ft 5in	27ft 5in	27ft 5in
Length	29ft	20ft 10in	20ft 10in	21ft	21ft	20ft 10in
Height	11ft 6in	9ft 4⅛in	9ft 4⅛in	9ft	9ft 10½in	9ft 5in
Weight	1,200lb	1,230lb	1,150lb	1,200lb	1,200lb	1,200lb
Max speed at sea level	N/A	91mph	96mph	135mph	92mph	90mph

Designing the S.E.5

In designing the S.E.5 Henry Folland took significant inspiration from the line of S.E. aeroplanes over which he had presided since Geoffrey de Havilland's departure. In this he was supported by Kenworthy as chief draughtsman on the project. Their exhaustive research and design work was overseen by Major Frederick Green as Chief Engineer at the Royal Aircraft Factory and Stanley Hiscocks as the Chief Draughtsman, both reporting to O'Gorman initially then later Henry Fowler, who came in as the new superintendent post-Burbidge.

Folland and Kenworthy also relied heavily upon input from Frank Goodden, who was one of the most experienced airmen in the United Kingdom, having cut his teeth flying balloons and airships at Hendon before qualifying on aeroplanes in 1913 and becoming Farnborough's leading test pilot in 1914.

It was agreed that aerodynamic efficiency was of paramount importance, and Folland expended enormous efforts in the wind tunnel at Farnborough honing the streamlining of his new creation. Freed from the constraints of a flat, circular rotary engine at the front of the fuselage, numerous sleek cowlings were tried with which to envelop the Hispano-Suiza.

A variety of aerodynamic fairings, based upon lessons learned from the S.E.4 record plane, were tried to ease the passage of air over drag-inducing areas such as the wing roots and other extremities – although in many cases the gains made were too small to justify either the increased manufacturing cost or the additional burden upon the men who would be servicing them in the field.

The upper and lower wings were of equal span, designed using the standard RAF15 pattern aerofoil section. They were rigged in a single bay, as the best compromise to achieve strength and aerodynamic cleanliness using the flat, aerodynamic Rafwires. A forward stagger between the top and bottom wings was set at 4° and wingtips were flared outwards over the ailerons used for lateral control on both the top and bottom wings, their elegant shape being

ABOVE Henry Folland's notebook for the S.E.5 shows the original fuselage bracing and predicted weights and loads. *(Farnborough Air Sciences Trust)*

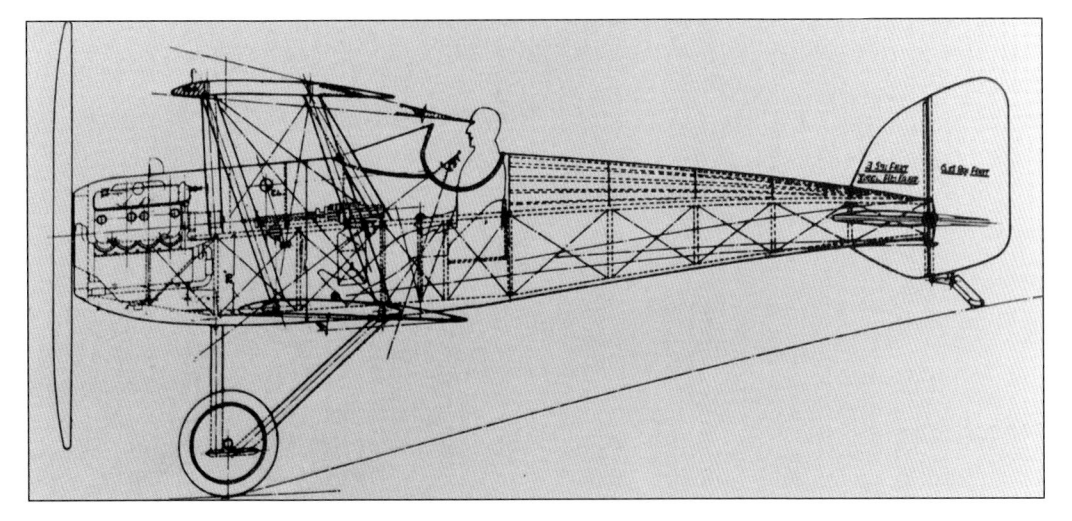

LEFT The original plans for the S.E.5 were laid out through the summer of 1916. *(Farnborough Air Sciences Trust)*

THE S.E.5 STORY

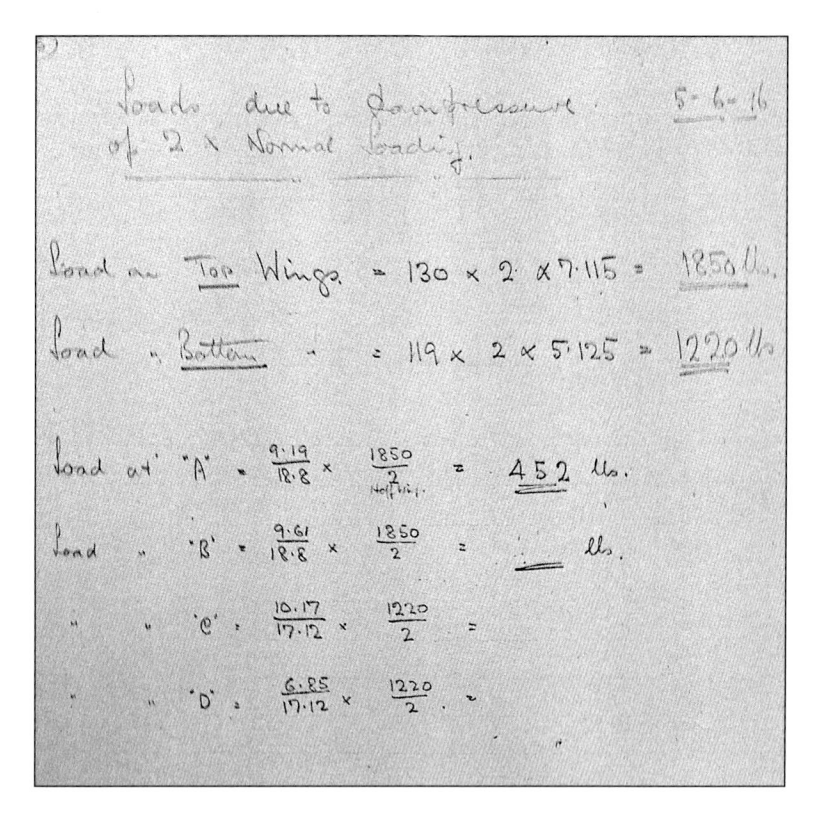

ABOVE Folland's calculations of the wing loading for his new fighter – an area that dogged the S.E.5/5a for some time. *(Farnborough Air Sciences Trust)*

BELOW SPAD eventually fitted a gun to fire through the propeller boss – the short-lived S.XII 'SPAD Canone', a type that found favour with Guynemer. *(Aviation Images)*

from 0° to 4° and finally back to 3½° to balance stability with manoeuvrability. Later, in the wind tunnel, it became apparent that the design lacked sufficient stability and a rethink was required. Eventually the wings were fixed with 5° of dihedral, requiring them to be moved forwards by 5in to compensate for the change in the centre of gravity. The stagger angle between the top and the bottom wing also increased to 5°.

The driving force behind the wing layout was that most air-to-air combat involved tail-chasing in a steep bank, and an aeroplane that would remain stable in such manoeuvres would be a better gun platform. An added bonus was that the aeroplane would naturally return to straight and level flight without any input from the controls, meaning that a pilot who was wounded, blinded by cloud or disoriented could allow his mount to fly itself out of trouble.

Triangular cut-outs were made in the bottom wings to allow the pilot downward vision, while his seating position was much higher than in most contemporary designs to give the best possible all-round view. The fuselage itself was a wire-braced box-girder made from spruce, which was slightly narrower than other contemporary designs, including the SPAD.

The benefits of this slender shape were two-fold: less wind resistance, to wring more speed from the design while also affording the pilot a reasonably good all-round view. The sides of the forward part of the fuselage were made of plywood, and the fuel tank, mounted on the upper longerons of the frame, was shaped to form the top of the fuselage.

Another major consideration was the armament, and initially Folland's design focused upon the idea of using a gear-driven Hispano-Suiza engine to offset the propeller, thereby allowing a Lewis machine gun to sit between the two banks of cylinders, firing through a hollow propeller shaft. This configuration would have saved considerable weight because there would be no need for an interrupter gear to be fitted. However, this idea was soon abandoned when it became clear that geared Hispanos were in short supply and as yet lacking in reliability. Rather than adding complexity to the design, a single Vickers machine gun was decided upon. This was to be mounted within an aerodynamic 'hump' on top of the engine cowling and would use the new Constantinesco CC hydraulic interrupter gear.

Eventually SPAD would produce a front-line fighter with a gun mounted between the cylinder banks of a gear-driven Hispano. In 1917 its updated S.VII scout, the S.XII, placed a 37mm Puteaux cannon on the engine with its muzzle in the propeller shaft and its breech between the pilot's legs – offering him just one shot at a time but with exponentially greater destructive power than a stream of .303 calibre bullets. Few pilots were good enough shots to make use of it, however, and the S.XII was soon killed off.

The most troublesome element in the S.E.5's design was its tail section and rudder, which from the outset Folland intended should be equipped with a means by which the pilot could alter the trim from inside the cockpit. His original design for the vertical surfaces of the tail proved insufficient in the wind tunnel, which prompted John Kennard to try using his own tail design from the abandoned F.E.10, featuring a dorsal and ventral fin, with a steerable tail skid separate from the rudder but operated by the rudder pedals.

The completed drawings and calculations were submitted to the War Office in August 1916, complete with draughtsman's tooling diagrams for every component. In September the War Office responded with an order for three S.E.5 prototypes to be built, which were allocated the serial numbers A4561, A4562 and A4563.

Intriguingly, one of the consequences of the Burbidge Committee report was that the Royal Aircraft Factory was no longer permitted to manufacture aeroplanes at the Farnborough facility – even as prototypes. This detail appears to have been studiously ignored.

Not only were the three prototypes ordered but so was an initial 'pre-production' run of 24 airframes, with the War Office issuing a very specific contract – perhaps at the request of Henry Fowler to ensure that the Royal Aircraft Factory did not carry the can alone for breaking with Burbidge.

With the formalities thereby complete, two Hispano-Suiza 8Aa 150hp direct drive engines were delivered to Farnborough swiftly afterwards and construction work on the S.E.5 prototypes began in earnest. After the required inspections and static running the first completed prototype, serial A4561, was wheeled out on to the grass at Farnborough and prepared for flight on 20 November 1916.

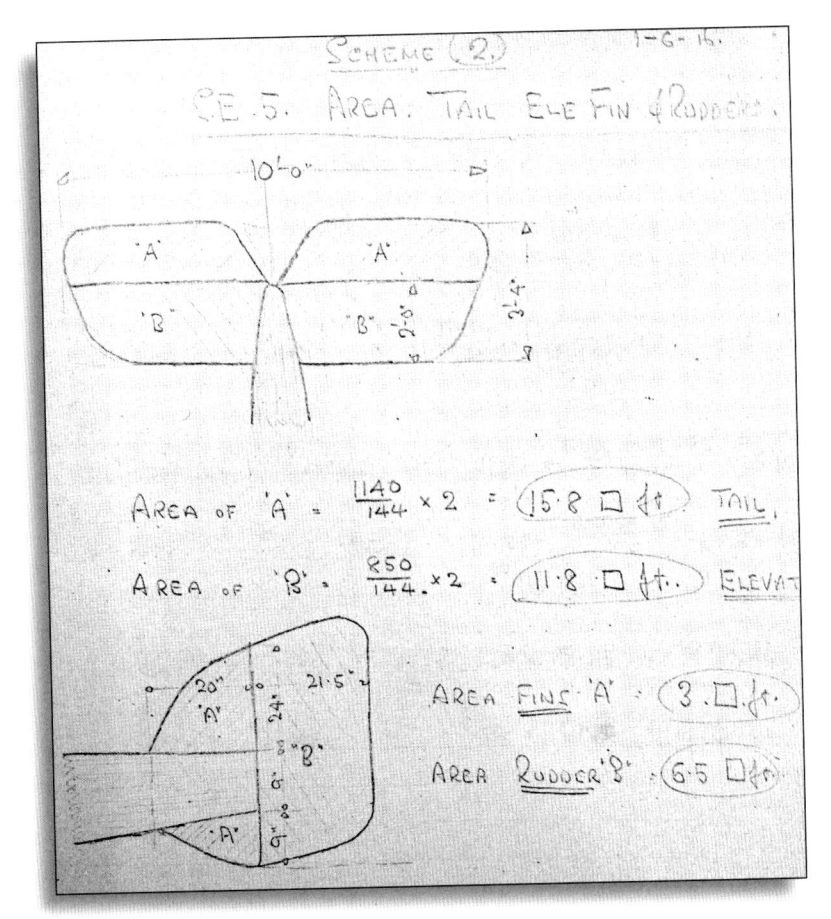

Without guns or windscreen, her freshly doped canvas unblemished by national or unit markings save for the red, white and blue rudder, the S.E.5 made a handsome sight. She would be flown by the man who was in part responsible for the programme, Major Frank

ABOVE One of Folland's sketches for the tail assembly, 1916. *(Farnborough Air Sciences Trust)*

BELOW As chief test pilot and uncredited member of the design team, Major Frank Goodden would lead the testing programme of the S.E.5. *(Aviation Images)*

RIGHT The first prototype S.E.5 is rolled out for its maiden flight at Farnborough.
(Farnborough Air Sciences Trust)

Goodden, and his presence in the cockpit would have given some additional confidence to Folland, Kenworthy and the rest of the engineering team who gathered to see their creation take flight.

Goodden had a clear head and a capacity to analyse an aeroplane's behaviour that very few airmen possessed in 1916. His reputation as a test pilot had been built upon teaching pilots that their worst nightmare, a spin, could in fact be saved if approached calmly. In this way, and through his personal example, he was able to restore confidence in the promising F.E.8 design when many pilots believed that it was a death trap. Since that time he had been relied upon to finesse the handling characteristics of many different types that were built at Farnborough, of which the S.E.5 would be his last and undeniably his greatest. Sadly for all concerned the Hispano-Suiza could not be coaxed into life and in the end the first test flight was delayed by 24 hours.

On 21 November the engine behaved itself. A small auxiliary petrol tap had been fitted and had not been opened prior to the first attempt. With this slightly embarrassing fault cured the engine was warmed up and some last-minute ground running was made before the S.E.5's nose swung into the wind at around 10:00am.

Goodden opened the throttle. Without weapons or much of a load the sleek, olive-coloured S.E.5 was airborne in no time at all for what would be an uneventful 20-minute acclimatisation flight. On this first outing Goodden's main concerns would be centred upon checking that the bias in the rigging and the gearing of the control surfaces were set accurately and that the machine was sufficiently balanced to continue with her test programme without undue delay.

Returning gently to earth, Goodden taxied in and the new machine was surrounded by expectant faces, not least those of Folland and Kenworthy. The post-flight checks were made and Goodden gathered his thoughts before he spoke with a satisfied grin: 'She's a pixie!' he said.

Albert Ball and the S.E.5

No matter how solid the preparations had been, such a successful maiden flight for the S.E.5 would have been a cause for relief not only through its core design team but also throughout the Royal Aircraft Factory. Its performance validated both the hard work done by the engineers and the practices and methods of the Factory, as established under Mervyn O'Gorman.

As such it was another finger in the eye of Noel Pemberton Billing, and thus doubtless a much-needed morale booster among the Farnborough faithful. Everything up to the maiden flight had gone to plan, but on the very next day the development of the S.E.5 took a sharp tangent.

It is no great overstatement to say that the ten-minute flight made by A4561 on 22 November would come to have almost as great an impact upon the S.E.5's future as all the preceding months of development work combined. It was not Frank Goodden who climbed into the cockpit; it was instead the greatest hero of the Royal Flying Corps and arguably the most popular man in Britain at that moment in time: Captain Albert Ball.

Ball arrived at Farnborough just days after receiving his third Distinguished Service Order in an investiture at Buckingham Palace in recognition of his bringing down 31 enemy aeroplanes between May and September 1916. The British public whipped itself into a frenzy of adulation over the cherubically short, stocky and handsome youth, and it is clear that even among battle-hardened pilots there was little else but admiration. With his standing at such an incredible height, there is no doubting that his endorsement of the S.E.5 would go a long way towards repairing the damage done to the Royal Aircraft Factory's reputation over the previous 12 months.

Ball's actual comments after the flight have not been recorded, but there was no suggestion that the word 'pixie' entered into his opinion. He took an instant dislike to the S.E.5 and proceeded to lobby hard against it in almost every conversation and piece of correspondence possible. At a time when the great and the good were lining up to bask in Ball's reflected glory, he wasted no opportunity to talk down the Royal Aircraft Factory and its new fighting scout.

There are many reasons why Ball took such a profound and voluble dislike to the S.E.5. Firstly, he had been assigned to fly the B.E.2 early in his front-line career, an aeroplane that he detested and blamed the Royal Aircraft Factory for inflicting upon him. Secondly, all but one of Ball's colossal tally of victories had been achieved while flying the bantamweight Nieuport scouts, which were outgunned and under-powered next to their German opponents but were incredibly manoeuvrable. In comparison to the Nieuport, the S.E.5 would doubtless have felt lethargic in its handling.

Whether or not the Royal Aircraft Factory was aware, there was also a third reason why Ball should want to snuff out the S.E.5 programme. The young hero of the hour was personally and deeply involved in a rival project intended to meet the required specification and win the supply of Hispano-Suiza engines.

Ball's father, Albert Sr, was an Alderman of Nottingham and also a director of the Austin Motor Company in Birmingham. A sharp businessman and a skilled politician, the elder Ball played every card that life dealt him to the fullest, and that included his son's unique status. Long before young Albert's rise to fame there had been correspondence between father and son about the possibility of Austin developing a spectacular new aeroplane for the war effort. The interest of father and son in Austin was entirely mutual, for not only did Albert Sr sit on the board but he also made young Albert a shareholder.

Through the summer months of 1916, while

ABOVE Albert Ball with his mother, sister and girlfriend on the way to Buckingham Palace in November 1916. *(Getty/Hulton)*

BELOW Ball rose to fame flying lightweight Nieuport scouts that were far removed from the S.E.5 in their handling. *(Imperial War Museum)*

building his legend in the sky, the gifted airman had devoted considerable amounts of time on the ground to designing a new fighter to be powered by the Hispano-Suiza engine. At the same time, and doubtless encouraged from the boardroom by Albert Ball Sr, Austin had begun work on extending its Longbridge factory for increased production, and since 1915 had already been contracted by the Royal Aircraft Factory to build examples of several aeroplanes – notably the R.E.7 and R.E.8 reconnaissance machines. The company's new purpose-built facility was constructed at the junction of Lickey Road and the A38 Bristol Road in June 1916, with an airfield alongside on land that had been levelled for the purpose.

When young Albert returned from France for some long-overdue leave in October 1916 he set to work with the designers at Austin to turn his ideas and their industrial muscle into a world-beating – and doubtless profitable – aeroplane. So it was that by the time Ball arrived in Farnborough and tested the new S.E.5 he had already got clearance from General Sir David Henderson, the head of Military Aeronautics, to push ahead with his design as a rival to the Royal Aircraft Factory. On 20 November Austin declared itself ready to commit to full-scale production in 1917, and submitted its designs to the War Office on 27 November. In this light, when Albert Ball climbed aboard the S.E.5 on 22 November he could scarcely have been expected to offer an unbiased opinion of it!

Whatever the motives behind Ball's negative response to the S.E.5, he did offer some suggestions to the Royal Aircraft Factory for improving the design at its prototype stage. One was a faired headrest for the pilot and the other was a Lewis gun mounted on the centre section of the upper wing, as had been standard fitment on the Nieuport scouts with which Ball had cut a swathe through the German Air Service.

The Lewis gun made sense for two reasons. One was that Ball's favourite method of attack was to fly into the blind spot underneath the tail of an enemy two-seater, pull the Lewis down on its sliding Foster mount to fire upwards and thus dispatch his victims before they knew he was there. The other was that a single machine gun was no longer sufficient for fighting the two-gun Albatros scouts that had begun to proliferate on the German side of the lines.

The Albatros used a mechanical interrupter gear to allow the two machine guns to fire through its propeller arc. The S.E.5 would use the new and largely unproven Colley-Constantinesco 'CC' gear. Fitting the Lewis would double the S.E.5's firepower without over-burdening the Constantinesco gear, putting it on an equal footing with the Albatros for dogfighting while giving experts like Ball the opportunity to continue hunting their prey from the blind spot.

The fitting of the Lewis gun and mount was no small undertaking, however. Bracing the wing for the extra weight meant deleting the header tank from inside the upper port wing and replacing it with a streamlined example mounted above the port upper wing root. The windscreen was also extended to allow the Foster mounting to be secured.

Tested to destruction

One week after the first S.E.5 prototype, A4561, was rolled out of the Farnborough workshops she was joined by the second prototype, A4562. At first the only obvious difference between the two aeroplanes was that the first utilised an engine-driven air pump while the second had a wind-driven unit mounted beneath the cockpit.

The second prototype suffered fairly significant damage in a landing accident within

BELOW The over-wing Lewis gun on its Foster mount on the Shuttleworth Collection's S.E.5a – an addition suggested by Albert Ball. *(Author)*

days of her completion, sending her back into the workshops. She emerged in December after having been fitted with all and any changes that had been suggested by pilots taking part in the evaluation programme, such as enlarging the windscreen to allow better access to the Vickers gun if it should jam.

In this form, Frank Goodden took off from Farnborough in A4562 on Christmas Eve 1916 and set course for Saint Omer airfield in France. Here he would be joined by Lieutenant Frederick Selous of 19 Squadron RFC, who brought with him one of the new SPAD S.VIIs with which the unit was being equipped, and Lieutenant Roderick Hill from 60 Squadron, who arrived in one of his unit's Nieuport 17 scouts.

On Boxing Day the pilots set about assessing how these three types measured up to one another. Selous' report was as follows:

'Control Elevator: The S.E.5 is slightly lighter in the elevator than the SPAD but the machine is harder to keep in a steep dive.

'Laterally: There is not any difference between the S.E.5 and the SPAD.

'View: The view in all directions is very good [in the S.E.5], much better than the SPAD, especially forwards and downwards.

'Climb and Speed: This cannot be judged accurately without flying the machines together, but the S.E.5 has a much greater range of speed than the SPAD and will fly at 45mph.

'General Flying: Although the S.E.5 is stable it can be manoeuvred quite as well as the SPAD. The S.E.5 can be landed slower than the SPAD and has a much flatter glide.'

Roderick Hill came from Albert Ball's former squadron and flew the type in which the great hero of the hour held such store for its deft handling. Unlike his illustrious comrade, Hill had very few reservations about the S.E.5, saying:

'The S.E.5 has, in my opinion, certain advantages over the Nieuport and the SPAD: its speed is good; it lands as slowly as the Nieuport and more slowly than the SPAD; it is stronger than the SPAD; its gun mounting is superior. Its disadvantage with respect to the Nieuport is that it cannot be manoeuvred with quite the same rapidity, although at high altitudes, manoeuvres should be possible with a much smaller loss of height.'

As a result of the feedback from Selous and Hill a number of detail changes were incorporated within the S.E.5's cockpit layout. The tailplane trim wheel gained a knob for ease of use with gauntleted hands at altitude, the gun trigger levers were set on to adjustable mountings to be placed where the pilot preferred, an extended loading handle was fitted to the Vickers gun, the release lever for the Lewis gun was repositioned and storage for extra Lewis gun magazines was built into the cockpit. An engine decelerator was also fitted for emergency use.

ABOVE A SPAD S.VII of the Royal Flying Corps was used to benchmark performance of the S.E.5. *(Alamy)*

ABOVE Ergonomic improvements in the cockpit were the main focus of the RFC pilots who tested the S.E.5 prototype over Christmas 1916. *(Darren Harbar)*

BELOW The square wingtips giving a span of 26ft 7in are what distinguish the S.E.5a from the S.E.5 – not, as is often reported, the 200hp engine. *(Darren Harbar)*

Another order for 50 more production models to be built at Farnborough was made on the strength of the S.E.5's performance in December. While the first two prototypes, A4561 and A4562, were fitted with the requested modifications the third, A4563, was completed and fitted with the first 200hp Hispano to arrive at Farnborough. A reduction gear was needed to give the propeller a fighting chance of managing the increased power. This gear raised the propeller hub and thereby the thrust line of the engine, allowing the fitment of a larger propeller to maximise the effectiveness of the increased power.

A4563 was soon joined on the flight line by the revised A4562, now fully equipped with the requested changes from the testing programme, and on 28 January 1917 Frank Goodden went up in it on a routine flight and indulged in some aerobatic manoeuvres while he was returning to Farnborough. Flying southbound over the village of Cove at around 1,500ft, the port wing cell collapsed as he pulled out after a loop. Goodden was seen to remove his helmet and goggles and stand up in the cockpit as the aeroplane fell, his intention possibly being to jump clear before impact, but he was still on board when it hit the ground and was killed.

An immediate investigation was launched into the cause of the catastrophic wing failure, and it was discovered that the wings of A4561 were also close to breaking point in the main spar. The reason was found to be the design of the compression ribs which carried too much vertical flex, passing this through to the spar and weakening it over time. A simple fix consisting of plywood webbing to bolster the compression ribs was effected and proved to solve the problem.

Further research into the integrity of the wings revealed that they could withstand forces of 5.5g before breaking. This was deemed insufficient and further design work was carried out. The spar was made thicker and it was also proven that the greatest point of inherent weakness lay in the amount of flex where it increased towards the wingtip, beyond the interplane struts. Reducing the wingspan from 28ft to 26ft 7in by squaring off the elegantly tapered wingtips was a simple yet effective solution to the problem. A point of history is that aeroplanes fitted with these redesigned wings were considered to be of a later specification and thus named S.E.5a.

Frank Goodden's loss and the subsequent investigation bequeathed the S.E.5a with the structural integrity for which it was subsequently renowned and which would go on to save many hundreds of airmen's lives in battle. This came as no consolation to Henry Folland, however, who held himself responsible for Goodden's demise and resigned from the Royal Aircraft Factory. Meanwhile the design that Goodden, Folland and Kenworthy had developed was now being pressed onward towards its debut in battle.

To war with 56 Squadron

At the end of November 1916 the British Army was on the front foot in France, having recovered from its catastrophic losses on the first day of the Battle of the Somme on 1 July to grind its way through the German Army's resolve over the weeks and months that followed. As soon as the arrival of spring weather ended the enforced break in operations, Britain's commander-in-chief, Field Marshal Sir Douglas Haig, was determined to pick up where he had left off.

Having started the war with a dismissive attitude towards the value of aviation, Haig now saw that it had a vital role to play and, while not fluent in aviation matters, he could see that the Germans had established superiority in terms of tactics and technology. Thus Haig demanded that the commander of the Royal Flying Corps in France, Major-General Hugh Trenchard, should have sufficient strength to take on the German threat by the time the new offensive began.

Trenchard's nickname was 'Boom'. In part the name was inspired by his manner of speech, which was likened by many to the firing of a large calibre artillery piece. It was also coined as a result of his explosive temper and, in early 1917, Trenchard had plenty to be angry about.

Since putting forward his optimum specification at the start of 1916, he had gained confidence that new designs including the S.E.5, the Bristol Fighter and the Sopwith Camel would be superior to their German counterparts. The problem was that there were innumerable delays caused by material shortages, flaws in design and a rash of industrial disputes and wildcat strikes in the factories.

Despite the best efforts of the Burbidge Committee, the lines of supply also remained chaotic, ensuring that delivery dates slipped further and further behind. Haig and the French armies under General Nivelle had meanwhile committed to launching a three-pronged assault around the town of Arras in April 1917. This massive undertaking would see the Canadian armies take Vimy Ridge as a prelude to the French making a major push in the Chemin des Dames region – the Nivelle Offensive. As a diversion, the British would attack simultaneously, aiming for the town or Arras.

It was a vast and complex plan that would be utterly dependent upon the eyes of its airborne artillery support and reconnaissance aeroplanes. As the countdown gathered pace, Trenchard was painfully aware that he would

ABOVE Captain Albert Ball in the cockpit of his much-modified S.E.5 at London Colney. *(Imperial War Museum)*

BELOW 'Boom' Trenchard (left) was fighting the war upon shifting sands of technology that nobody had ever seen before. *(Imperial War Museum)*

ABOVE The Bristol F2 Fighter was the first of a new generation of aeroplanes to arrive in France and would serve until the 1930s – although its debut over Arras was disastrous. *(Author)*

be forced to expose his young airmen to significant losses. The German fighting units – the *Jagdstaffeln* – were now fully equipped with the magnificent two-gun Albatros D.II and D.III scouts which had the measure of virtually all the Allied types ranged against them.

The Royal Flying Corps could muster only

BELOW Only the handful of Sopwith Triplanes made available by the Royal Naval Air Service could really be counted as first-class fighters at the start of the Battle of Arras. *(Shutterstock)*

24 squadrons in total, of which just eight were fighter squadrons intended to defend the artillery spotters and reconnaissance machines upon which Haig's attack would depend. Of these fighter units, just two were equipped with the most modern British design at the front, the Sopwith Pup, while the French Nieuport and the SPAD S.VII equipped a further two squadrons apiece. The rest of his fighters would be obsolescent 'pusher' designs such as the D.H.2 and F.E.8 that had no business at all in trying to tackle the Albatros.

A single composite squadron of Sopwith Pups and the brilliant new Sopwith Triplane was thrown into the mix by the Royal Naval Air Service, but the best that Trenchard could hope for was to hold out until the next generation of fighting machines arrived. Delays at Sopwith caused by the outstanding orders for Pups and Triplanes meant that the Camel would not be available until summer, which left him with a maximum of one squadron of Bristol Fighters and one squadron of S.E.5s to turn the tide.

The Bristol Fighters were first to arrive, with the newly formed 48 Squadron under the command of Captain William Leefe Robinson. On 5 April 1917 a formation of six Bristol F2A Fighters made the first patrol over enemy lines for this new machine and immediately found themselves under attack from the Albatros scouts of Manfred von Richthofen's *Jasta* 11. As they had been advised, the formation held steady to give its rear gunners a chance to bring down the German machines. This was a fatal error: four out of the six Bristols were shot down, and confidence in the 'Brisfit' plummeted.

Two days later, less than 48 hours before the Battle of Arras began, the first S.E.5s touched down in France. So began the story of the unit that would be most closely associated with the successes of the new machine: 56 Squadron.

The first seeds of 56 Squadron had been sown during the summer of 1916 when a small detachment of ground staff gathered in Gosport. When sufficient manpower had been built up the unit relocated to London Colney airfield near St Albans, and in February 1917 a new commanding officer was appointed. Major Richard Graham Blomfield was an experienced commander who had been tasked with turning 56 Squadron into an elite fighting force –

albeit one that had no front-line aeroplanes on strength. After the War Office cancelled its order of Sopwith Triplanes for the RFC in horse-trading with the Admiralty, which preferred the unconventional fighters, the best currently available to him was the SPAD S.VII. At least one of these machines was delivered to London Colney, but ultimately it was decided that 56 Squadron would take the new S.E.5 into battle – and Blomfield was given every opportunity to make it a successful debut.

With the pick of available men to act as flight commanders, Blomfield's first real coup was to get hold of Captain Albert Ball. Throughout the winter months, Ball had been on Home Establishment duties such as gunnery tuition. These were not the sort of tasks to which Ball warmed and he had used his celebrity status to spend many hours in the company of everyone up to and including the new Prime Minister, David Lloyd George, lobbying for a return to active duty. Ball's time as an instructor was not without profit, however, for it allowed him to act as talent-spotter. It was through Ball's headhunting that future stars such as Arthur Rhys Davids were plucked from obscurity to join what was becoming known, via the jungle drums of the Royal Flying Corps, as a 'crack' squadron tasked with taking the fight to the Germans.

No unit could be entirely filled with 'crack' pilots, however – even 56 Squadron. In 1953 Gerald Maxwell recounted his own introduction to the unit as a young lieutenant and how he fell far short of expectations among the senior men of '56':

'When I was posted to No 56 Squadron at London Colney I had done seven hours' solo and Major Blomfield was furious with the Air Ministry for posting a brand new inexperienced pilot to his crack squadron, full of chaps with lots of experience like Albert Ball, and specially chosen to fly the new super fighter, the S.E.5.

'However, after a few days, when the flight commanders were asked to choose the pilots for their flights, Captain Ball said "I'll have that chap with the Scottish bonnet." This was luckily me because I was wearing my Lovat Scouts bonnet; I had served at Suvla Bay, Gallipoli, with the Lovat Scouts, which regiment my uncle had raised in the Boer War.'

Readers will also recall that Ball had been extremely busy denigrating the S.E.5 project at every opportunity – while pushing for the new design that he had been working on with Austin to replace it. Up until December only 74 production S.E.5s had been ordered, and Ball was convinced that his design would be a better use for the Hispano-Suiza engine – writing to his mother that:

'If they are found to be any better than any others we get a big order. That is left for me. I told Austin's that I was surprised at their calling the machine the Austin and forgetting that it

ABOVE The hard-pressed Royal Flying Corps squadrons were reliant on outdated machines like the D.H.2 until the latest generation of fighting scouts like the S.E.5 arrived, resulting in 'Bloody April'. *(Getty Images)*

ABOVE The brand new S.E.5s in line at London Colney as 56 Squadron works up to readiness.
(Imperial War Museum)

was to be called the A.B. or Austin-Ball. So much for that I saw Lord Northcliffe and he is going to put in a word for me and my machine.

'I want a bit of cash from Austin's or they will not have the big job when it comes and come it will.'

It would appear that Austin soon acquiesced to Ball's demands, with payment of £1,000 (the equivalent of perhaps £105,000 today) plus an agreement to establish a motor dealership and a supply of cars. The new aeroplane design meanwhile became known as the Austin-Ball A.F.B.1, and it was understood by Ball that he was to remain with 56 Squadron only for a matter of weeks until he had proven the value of the Austin prototype. He would then return to England in order to lead the new machine's development programme.

On 14 March 1917 the first of the production models of the S.E.5 was accepted by the Royal Flying Corps and Ball went to collect it the very next day. At London Colney, Ball gently brought A4850 down on to the runway then immediately had it wheeled into the hangar under the supervision of the squadron's chief engineering officer, Hubert Charles:

'When he started flying the thing around London Colney, before landing, everybody couldn't believe it – that this was the S.E.5 fighter?' Charles later remembered. 'The thing looked hopeless! It was obviously slow and Ball obviously didn't want to do any aerobatics on it. When he landed it was boiling. The paint was all stuck to the outside of the cylinder block. The very first thing we did was to take the radiator off and wash it out backwards with a mixture of weak washing soda water and wire and fit it with a wire mesh filter bag in the header tank, so that if any more paint came out of the water jacket it wouldn't block the radiator, washed out the water jacket and put the whole thing back.'

Most of the issues that Ball had taken with the new machine stemmed from further modifications that had been made to the S.E.5's design between the prototype and production stages. The wings of A4850 were still of the original 28ft span with the tapering shape that denoted an S.E.5, although the strengthened compression rib bracing and thicker wing spar had been fitted, but other changes had also been effected and few met with Ball's approval.

The windscreen was now a semi-enclosed canopy, intended to reduce the buffeting wind when pilots pulled down the Lewis gun to change ammunition drums or to fire upwards at the enemy. The pilot's seat was also a much more ornate affair, being adjustable for height and reach and carrying 0.5in armour plate around it for maximum pilot protection.

None of this mattered a hoot to Albert Ball, and he immediately set about modifying A4850 with the assistance of Hubert Charles. The 'greenhouse' windscreen was the first thing to go, being replaced with a small aeroscreen taken from an Avro 504K trainer. The next thing to go was the Vickers gun and its synchronising gear, which Ball mistrusted. Instead a second Lewis gun was fitted in between his legs, firing obliquely through the cockpit floor.

The main fuel tank was removed and, with the

Vickers gun deleted, was replaced by a bigger tank for better endurance. A new upper-wing centre section was made from plywood with a larger cut-out to increase visibility and with the external gravity tank fitted inside the leading edge – as per the original design. While cleaning up the aerodynamics in this way, Ball also chose to swap the standard 700mm x 100mm undercarriage wheels for a pair of narrower 700mm x 75mm wheels from an old Bristol Scout. The adjustable and armour-plated pilot's seat was thrown out and into its place a simple plank was fitted on to which a standard wicker seat was fixed, lowering the pilot into the fuselage. Finally, a streamlined fairing with a headrest was fitted behind the cockpit, as Ball had suggested in November.

The resulting aeroplane looked much more like the later S.E.5a than those of the rest of the squadron, which mostly retained their factory specification. One or two pilots elected to at least get rid of the 'greenhouse' windscreens, but none of the modifications had been approved and few but Albert Ball had the confidence to go ahead with any changes.

Despite this, the very clear disappointment shown towards the S.E.5 permeated among the rest of the pilots fairly quickly. Another of the pilots based at London Colney was Lieutenant Cecil Lewis, whose own misgivings were focused upon the combination of the synchronised Vickers gun with the wing-mounted Lewis gun. Not knowing that the arrangement was Ball's suggestion, the young pilot felt that the decision to place the guns in this way was 'a typical [Royal Aircraft] Factory invention that could never have been devised by a pilot who had combat experience.'

The Royal Aircraft Factory was well aware of the fact that 56 Squadron was getting spooked by the S.E.5 and thus dispatched its new chief test pilot, Roderick Hill, to London Colney. Taking one of the regular aeroplanes from the line, Hill performed a 20-minute flying display of tub-thumping bravura. Doubtless there were many among his audience who knew that the wing failure of an S.E.5 had killed his predecessor and Hill performed a full repertoire: dive and zoom, stall, spin, loop and corkscrew turns at the very limit of its abilities.

With at least some of the pilots' jitters settled, all of 56 Squadron's complement of S.E.5s had been delivered by 30 March. On

ABOVE LEFT The pilots of 56 Squadron universally disliked the 'greenhouse' semi-enclosed canopy with which the S.E.5 was delivered.
(Imperial War Museum)

ABOVE Albert Ball shows off the bare plywood centre section, headrest and single Lewis gun fitted to his personal mount.
(Imperial War Museum)

BELOW The view looking out over what was London Colney airfield has changed little over a century, despite the noisy presence of the M25 nearby.
(Author)

35

THE S.E.5 STORY

ABOVE Only a minority of S.E.5s were modified from standard before departing for France. *(Imperial War Museum)*

7 April, two days before the Battle of Arras began, the squadron was ordered to transfer from its home at London Colney to Saint Omer and then onwards to its new operating base at Vert Galant. Cecil Lewis was handed the job of leading the squadron along the delivery route, which would see the squadron fly to Hawkinge on the Kent coast to refuel and confirm that they were fit for the cross-Channel leg. Lewis was determined that 56 Squadron should become the first unit to land in France with as many aeroplanes as had taken off in England and, thanks to the reliability of the Hispano-Suiza engines, this ambition was fulfilled.

Upon their arrival at Vert Galant, the men of 56 Squadron were almost immediately inundated with visits from the 'top brass', starting with Brigadier-General Robert Brooke-Popham, the Quartermaster-General of the Royal Flying Corps. His was the responsibility to ensure that the squadrons in the front line were properly equipped and prepared for action, and he must have been severely taken aback by the level of discontent about the S.E.5.

Brooke-Popham studied the alterations that had been made to date, particularly those on Ball's A4850. It was clear to him that the S.E.5 design had issues and that Ball's modifications went a long way towards resolving them – although implementing these same changes to the other 12 aeroplanes would take time, not least because Hubert Charles and the engineering team would not arrive at Vert Galant before the 16th. So it was that Brooke-Popham prepared an order that was sent out the following day:

1. The following Alterations will be made to the S.E.5s of 56 Squadron:
   a. The present windscreens will be taken away and a simple three-ply cowling with an Avro windscreen at the rear will be substituted, similar to the sample machine I was shown yesterday.
   b. The present adjustable and armoured seat will be taken out and a simple board fitted across. This should be lower than the lowest position of the present seat.
   c. The gun mounting for the Lewis gun must be made to fit better and the slide lengthened by about 2 inches so that cover from the Avro windscreen is afforded when changing drums. No.2 Aircraft Depot will assist the squadron in making extensions for the slides.
2. The squadron commander will be given a free hand as regards details of the above alterations provided that all twelve machines of the squadron are the same.
   Please note that the Vickers gun is to be left where it is. The design of the two Lewis guns that is in Capt. Ball's machine is not approved, but this machine need not be altered back again.
3. Instructions regarding the removal of the gravity tank on the top plane will be given as soon as certain information has been obtained from England.

The following day saw General Trenchard himself visit Vert Galant – flying in aboard an R.E.8 that was seconded as his personal transport, no doubt in part to inspire the troops to believe that this new reconnaissance aeroplane was not the complete disaster that was being rumoured.

His arrival was not a specific trip to visit 56 Squadron but rather part of his 'eve of battle' tour of all the airfields on the day before the troops went over the top for Arras. It was already clear that the S.E.5s of 56 Squadron would play no part in the early stages of the battle, but Vert Galant was also home to the SPAD S.VIIs of 19 Squadron and the Sopwith Pups of 66 Squadron that would soon be in the thick of the action.

Trenchard's priorities towards the other squadrons did not prevent Albert Ball from buttonholing the general to complain about the S.E.5 and, doubtless, to press his case for the Austin fighter. 'Boom' was clearly frustrated at the extent of the work that was needed to make 56 Squadron ready for battle and singled out the 'greenhouse' windscreen as a particular bugbear at a time when he needed every available pilot.

Despite this accord, Ball was clearly unsatisfied with the amount of time he was able to hold Trenchard's ear at Vert Galant, and gave chase to the general's party after it left for the next airfield, Le Hameau. Making the most of his opportunity to rejoin Trenchard over afternoon tea, Ball requested that until the prototype Austin became available he be given a Nieuport scout with which to pursue the enemy on a roving commission, while continuing to fly the S.E.5 to perform his duties as a flight leader.

None of this was going to get 56 Squadron into action any faster. Brooke-Popham revised his previous order by stating that Ball was not permitted to keep his downward-firing Lewis gun and must have the synchronised Vickers reinstalled so that all of 56 Squadron's S.E.5s were at the same specification. It would take more than two weeks for them to be ready – during which time the Royal Flying Corps suffered its most grievous losses of the war to date in the darkest days of 'Bloody April'.

Trenchard's misgivings in the lead-up to the Battle of Arras had been well founded. The skies over Arras were being turned into a slaughterhouse by the numerically inferior but tactically brilliant German *Jagdstaffeln*. In the five days leading up to the attack on Vimy Ridge, the Royal Flying Corps lost 75 aeroplanes – a quarter of its front-line force – with 13 aircrew wounded and 92 dead or missing.

As the battle for Vimy Ridge reached a crescendo and the larger assault on Arras was unleashed, so the numbers of British aeroplanes falling in flames over the Front continued to rise. In total the month of April would see nearly 250 machines shot down with the loss of 400 men – a fraction of the carnage going on down below, but as a corps and at squadron level it was a holocaust. Not only were the losses great but, worse, they were being inflicted by a relatively modest number of Albatros scouts – just five *Jagdstaffeln*. This meant that huge personal scores were being accumulated by the German 'aces' led by Kurt Wolff, with 23 victories in April, Manfred von Richthofen with 22 and Karl-Emil Schäfer with 21.

Not only were individual German pilots able to build their scores but, thanks to the unique liveries that they applied to their personal aeroplanes, it was all too clear who the most dangerous among them was. Any British pilot who found himself with an all-red Albatros on his tail knew that it was the 'Red Baron' and this knowledge often caused pilots and observers to lose heart, handing their attacker an additional advantage that was eagerly accepted.

What the Royal Flying Corps desperately needed was a British answer to the Red Baron – an inspiration to the men who were under the insatiable guns of the Albatroses – and into that role Captain Albert Ball was preparing to step. As 56 Squadron grew closer to combat readiness, so the mercurial

ABOVE Outgunned and underpowered, the two squadrons of Sopwith Pups were the best of the fighters available to the RFC until the S.E.5 was combat-ready. *(Shutterstock)*

ABOVE **Pictured at the height of their powers in April 1917, Manfred von Richthofen (centre) flanked by (left to right)** Vizefeldwebel **Sebastian Festner,** Leutnant **Karl-Emil Schäfer,** Leutnant **Lothar von Richthofen,** Leutnant **Kurt Wolff and Richthofen's prized Great Dane, Moritz.** (Imperial War Museum).

20-year-old's sense of duty and patriotism took hold of him. Trenchard had granted his request for a Nieuport for solo flying and the S.E.5s of 56 Squadron had been modified to his specification, meaning that his griping was stifled significantly and he was able to focus on the job in hand.

An extra modification that Ball added was a pair of exhaust pipes taken from the Hispano-engined SPADs operated by 19 Squadron. Rather than a small outlet pipe poking out of the manifold, the SPAD pipes ran back down the fuselage on either side to behind the cockpit, cleaning up the aerodynamics and providing heat into the cockpit. As a finishing touch Ball painted the radiator and metal parts of his S.E.5's cowling bright red – he wanted the beleaguered Royal Flying Corps to rally to him, and to be seen to challenge the Red Baron directly.

At 10:18 on the morning of 22 April, Ball led five S.E.5s out for their first active patrol. Although Ball pursued an Albatros two-seater and fired off three drums of ammunition from the Lewis gun the enemy machine got away. The following morning Ball took off alone in his Nieuport and at 06:45 he dived on a pair of two-seat Albatroses (or, in period airmen's parlance, 'Albatri'), sending one down in flames for 56 Squadron's first victory. Minutes later he attacked another two-seat Albatros and overshot, the enemy pilot instead raking the Nieuport with bullets which put the little French machine out of action for nearly a week.

A little more than three hours after this narrow escape, Ball took off alone in his red-nosed S.E.5 A4850, attacking another two-seat Albatros but suffering a jammed Lewis gun, forcing him to land at Le Hameau for repairs, rearming and refuelling. An hour later he dived upon a patrol of five Albatros scouts and shot their leader down in flames. The four remaining aircraft swarmed around Ball, but he used the S.E.5's inherent strength and diving speed to leave them furiously impotent in his wake.

Ball's confidence in the S.E.5 grew, and so too did that of the squadron. Lieutenants Barlow, Crowe and Kay became the first men besides Ball to score a victory for 56 Squadron when they shared in the destruction of another two-seater. Soon both two-seaters and the dreaded Albatros single-seaters were beginning to fall under the guns of the S.E.5s. Barely a week after going into battle, spirits were so high that Crowe took the opportunity to dive down upon Douai airfield, home of Manfred von Richthofen's *Jasta* 11, to take a look at the lair of the 'Red Baron', thumbing his nose at the superiority of the Albatros.

On 30 April the squadron suffered its first loss when Maurice Kay was cornered by two

LEFT **Ball, who always chose to fly bareheaded, ready for the off in A4580.** (Getty Images)

Albatroses and sent spinning down to crash in flames. The performance of the S.E.5s was generally strong but there were too many gun stoppages for comfort, being blamed on a combination of poor-quality ammunition and faults with the Constantinesco interrupter gear.

Despite these problems 56 Squadron was performing well and in a period of 14 frenetic days – of which three were completely washed out by poor weather – Albert Ball put in claims for 13 German aeroplanes. The cost to Ball was considerable, for he was in many ways fighting in an environment very much different to that in which he had shot to prominence the previous year. The intensity of the air battles had been magnified many times since then, and he was confronting an enemy who flew with a heavy tactical advantage.

Increasingly, the German scouts flew as a unit of between one and four full *Jagdstaffeln*, up to 40 aircraft at a time, against which a lone hunter such as Ball was living on borrowed time. He took exceptional risks, as evidenced when time and again he returned to Vert Galant with his aircraft shot to pieces around him. The innate strength of the S.E.5 and its rugged construction may have limited its aerobatic prowess, but Ball had good reason to be thankful for its yeoman-like build.

Ball had played a captain's innings and delivered all that could have been hoped of him but on the evening of 7 May his luck ran out leading an 11-strong formation of S.E.5s on patrol, crossing the lines at 7,000ft in the direction of Cambrai. Bad weather was rolling in and, in anticipation of a day of no flying to follow, the sky was full of observation aeroplanes trying to capture a final picture of the situation on the ground, and predatory scouts seeking opportunities to stop them.

In these conditions the 56 Squadron formation broke apart and its pilots found themselves embroiled in numerous combats. Crowe, flying S.E.5 A4860, was one of several pilots to find himself alone and under attack, his goggles being shot off before he used the

ABOVE Brave to the last: the windscreen taken from Albert Ball's 'spare' S.E.5, A8898, after he had flown head-on to attack an Albatros on 6 May 1917 – such risk-taking was a sign that he should not have been at the Front. *(Author)*

LEFT Ball sits in S.E.5a A8907 with the revised wings fitted, delivered to 56 Squadron on the morning of 7 May 1917. *(Aviation Images)*

39

THE S.E.5 STORY

RIGHT **Albert Ball Sr bought the field in which his son fell and erected markers where the nose and tail of the aeroplane lay. One still remains.** *(Author)*

S.E.5's superior dive to get away. Climbing hard to get back into the fray, he found another lone S.E.5 and discovered it was Ball, flying his red-nosed A4850, who fired two red flares as the signal to attack and led Crowe down through the cloud to pounce on a lone Albatros scout.

Both S.E.5s fired at the Albatros but a whirling dogfight broke out and Crowe lost sight of the other two aeroplanes as they disappeared into a wall of cloud. Minutes later, Ball's S.E.5 dropped out of the bottom of the cloud over the village of Annœullin, inverted and in a shallow dive with its engine off. At an altitude of just 200ft there was no prospect of rescuing the situation and the S.E.5 hit the ground, causing Ball terrible injuries from which he died just moments after his body was pulled from the wreckage.

In total six of the eleven S.E.5s failed to return from Albert Ball's last flight. Crowe and Rhys Davids crash-landed their severely damaged aeroplanes behind the British lines without injury. Leach and Meintjes had both crashed and were wounded. Ball and Chatworth-Musters were dead. It was a savage blow to the confidence of the squadron, among whom a number of men chose to blame the S.E.5.

The hard truth, however, was that the squadron had yet to adapt to the realities of aerial fighting in 1917. Individual brilliance had been overpowered by effective formations of fighters finding a tactical advantage before launching a unified attack. It was a cold and efficient way of fighting that Ball could never have stood for – but at which the S.E.5a would soon prove to be perfectly suited as it started to arrive in greater numbers. A different kind of war would now be fought – requiring no less courage from individual pilots than it ever did, but relying on effective teamwork to deliver success.

Mass production

Throughout April and May 1917 the third and final S.E.5 prototype, A4563, was slowly but surely upgraded from the original specification to the latest, refining the modifications made

BELOW **Workers celebrate the construction of the 1,000th S.E.5a at Vickers' Weybridge factory, Brooklands.** *(Brooklands Museum)*

by 56 Squadron in the field. Among the many changes to her specification were the shorter-span S.E.5a wings, the revised upper centre section, the lengthened Foster mount, the pilot's headrest and fairing, the simplified and lightened cockpit details, the new top fuselage decking with a small windscreen and the long SPAD-type exhausts. She was also fitted with the new 200hp Hispano-Suiza engine, driving a four-bladed propeller through a 24:41 reduction gear. Pilot-operated shutters were added to the enlarged radiator in order to maintain optimum temperatures for longer, and this third prototype became in effect the benchmark for all production models to follow.

At Farnborough the construction of a second short-run production batch of 50 airframes, serials A8898 to A8947, had been ordered in December 1916. These aircraft were built with the shorter-span S.E.5a wings and featured adjustable shutters over the top half of the radiator to try and maintain engine temperature at altitude. All of these Farnborough S.E.5s retained the 'greenhouse' cockpit canopy and armour-plated adjustable seat, but while most were fitted with the original 150hp direct-drive engine, 19 airframes were fitted with 200hp Hispano-Suizas built at factories in France and at the Wolseley factory in Birmingham. The first new machines reached 56 Squadron on 7 May and the last was delivered to the Royal Flying Corps by the end of June.

ABOVE Then and now: the grass area to the right of this shot is where the original Royal Aircraft Factory buildings, workshops and hangars stood. *(Author/Imperial War Museum)*

BELOW Then and now: the Martinsyde factory became the Lion paper works and is now a retail park. *(Historic England/Author)*

ABOVE Then and now: after many years with British Aerospace, the Vickers factory at Brooklands made way for a landscaped business park. *(Historic England/Author)*

BELOW Then and now: the roundabout marks the junction of Lickey Road and the A38, with the aircraft factory and airfield now a residential and retail area. *(Historic England/Author)*

By that stage volume manufacturing of the S.E.5a had already begun. On 1 February the Martinsyde company received the first volume order, number 87/A/1616, for 200 aeroplanes to be built at its factory in Woking. On 6 April, the day that 56 Squadron flew out to France, Vickers received contract number 87/A/1627 for 200 aircraft (serials B501 to B700) to be built in its factory at Brooklands racetrack.

These two factories lay less than five miles apart and both were within easy reach of Farnborough, making logistics significantly easier. Managing the mass production of weaponry became an increasingly important consideration for aircraft production as shortages and delays in materials combined with an increasingly restless workforce. The material shortages were largely down to the effectiveness of the unrestricted U-boat campaign that the German Navy launched in January 1917. The target put forward by Admiral von Holtzendorff was to sink 600,000 tons of shipping each month. German intelligence suggested that if merchant shipping was sunk at such a rate, Britain would be forced to sue for peace within six months.

The campaign was launched with 46 U-boats in the High Seas Fleet (23 in Flanders and 23 in the Mediterranean) supported by ten in the Baltic and three based at Constantinople. The commitment to this campaign also launched a fresh round of U-boat construction, ensuring that at least 120 submarines would be available for the rest of 1917. In February 1917 nearly 500,000 tons of British merchant shipping was sunk, with a similar figure being reached in March. A staggering 860,000 tons was sunk in April, averaging 13 ships per day, and the campaign rolled onward with 600,000 tons being sunk in May and 700,000 in June.

The supplies most badly affected by the U-boat campaign were of wood for the construction of airframes. This was Douglas fir and Sitka spruce that was sourced from the forests of British Columbia, Oregon and Washington – their timber being the ideal combination of strength, weight and durability. Few trees indigenous to Britain or her colonies could replicate the performance of these North American woods in aeroplane production, and even these required very careful handling indeed.

In perfect conditions trees should be felled in winter, when they are mature and when the sap is at rest, to minimise the warping and twisting caused as it dries. In order to deliver the torsional strength needed, the wood also needed to be 'rift sawn' parallel to its thickness – neither the cheapest nor the most efficient way of cutting wood. It must then be seasoned – dried out – to a very specific degree where 15% of the timber's natural moisture remains. Wood that was too dry would be too brittle and wood that was too moist would warp and lose strength. It was a true juggling act.

It was therefore a grave threat to aeroplane production that, as the demand for these woods increased, so the available supplies were cut drastically by the U-boat campaign. A rise in the incidence of timber that was too young, badly seasoned and badly cut began to find its way into the supply chain. At best this wood got rejected and caused delays in production. At worst it would be deemed 'close enough' and ended with the catastrophic failure of a wing section at 15,000ft.

Nor was the delivery of raw materials the only headache in the aircraft industry in 1917. Even if all the required supplies reached the factories, there was still the workforce to contend with. As workers grew hungrier and more hard pressed,

ABOVE Then and now: behind the façade of a modern retail park, hints of the Vickers Crayford factory still remain.
(Historic England/Author)

BELOW Then and now: the Air Navigation Company factory in Addlestone took on many and varied uses before being pulled down for a business park.
(Historic England/Author)

ABOVE **Then and now: most of the Wolseley factory floor remains in Adderley Park, Birmingham, where it's used as a truck park and recycling dump, but only a handful of buildings still stand.**
(Historic England/Author)

and as the processes of manufacturing took a toll on their health, they grew increasingly militant. They started to down tools over the food and coal shortages in Britain and over the wrongful dismissal of their shop stewards, at a cost of 281,600 days' production. Further down the supply chain, a steel strike in Sheffield created a shortage of crankshafts and airframe components and, at various times, the sheet metal workers and the woodworkers came out over pay and conditions.

Throughout 1917 and into 1918 it was quite common to see strike action take more than 50,000 workers away from their posts. In addition alcoholism remained a major bugbear amongst the workforce, despite the introduction of restrictions on the opening hours for licensed premises to lunch (12:00 to 14:00) and later to supper (18:30 to 21:30). When problems continued a 'No Treating Order' was brought in, banning the purchase of rounds of drinks, and a drastic increase in taxation of alcohol saw prices rise five-fold from 1914 to 1918.

Alcohol was not the only issue confronting factory foremen in 1917. A much smaller but no less problematic minority preferred to self-medicate using cocaine or opium, relatively mild restrictions on the ownership and use of psychoactive drugs only coming into force in 1916, and the sale of such drugs in 'medical kits' being continued throughout the war.

Production of the S.E.5a nevertheless continued to escalate through 1917–18 despite the many and varied obstacles to be overcome.

Alongside Vickers at Brooklands and Martinsyde in Woking, new contracts were placed with the Air Navigation Company at Addlestone in Surrey, with Vickers at its Crayford works in East London, with Wolseley at its factory in Adderley Park, Birmingham, and with the Austin Motor Company.

Austin's dream of producing the Austin-Ball scout did not long outlive Albert Ball himself. The prototype Austin-Ball A.F.B.1 carrying serial number B9909 was completed on 22 May 1917 and sent to the evaluation facility at Martlesham Heath a few days later. Here it was flown for a total of 27 hours and 25 minutes, and while it showed a significantly improved increase in climb, speed and ceiling over a standard S.E.5a, these virtues were only achieved at a cost of poor endurance and turning ability.

The design was not without promise but was not deemed to be of sufficient value to derail the S.E.5a. It is interesting to note, however, that many of the design features of the A.F.B.1 did eventually make their way to the Front in the design of the Hispano-engined Sopwith 5.F1 Dolphin. In fact, a late development of the A.F.B.1 at Martlesham was the trial of a set of two-bay wings staggered backwards that looked uncommonly similar to those of the Dolphin – which became arguably the best Hispano-engined fighter of the war.

With no small amount of irony, however, Austin's vast production facilities at Longbridge were eventually put to work in building the S.E.5a. In the end no other factory came close

LEFT The Austin-Ball A.F.B.1 prototype showed insufficient promise to derail production of the S.E.5a and was quietly forgotten.
(Imperial War Museum)

RIGHT Sharing many similarities with the Austin design – which was also fitted with rear-staggered wings under trial – the Sopwith 5.F1 Dolphin was the best Hispano-engined fighter of the war. *(Author)*

to building as many examples of the type after Austin's initial order for 350 aeroplanes swelled to a total of 1,550. The delivery schedule began at an agreed one aeroplane per day, rising to a peak of 30 per week, a record being set when 63 were built in the first week of June 1918.

One of the great advantages of Austin's modern and purpose-built facility was its doping room. The treatment of an aeroplane's linen skin involved the application of six coats of dope – a varnish made of acetone, benzene and tetrachloroethane dissolved in cellulose – which waterproofed and protected the skin as well as pulling it taut to add strength and streamline the structure. The downside of dope was that it was a deadly poison giving off fumes that attacked the lungs, liver and kidneys of anyone exposed to it. Austin therefore built a fully ventilated and temperature-controlled doping facility at Longbridge – not all factory workers would be so lucky.

Each of the contracted factories would receive detailed and fastidious drawings for S.E.5 components from the Royal Aircraft

RIGHT A young worker applying dope to an S.E.5a at Austin's Longbridge factory in 1918.
(Imperial War Museum)

45

THE S.E.5 STORY

Factory to ensure uniformity, fit and finish of their output. The National Archive in Kew holds no fewer than 425 individual documents, some running at up to more than ten pages, detailing every wooden, wire and metal component in a single aeroplane. This approach worked, and virtually eradicated the sorts of quality issues and delays that other types were subject to when built under contract.

If the German naval blockade and outbreaks of workplace delinquency weren't sufficient grounds for delay, the Royal Aircraft Factory itself also shouldered some responsibility. Tinkering with the design of the S.E.5a continued long after contracts were in place for volume production – indeed, Sir Herbert Austin wrote a letter of complaint to the Department of Aeronautical Supplies detailing 100 such changes in the period from June to December 1917, concluding that 'today we cannot foresee what is likely to happen at the end of next week'. Further compounding the problems confronting the factories were the endless delays in the supply of Hispano-Suiza engines, detailed in Chapter Three.

Yet despite every obstacle, production of the S.E.5a saw 828 aeroplanes completed in 1917 and 4,377 completed in 1918. In total just over 2,900 S.E.5s of all types were delivered before the Armistice, of which 1,999 aeroplanes were dispatched to France at the disposal of the RFC/RAF, the Australian Flying Corps and United States Army Air Service; 172 more went to the Middle East Brigade and 74 seconded to Home Defence duties.

ABOVE AND BELOW Then and now: workers at the Austin factory in Longbridge and the site of their workplace today. *(Author/Imperial War Museum)*

ABOVE Fuselages under construction in the Vickers Weybridge factory at Brooklands. *(Brooklands Museum)*

BELOW One week's work: completed S.E.5a airframes stand on the start line at Brooklands, ready for onward transportation. *(Brooklands Museum)*

S.E.5/S.E.5A PRODUCTION BATCHES

Serial run	Factory
A4561–A4563 (3 S.E.5/5a prototypes)	Royal Aircraft Factory, Farnborough
A4845–A4868 (24 S.E.5)	Royal Aircraft Factory, Farnborough
A8898–A8947 (50 S.E.5a)	Royal Aircraft Factory, Farnborough
B1–B200 (200 S.E.5a)	Martinsyde Ltd, Woking and Brooklands
B501–B700 (200 S.E.5a)	Vickers Ltd, Brooklands
B4851–B4900 (50 S.E.5a)	Royal Aircraft Factory, Farnborough
B8231–B8580 (350 S.E.5a)	Austin Motor Company, Longbridge
C1051–C1150 (100 S.E.5a)	Royal Aircraft Factory, Farnborough
C1751–C1950 (200 S.E.5a)	Air Navigation Company, Addlestone
C5301–C5450 (150 S.E.5a)	Vickers Ltd, Crayford
C6351–C6850 (500 S.E.5a)	Wolseley Motors, Adderley Park
C8861–C9310 (540 S.E.5a)	Austin Motor Company, Longbridge
C9486–C9635 (150 S.E.5a)	Vickers Ltd, Brooklands
D201–D300 (100 S.E.5a)	Vickers Ltd, Brooklands
D301–D450 (150 S.E.5a)	Vickers Ltd, Crayford
D3426–D3575 (150 S.E.5a)	Vickers Ltd, Brooklands
D3911– D4011 (100 S.E.5a)	Martinsyde Ltd, Woking and Brooklands
D6851–D7000 (150 S.E.5a)	Wolseley Motors, Adderley Park
D7001–D7025 (25 S.E.5a)	Royal Aircraft Factory, Farnborough
D8431–D8580 (150 S.E.5a)	Vickers Ltd, Crayford
E1251–E1400 (150 S.E.5a)	Vickers Ltd, Crayford
E3154–E3253 (100 S.E.5a)	Martinsyde Ltd, Woking and Brooklands
E3904–E4103 (200 S.E.5a)	Vickers Ltd, Brooklands
E5837–E5936 (100 S.E.5a)	Austin Motor Company, Longbridge
E5937–E6036 (100 S.E.5a)	Air Navigation Company, Addlestone
F551–F615 (65 S.E.5a)	Vickers Ltd, Crayford
F851–F950 (100 S.E.5a)	Wolseley Motors, Adderley Park
F5248–F5348 (100 S.E.5a)	Martinsyde Ltd, Woking and Brooklands
F5449–F5698 (200 S.E.5a)	Vickers Ltd, Brooklands
F7751–F7782 (32 S.E.5a)	Wolseley Motors, Adderley Park
F7951–F8200 (250 S.E.5a)	Austin Motor Company, Longbridge
F8946–F9145 (200 S.E.5a)	Vickers Ltd, Brooklands
H634–H711 (77 S.E.5a)	Air Navigation Company, Addlestone

Additional aeroplanes were built from salvaged airframes; this list includes only newly-built machines.

With a final contract being placed with the Curtiss Aeroplane and Motor Company in Buffalo, New York, adding 57 more, the total production of S.E.5 and S.E.5a numbered 5,205 aeroplanes. The cost (less its guns, instruments and engine) was £1,063 10s – about £111,700 today. The 200hp Hispano-Suiza engine was an additional £1,004 (£105,400 today), with the equivalent Wolseley Viper costing £814 (£85,500).

Home Defence and the Royal Air Force

The overwhelming majority of S.E.5s to see service did so on the Western Front, but the type was active in all theatres throughout the final 18 months of the Great War. Its first deployment away from France came in July 1917 after the first daylight raids on London had been carried out by the Gotha G.IV bombers of *Kagohl* 3.

In its first raid on Britain the *England Geschwader* had focused its efforts on the Kentish port town of Folkestone, and were left almost completely unmolested by defences that included B.E.2 and B.E.12 aeroplanes scrambled from the airfields at Manston, Rochford, Stow Maries and Westgate to intercept them. The devastation wrought on the town's vulnerable streets was unprecedented and bloody.

When they returned on 13 June, the bombers made for their ultimate target: London. In total 17 bombers reached the British capital from 22 that had set out from their airfield at Gontrode in Belgium, with one Gotha making a diversionary raid on Margate. They carried half their maximum payload, mainly consisting of 12½kg and 50kg bombs, and approached the city from the north, crossing Epping Forest and heading for the docks and industrial east of the city.

While Londoners watched on entranced by the spectacle – most believing that these were friendly machines in the sky overhead – the bombs began to rain down on Stoke

LEFT Londoners show off their improvised bomb shelter, 1917. *(Getty/Topical Press Agency)*

Newington, Liverpool Street railway station, Bethnal Green, the Royal Albert Docks, Barking, East Ham, Stratford, Islington and Aldgate. The most savage blow was struck by a single 50kg bomb that drove down into the Upper North Street School in Poplar. Although the bomb was split in half upon impact the detonation was catastrophic, killing 18 children and seriously injuring 33 more, with scores more children among the walking wounded. In total 594 people were killed or severely injured.

The impact upon the British psyche – and that of London in particular – was profound and unnerving. In the East End, businesses owned and run by people with Germanic-sounding names were hounded out, as were almost any traders and families of foreign extraction. There was widespread violence and looting that held all the hallmarks of open rebellion in the streets, and public support for the war was stretched to breaking point.

The British government, the Royal Flying Corps and the Admiralty had been repeatedly warned that its defences against such an attack were woefully inadequate. As part of the frantic public relations exercise that was required to restore order, it was decided to bring a front-line squadron back to defend London as a stopgap measure while work began feverishly to evolve solutions to the Gotha threat. The squadron selected was 56 Squadron, with its S.E.5s.

General Trenchard and Field Marshal Haig were incensed at the request. The Battle of Arras was still being fought and preparations were well advanced to strike out again with

ABOVE A Gotha G.IV bomber. Formations of the *England Geschwader* wrought havoc upon London and the south-east of England, ultimately prompting the formation of the Royal Air Force. *(Imperial War Museum)*

BELOW Schoolgirls lay flowers on the grave of another child, victim of the Folkestone raid of 25 May 1917. *(Getty/Topical Images)*

LEFT S.E.5a of Lieutenant K. Muspratt, 56 Squadron, basks in the sunshine at RAF Bekesbourne, June 1917.
(Imperial War Museum)

ABOVE Bekesbourne aerodrome as it looks today. A large memorial stone dedicated to its role in the defence of London now stands next to the houses. *(Author)*

BELOW Today known as London Southend Airport, Rochford was a Home Defence airfield from 1915 until 1920, recommissioned in 1939 and playing a vital role in the Battle of Britain and D-Day. *(London Southend Airport)*

BELOW RIGHT The Hotel Cecil was home to the Air Board, and was nicknamed 'Bolo House' for its poisonous atmosphere. *(Author)*

a new offensive in Flanders: the third Battle of Ypres. Yet they could offer little argument against the turmoil in the streets and reluctantly sent 56 Squadron back, as much for the purposes of propaganda as for their contribution to warding off the marauding bombers. The 12 pilots chosen to fly back were 'elated', in the words of Cecil Lewis, who was among the detachment. After their gruelling first few weeks in the line of fire in France, with the loss of Albert Ball chief among their concerns, the prospect of defending London appeared to be light relief, and was treated as such.

The squadron was to be based at Bekesbourne airfield in Kent, with 'B' Flight later transferring to Rochford – today known as London Southend Airport – to cover both sides of the Thames Estuary. The pilots remembered this period fondly for its many dinner dances and other social occasions on the airfield. In the event, however, weather conditions and serviceability issues kept the Gothas grounded and no raids were launched against London before 56 Squadron returned to the front line on 7 July – the very same day that the next Gotha raid took place.

In the rush to build a more effective long-term system of defence against air raids, it was clear that much greater cooperation was needed between the factions of Army and Navy. In a governmental report commissioned into the organisation of the air war as a whole, brought about by the failure to prevent air raids on London, General Jan Smuts recorded that the rivalry between the two services was disastrous.

In his report of 17 August 1917, Smuts believed that the British should be able to launch strategic aerial bombing attacks on enemy cities in the same way as the Germans. In addition to this target, and to improve the standard of air defence for London as well as better utilising both Royal Flying Corps and Royal Naval Air Service resources in France, he recommended a new air service be formed that would be on a level with the Army and Royal Navy – as well as ending the toxic inter-service rivalries that at times had adversely affected aircraft procurement. (The Air Board, presiding over all matters of aviation, was housed in the Hotel Cecil on the Strand, a short walk from both the War Office and the Admiralty. Such was the toxic atmosphere of inter-service antagonism in the building that it became known as Bolo House – named after the celebrated French traitor, Bolo Pasha.)

The Royal Air Force was finally formed as an entity in its own right on 1 April 1918. In the meantime, construction of an 'operations room' in which incoming air raids could be tracked and defending fighters launched and plotted was completed in the basement of the Hotel Cecil as one of a number of improvements to air raid warning and rapid response techniques.

The S.E.5 was originally considered to be a potential air-defence fighter to replace the slow and under-equipped Sopwith Pups and B.E.2/B.E.12 types that were previously used to defend London from attack. In January 1918, 61 Squadron was equipped with S.E.5s for dedicated Home Defence duties, followed by 143 Squadron the following month. By that time the Gothas had switched to night-time raids and the S.E. proved less suited to the role, offering its pilots less forward visibility for night-time landings and its engines – both the Hispano and Wolseley Viper – requiring too long to warm up before being scrambled to intercept an incoming raid. In the end they were replaced by Sopwith Camels.

Service in foreign fields

As well as the chill and wet of Northern Europe, the S.E.5 went to war in much hotter climes. The desert between Egypt and Palestine was a harsh environment for any turn-of-the-century machine, and aeroplanes were particularly vulnerable. Nevertheless, when the Egyptian Expeditionary Force broke out of Gaza in the spring of 1917 a new theatre for aerial warfare was soon established.

Throughout October 1918, 111 and 145 Squadrons were equipped with S.E.5a aircraft primarily for ground strafing duties and escort work, including bombing missions. Their heaviest workload came during the final push towards Damascus, when they were heavily engaged in hitting the fleeing Turkish Army and tackling points of resistance.

The S.E.5 had already been tested in the desert by 72 Squadron, operating from Samarra on the banks of the Tigris in Mesopotamia. From here, the fighters would be worked primarily in ground-attack roles as they pressed the retreating Turks towards the Persian border. Little aerial opposition was encountered, with the climate and local tribesmen proving to be the greatest threat to life and limb.

In sharp contrast to the relatively empty skies over Arabia, the campaign in Macedonia was considerably busier for fighter pilots. A heavy toll was taken on the outdated machinery used by the Royal Flying Corps in 1917, with the result that S.E.5as were dispatched in January 1918 to stem the flow and meet the primarily German opposition on equal terms. Despite frequent parts shortages, the conflict was resolved with the defeat of Bulgaria in September 1918.

ABOVE Cecil Lewis with his S.E.5a at Rochford modified for night flying with flame-damping exhaust mufflers and a disruptive camouflage of grey squares. *(RAF Museum)*

BELOW Hispano-engined S.E.5a of 111 Squadron in Palestine, October 1918. *(Getty/Imperial War Museum)*

THE S.E.5 STORY

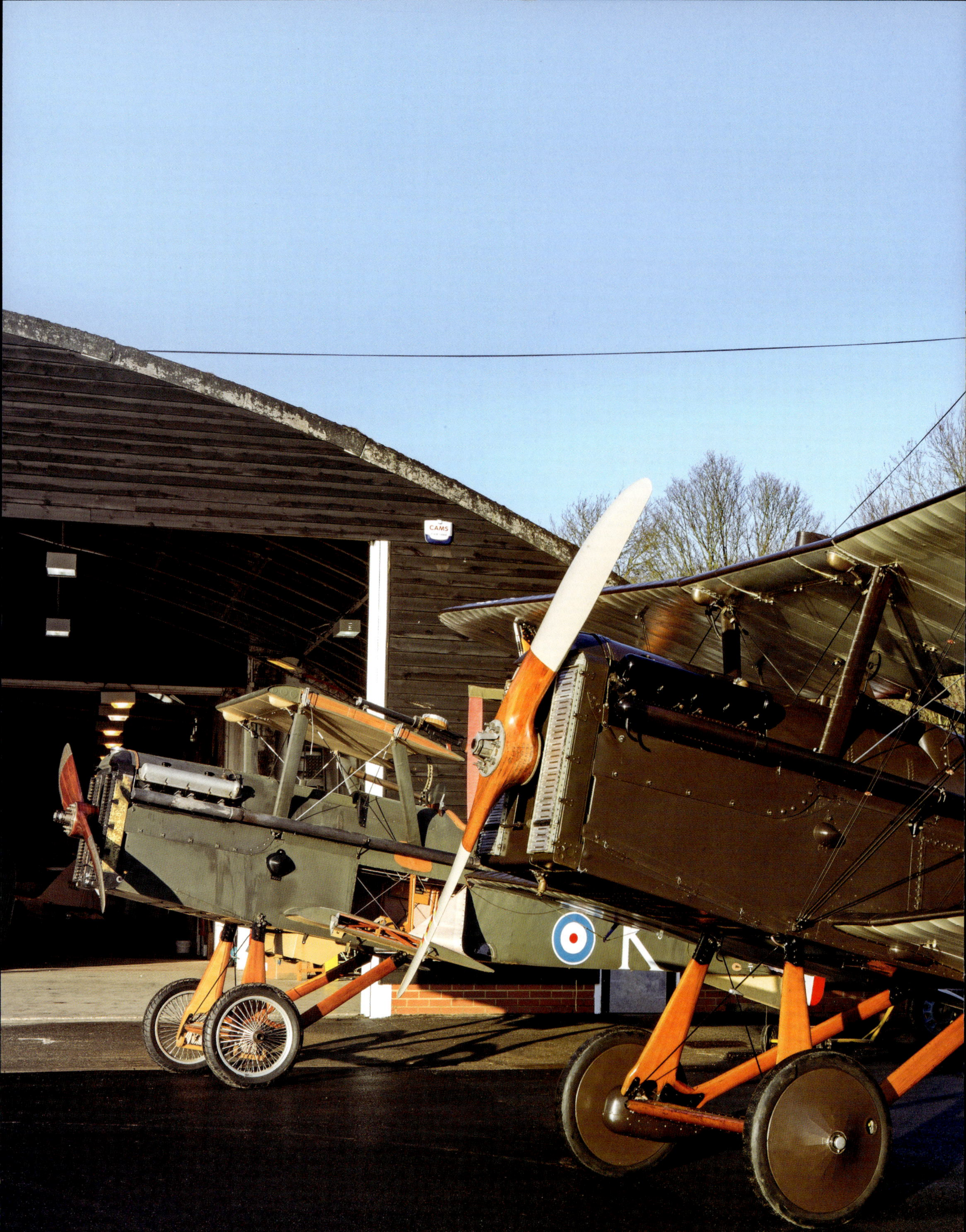
CAMS

Chapter Two

Restore to flight

A century after the type went into service and 90 years since the majority of survivors faded away, the likelihood of an original and previously unseen Royal Aircraft Factory S.E.5 undergoing restoration to flying status is, it must be admitted, an infinitesimally small one. With just eight original examples of all types known in existence, there is much less possibility of any other 'lost' aeroplanes coming to light than might be the case with a later Spitfire, or even a Hawker Hurricane.

OPPOSITE The Shuttleworth Collection's G-EBIA/F-904 stands next to an authentic recreation S.E.5a as it's prepared for flying duties in the workshop at Old Warden. *(Darren Harbar)*

ABOVE Recreations that are authentic in every detail, such as those built by the Vintage Aviator Limited, cannot be considered 'replicas' in the eyes of the experts. *(Phil Makanna)*

Components of an airframe that was a wooden structure, bound together using cheap mild steel and covered in linen are not likely to have been squirreled away in the same way as those of metal aeroplanes. They will have been discarded or else used for firewood or to build an allotment shed rather than preserved as pieces of timber and tarpaulin cloth.

A much more likely increase in the active population of S.E.5s around the world would therefore come from an authentic reproduction – a 'tool-room copy', if you prefer – of which there are already several fine examples in existence. It has been proven that a brand new S.E.5 can be built that is all-but indistinguishable from its illustrious ancestor throughout the airframe, which is why the majority of the focus in this chapter unashamedly concentrates on these recreations.

The total production of the Hispano-Suiza 'Monobloc' V8 engine reached 49,000 examples, of which many remain both in use and on static display. Thanks to the dedication of experts such as the Vintage Aviator Limited, it is entirely conceivable that more enthusiasts may choose to build or commission the build of authentic reproduction aeroplanes with an original engine – which meets with the approval of Rob Millinship, one of the longest-serving pilots at the Shuttleworth Collection:

'They produce absolutely beautiful new-build aeroplanes and they're not replicas – I get very cross when people call them replicas. If they were replicas, then my Pitts Special is a replica because I built it in my shed!' Rob laughed. 'They'd be replicas if they had Lycoming engines and were half the size and they'd got welded steel tube fuselages. The thing is that parts get worn and replaced, and nobody wants to be roaring round on too much 100-year-old metal – or even 70-year-old metal. Yet while a lot of World War One aeroplanes get called replicas, there's not one replica Spitfire flying – they're all original!'

LEFT A meticulously researched Bristol Scout, complete with original engine and components, coming in to land at Stow Maries Great War Aerodrome. *(Author)*

The only reservation that a pilot with significant experience of aeroplanes dating from World War One would raise is over their usefulness and ultimately their role in our modern safety-conscious society. In the pioneering days of flight, it was only to be expected that problems might cause an aeroplane to force land in a field, but in 2017 the aviation world is a vastly different place, with considerably different expectations among the public, insurance companies and other associated arbiters of modern mores.

'The problem is that all of these aeroplanes, both new-build and original, are as unreliable now as they were in 1916–17,' Millinship added. 'That's the big problem, because people think that because they're new-build aeroplanes they can be operated like a Cessna, and they can't. The engines are just as useless as they were a hundred years ago!'

The question of originality is one that dominates all historic vehicles in use on land, sea and air. Parts need replacing, structures require work doing through accident or design, thus reducing the originality of the vehicle with every repair. Yet the value of these vehicles – be it a classic Ferrari, a Riva powerboat, a Spitfire or an S.E.5 – is increasing dramatically each and every year. Billions of dollars are being invested in the sure and certain knowledge that they are increasing in value faster than almost any other asset in the world, be it art, property or gold.

'Values certainly aren't going down,' said Richard Grace, who has restored aeroplanes such as a rare Seafire Mk III and an Eberhart SE-5E. 'There's a certain accessibility level that will always cap the market, in my opinion, in that it will only be capped in relation to the value compared with cars, because you can't just buy an aeroplane, get in it and go flying, unfortunately. But definitely the right aeroplanes are going up in value all the time, "not the right" aeroplanes aren't.'

Provenance is the decisive factor in placing the value on any of these vehicles. Passion is the other: the passion of owners wishing to own and operate them and the passion of the general public to see them in action and to marvel at what they are and what they stand for. At events such as the dedicated flying displays held at Old Warden and Stow Maries in the UK, at Omaka and Masterton in New Zealand and Old Rhinebeck in the USA, as well as at prestige airshows and events like the Goodwood Revival worldwide, the sight and sound of genuine World War One technology is a genuine show-stopper.

Long may there be a ready supply of enthusiastic owners and dedicated engineers to ensure that these delights remain available for many generations to come.

ABOVE An Albatros under brooding skies at Stow Maries – a sight made possible by recreating long-lost designs and manufacturing techniques. *(Author)*

RIGHT Each year more vintage aeroplanes return to the sky – including a dramatic increase in the Hawker Hurricane population – and are seen as a shrewd investment. *(Shutterstock)*

55

RESTORE TO FLIGHT

ABOVE **Shuttleworth's S.E.5a stands ready at dawn alongside a Model 'T' Ford, one of the Collection's veteran vehicles.** *(Author)*

Shuttleworth's original masterpiece

Only one genuine S.E.5a has ever been restored to flight, this being F-904, civilian registration G-EBIA, which belongs within the Shuttleworth Collection and has been based at Old Warden Aerodrome for the last 40 years.

Relatively recent research undertaken by the Shuttleworth Collection has revealed that this aeroplane, built by Wolseley Motors at its Adderley Park factory in Birmingham, was issued to 84 Squadron in France early in November 1918. It was in action on 10 November, piloted by the squadron's commanding officer, Major C.E.M. Pickthorn MC, when he successfully destroyed a Fokker DVII in the vicinity of Chimay in Belgium.

RIGHT **The original reconstruction of F-904 took place at Farnborough in 1957–59.** *(Farnborough Air Sciences Trust)*

After the Armistice the aeroplane was stored and later disposed of, becoming one of 33 S.E.5as purchased by Major Jack Savage for his skywriting business (see Chapter Six) and was used for this purpose from 1924 until 1928, when it was put into store. In 1955 it was recovered from storage in the roof of the Armstrong-Whitworth flight shed at Baginton. It was in such a poor state that the restoration work would have been beyond the capabilities of the Old Warden team at that time, so the Royal Aircraft Establishment agreed to restore the aeroplane on behalf of the Shuttleworth Trust. Work began in 1957, and was undertaken by an array of voluntary workers: apprentices, enthusiasts and some 'old hands' – including craftsmen with long associations with the S.E.5 going back to the 1914–18 war. The work was completed by the end of 1959.

During the restoration the RAE installed an Hispano-Suiza engine in the aircraft which they sourced from the Science Museum, as they were unable to access a Wolseley Viper engine, which would have been originally fitted when it was built.

When the completed restoration was presented to the world on 4 August 1959, *Flight* magazine declared it to be something else entirely. Perhaps in error, its notice read: 'An S.E.5A replica built by R.A.E. apprentices made its first flight, at Farnborough on August 4, in the hands of A. Cdre. A.H. Wheeler.'

ABOVE Many of the 'apprentices' credited with rebuilding F-904 were men whose experience went back to when the aeroplane was first built. *(Farnborough Air Sciences Trust)*

BELOW Re-covering the wings with fresh Irish linen. *(Farnborough Air Sciences Trust)*

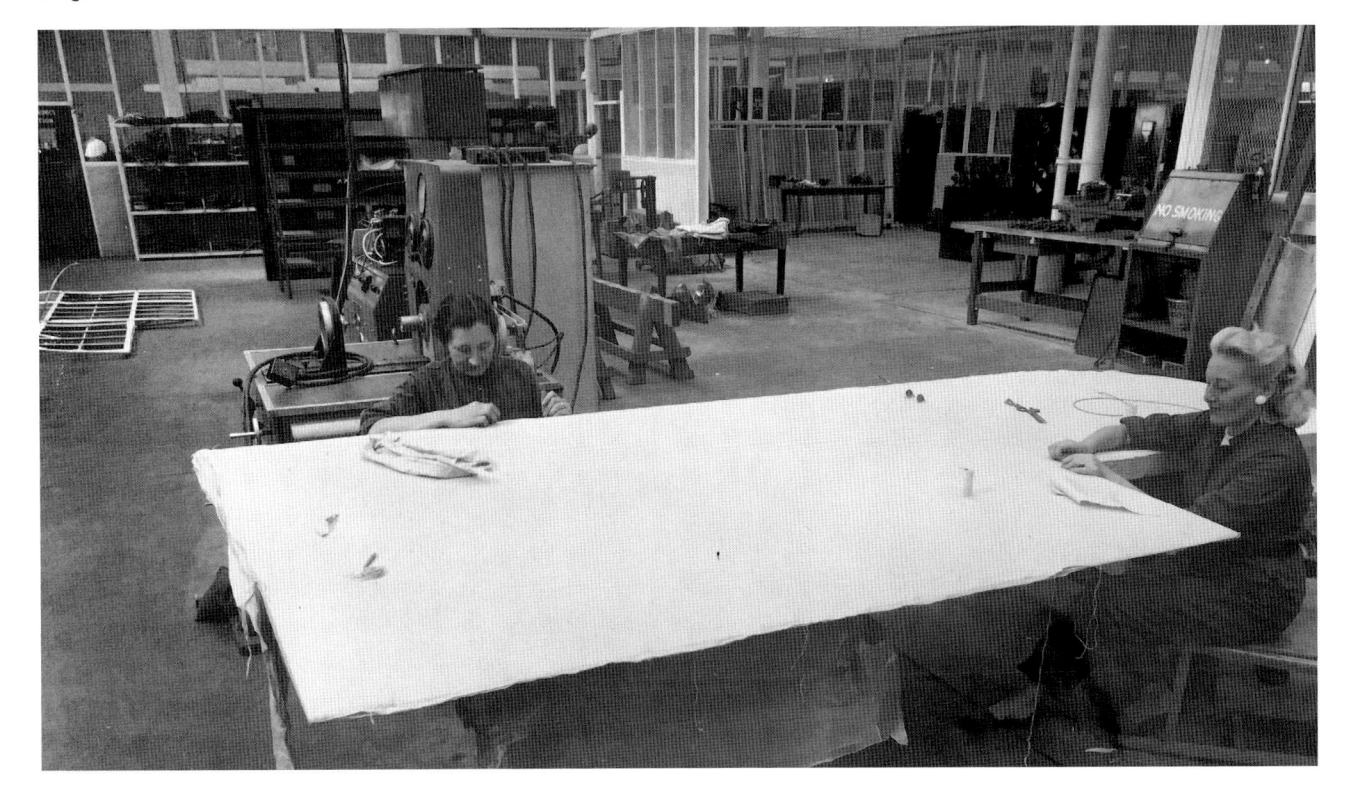

RIGHT The completed restoration breaks cover in 1959.
(Farnborough Air Sciences Trust)

LEFT Preparing for her maiden flight after restoration. Pilot Air Commodore Allen Wheeler owned a pair of S.E.5s in his youth and would later act as technical advisor to films such as *The Blue Max*. *(Farnborough Air Sciences Trust).*

By the early 1970s, F-904 had changed out of her original silver finish and been dressed with a much more appropriate colour scheme – that of an S.E.5a of 56 Squadron in 1917, with the famous blue and white wheel discs of 'B' Flight.

After 16 years of service, F-904 required a major overhaul when the crankshaft of her Hispano-Suiza engine sheared – a problem that would have been familiar to veterans of 1917–18. Once again she returned to Farnborough, by which time a Wolseley Viper engine had been sourced from the Science Museum and was made ready for installation. She then remained at Farnborough until 1977, when she returned to Old Warden, where she has remained ever since as the only genuine World War One aeroplane with combat history still flying in the world. Farnborough handed over its interests in the machine on 21 October 1992.

The ongoing career of F-904 in the front line of the Shuttleworth Collection is testament to the care with which she – like all the historic vehicles at Old Warden – is treated by the

LEFT Flying the colours of 56 Squadron, F-904 flies over the Royal Aircraft Establishment at Farnborough during the late 1970s.
(Farnborough Air Sciences Trust)

58
ROYAL AIRCRAFT FACTORY S.E.5 MANUAL

staff, volunteers and trustees. She was last given an extensive refurbishment in 2007, and more recently received her updated paintwork reflecting her origins on 84 Squadron, which she is likely to be carrying for the foreseeable future.

The return of an original

In the 1980s British airshows saw a second S.E.5 in the skies. There were even occasions when she visited F-904 at Old Warden to make a memorable pairing in the air – or, more often, on the ground, as her engine was not always particularly willing to get going to order!

She was not an S.E.5a but rather an SE-5E, one of 50 licence-built American versions of the type, which were originally built in the Austin factory at Longbridge before being shipped to the States, where they were significantly modified by the Eberhart Steel Products Company for the US Army Air Service. Fitted with plywood fuselage skins and 180hp direct-drive 'Wright-Hispano E' engines, the Eberhart SE-5E continued to serve until 1927, by which time the handful of aeroplanes not crashed or cannibalised were withdrawn and disposed of.

Airframe number 296, which had originally been given the serial B4863 at Austin's, was sold off and given the civil registration NC4488. She would reappear as one of the stars of Howard Hughes' epic movie *Hell's Angels*. Among the many illustrious names in her log and documentation, transatlantic record breaker Charles Lindberg, movie mogul Hughes and General Chuck Yeager stand out in particular. After her flying career was over the aeroplane was placed in the Wing and Wheels Museum in the USA, where she was discovered by celebrated British collector of historic cars and aircraft the Hon Patrick Lindsay.

The restoration to flying condition was undertaken by Tony Bianchi's Personal Plane Services operation at Booker airfield near High Wycombe, during which time it was converted back to something approaching S.E.5a specification with a linen skin on the fuselage, and given the registration G-BLXT. Paint and markings were applied to make it look like James McCudden's A4583 of 56 Squadron from late 1917, in which scheme it was subsequently displayed.

The untimely death of Pat Lindsay brought great sadness to the historic motor sport and aviation communities but did not curtail the SE-5E's flying career unduly. It was looked after by renowned aviator Henry Labouchere and then went to the Duxford-based Old Flying Machine Company, established by arguably the greatest display pilot in history, Ray Hanna.

'My brother Mark was instrumental in it happening, and he loved it,' remembered Sarah Hanna, who manages OFMC today. 'In the office we have a wonderful air-to-air picture of him flying it.'

Ownership of the SE-5E then passed to collector Doug Arnold, who jealously guarded a fleet of historic aircraft including numerous

ABOVE An Eberhart SE-5E in flight. *(USAF)*

BELOW The Hon Patrick Lindsay's SE-5E at Old Warden in the 1990s, wearing the colours of James McCudden's 56 Squadron aeroplane. *(Fotolibra)*

ABOVE Richard Grace has brought the remarkable SE-5E back to life with comparative technical ease. (Air Leasing)

Spitfires, Hawker Tempests and even a Lancaster bomber. When Arnold died in 1992 much of the collection disappeared into thin air, although the SE-5E was reportedly stored for many years inside a bunker at the former Greenham Common nuclear missile base. Under American ownership she was painted in the colours of the US Army Air Service but was never re-registered nor attempted to fly. Now, following her long hiatus, G-BLXT has returned to Britain and, still wearing its American markings, has been restored to flying condition by Richard Grace's Air Leasing operation at Sywell Airport in Northamptonshire.

'It didn't go missing for me at all, I knew where it was!' said Richard Grace, whose late father Nick shot to fame in the 1980s by restoring Spitfire Mk IX ML407, credited with the first air-to-air victory of the D-Day landings. Now Richard has followed in his father's illustrious footsteps and has been responsible for bringing a number of historically important types back to operational status.

'The S.E.5 just went off the radar when it was sold to a gentleman called Al Letcher and moved to America, but it never went on to the American register,' he said. 'It came back and sat in the nuclear bunker at Greenham Common for some time. A wooden aeroplane doesn't particularly mind a "not-bone-dry" environment. The story always goes that Al Letcher kept a paddling pool underneath it because he was worried about it drying out, but that's optimistic at best, I think!' Although G-BLXT was thus hidden away from view for many years, recommissioning it was a relatively straightforward job for experts in the field. 'It took more like two months – but that two months was over a two-year period,' Richard Grace added.

'We fairly swiftly figured out that the engine had some problems from being stored for some time and it was always a bit of a cantankerous engine when it was with the Hannas. So we knew that we had problems to solve there. So it was removed and taken to Paul Sharman at Vintech, who really is the maestro of engines of this ilk. He didn't go as deep into it as I think he went into it for PPS, when it was done for Patrick, so he inspected the bottom end which was in good shape, and it's really just had the top end and ancillaries overhauled. In doing that he found problems with magnetos, meshing and various types of thing that were mainly ignition and fuel related. There really is very little to go wrong. That's a real perk of the Hispano-Suiza – it's the simplest engine that I've ever seen anyway.'

Richard gave G-BLXT her maiden flight after restoration late in the afternoon of 21 October 2016. It is to be hoped that she becomes a regular performer at airshows in the 100th anniversary year of the type and for many years to come.

An Imperial Gift

Until relatively recently the number of airworthy Hawker Hurricanes worldwide could be counted on the fingers of one hand. The reason for this void in the international warbird community was that the skills required to construct a high-performance aeroplane from wood and linen had been lost. But one of the leading lights in regaining these lost arts was AJD Engineering – now known as Hawker Restorations. Small wonder, then, that it should be Hawker Restorations that took on a job of such complexity: recreating an S.E.5a from an assortment of original parts.

The basis for this build came from Australia and was one of the S.E.5a airframes sent out as part of the Imperial Gift programme, through which, in order to establish air forces in the British Dominions, the British government decided, in May 1919, to offer 100 aircraft each to Australia, New Zealand, South Africa, Canada and India. Additional aeroplanes would be donated in order to replace those presented by the efforts of local communities and individuals from the Dominions during the war. Only New Zealand initially refused the offer but subsequently accepted 33 airframes and sufficient engines to service them.

Each Dominion government was given a menu of pretty well every front-line fighter and bomber in service. Neither India nor New Zealand elected to accept the S.E.5 but Australia received 176 aeroplanes in total, including 35 S.E.5a airframes, together with 41 of the standard 200hp Wolseley Viper engines and one 180hp Viper. Subsequently South Africa received 22 S.E.5a airframes and 28 Wolseley Viper 200hp engines, while Canada received 12 airframes that were both S.E.5 and S.E.5a together with 16 of the 200hp Viper engines.

The Australian allocation was for S.E.5a serial numbers D369, D370, D371, C1916, C1917, E3169, E3170, E3171, D8471, D8473, D8474, D8475, D8476, D8477, D8480, D8482, D8486, D8488, D8490, D8491, D8495, B8567, C8994, C8995, C8996, F9106, F9107, F9110, F9113, F9119, F9122, F9131, F9143, F9144 and F9145. These were given Royal Australian Air Force serials A2-1 to A2-35 respectively. A2-2 was later converted to a two-seat trainer and re-serialled A2-36. Ten of the aeroplanes were never put together and were 'reduced to product' on 20 March 1928. These were A2-21 to A2-23, A2-27 and A2-29 to A2-34. The remainder were lost through natural wastage – *ie* written off in accidents – or subsequently 'destroyed by burning' or scrapped.

Hawker Restorations now has the most significant amount of components for its build from the remains of C8996, which was recorded as 'Components retained by Munitions Supply Board'. In 1992 she was rescued from the bush at Point Cook, which is where the Royal Australian Air Force Museum now resides. In its former guise as AJD Engineering, a recreation S.E.5a was built to order for the RAAF Museum and now stands in pride of place to represent the formation of the service.

While the completed replica travelled to Australia the remnants of C8996 made their way back to Hawker Engineering, where they formed the basis of a long-term project. Over time the rest of the components were gathered together. The engine now fitted was originally in an S.E.5a and had only run for 23 hours before being returned to England to be converted back to direct drive; it has remained unused ever since. The wings were found in Germany, having previously spent 50 years as partitions in a Norfolk chicken farm. There is evidence to show that they have been flown, and significant amounts of original fabric remain on two of them. The unused but original 1918 propeller was found in Edinburgh.

BELOW Replica of the Imperial Gift S.E.5a created by Hawker Restorations, which is now restoring the original aircraft. *(RAAF Museum)*

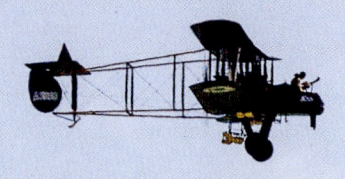

ABOVE **Two reproduction S.E.5as escort a reproduction F.E.2b in the skies over New Zealand.** *(Brian Harmer)*

BELOW **TVAL has now built five S.E.5a airframes, with three airworthy, one on permanent static display in the affiliated museum at Omaka and the fifth a restored original.** *(TVAL)*

Brand new S.E.5s from New Zealand

Those with a long-standing interest in Great War aviation will doubtless remember a time when thoughts of seeing most of the aeroplanes of that era in the sky would elicit a wistful sigh but not much else. How ponderous was a 'Quirk'? How terrifying was the front seat of an F.E.2b – particularly when standing up out of the cockpit to fire backwards over the upper wing?

The answer to these questions and many more besides have now been provided through the remarkable endeavours of the Vintage Aviator Limited. Thanks to TVAL, New Zealand has become the Jurassic Park of aeroplanes, where long-extinct species rise up off the runway on a regular basis, powered by the same engines that carried their illustrious ancestors into battle.

Utilising state-of-the-art computer technology has helped to ensure that the assemblies are identical to each other and able to fit more than one airframe. A great deal of time was then spent building suitable jigs for parts like ribs, elevators, ailerons, cockpit carlins, landing-gear legs and even entire wings. Bending and laminating was also needed to form parts like wingtip bows and elevator and aileron tips. A single part often required experimentation and study before it could successfully be produced. Potential pitfalls included checking how much 'overbending' was needed with the laminated wood components to end up with a part that matched the drawing exactly. Experiments on working with air-dried and kiln-dried timbers, and the properties of various types of glue, was all good data generated by the S.E.5a builds to go into future projects, and also provided a wealth of information that enabled TVAL to meet modern process standards.

Large pieces such as the interplane struts

were all hand-carved in 1917, but today can be cut much more rapidly and with greater precision by using a large CNC router which can then be hand finished. TVAL craftsman Murray Hunter said: 'Working with hand tools is a pleasure in itself, utilising skills that are largely gone in this day and age. First I made the profile shapes of the streamlined aerofoil struts at various points along the length of the strut, then marked the points on the bare timber. Then I planed the shape with a hand plane and finished each one with a compass plane and a spokeshave and finally with sandpaper. I must say that it's a pleasure to be working on these aircraft.'

Gene de Marco is general manager and chief pilot for the operation, which is based in Hood Aerodrome at Masterton on North Island. The S.E.5 was not the first choice that he would have made when starting out on full-scale production of Great War aeroplanes, having never been a fan of the type's perpendicular looks – joking that the cowling looked more like a 'doghouse' than a flying machine. There were also the many complexities of the S.E.5 design to consider: 'Ideally a fledgling company's first project choice should be a small, simple, easy-to-research and easy-to-build design, not the S.E.5a!' said Gene, an American aviator with more than 30 years of experience of all manner of Great War designs. Sure enough, there were a vast number of considerations when it came to manufacturing a brand new S.E.5, of which some were foreseen and others surprising.

'A very helpful resource was the Replicraft drawings produced by Jim Kiger,' Gene said. 'These nine large sheets gave us an outline of the entire project and we could then research each individual part using original Royal Aircraft Factory drawings. We've discovered a great deal of information on the S.E.5a that was previously unknown to many of us: triple vertical

ABOVE Combining modern computer-driven processes with hand tools and craftsmanship has allowed **TVAL** to work fast and accurately without losing period **'feel'**. *(TVAL)*

LEFT TVAL's trio of airworthy Hispano-powered S.E.5as on the flight line. *(Brian Harmer)*

ABOVE Hispano-Suiza crankcase fully serviced and ready to receive the cylinder blocks – a host of spares and tools have been manufactured to maintain these power plants. *(TVAL)*

BELOW TVAL's trio of S.E.5as have given good service over the last decade, including film appearances. *(TVAL)*

stabilisers, flaps, different wings, all sorts of engine installations and many other unique prototype and experimental designs. By process of elimination we started to pare down the huge number of original drawings to a workable set. As part of our manufacturing process and Civil Aviation Authority requirements we also ended up producing an aircraft specification, a drawing list, a drawing cross-reference – and of course a flight manual. Paperwork is a necessary burden at our workshop, maintaining compliance with CAA part 148 regulations. Keeping track of all the materials and manufacturing processes keeps us very busy.'

The focal point of the aeroplane that would give it final authenticity would be a correct period engine, and as with the build of the Shuttleworth Collection's example half a century earlier, the engine of choice was the Hispano-Suiza V8. While the Wolseley Viper confers some notable advantages when it comes to reliability and robust construction, it is an extremely rare engine in comparison with the Hispano – particularly the 180hp direct drive version that was licence-built in America for use in existing types such as the S.E.5 and SPAD, as well as being intended for home-grown designs.

Sufficient numbers of these engines still exist to make them a practical choice, having gone on to be used not only in aircraft manufacture in the 1920s but also in certain cars, such as the magnificent 1924 Béquet Delage. This car was originally a 2LCV model designed to the 2-litre Grand Prix regulations. French aviator Béquet obtained one of the cars and placed the lightweight 11-litre Hispano under its bonnet, the project being funded by perfumer Roland Coty, and it raced in *Formule Libre* events under the name *Le Coty Speciale*.

Despite the frailties of the Hispano engine in period, Gene de Marco and the TVAL team set about sourcing these engines with gusto while preparing the means with which to keep them running. Rather than build one single example of the S.E.5a the team decided to build three at once, meaning that problem-solving could be done relatively efficiently.

'These original engines were sourced from around the world,' said Gene. 'They were overhauled here in our workshop, and test-run prior to installation in the airframes. Special tools and replacement parts had to be made in order to facilitate the reconditioning process, and to ensure we have the ability to run and maintain these engines for years to come. The

ABOVE The abundance of Hispano-Suiza engines through the years led to many interesting projects, such as being fitted to this former Grand Prix car. *(Matt Howell)*

LEFT A TVAL-built Sopwith Snipe fires up at Stow Maries Great War Aerodrome. *(Author)*

RIGHT Original wing structure of S.E.5a E5668 undergoing restoration into a complete aeroplane at TVAL. *(TVAL)*

ABOVE AND RIGHT The newly built fuselage ready to receive the original components. *(TVAL)*

restoration process differed for each engine due to the unique condition of each 90-year-old powerplant.'

When it came to the finishing touches on the TVAL aeroplanes, many rediscovered processes meant the engineers had to master techniques such as the hand-splicing of cable, and the use of Irish linen for covering. Numerous detailed aluminium fairings such as those used on the landing gear and windscreen surrounds also had to be hand-formed, welded and made to fit. 'These time-consuming tasks are what makes the difference in an accurate reproduction,' said Gene de Marco. 'We like to think of them as "late model aircraft", just rolled off the new assembly line.'

The S.E.5as built at TVAL have been joined by all manner of types that have been revived through the painstaking work undertaken in New Zealand. As a result of these efforts, the skies are full of aeroplanes of British, French and German design throughout the airshow season, with spectacular set pieces allowing crowds the opportunity to see dogfights and trench strafing displays. Small wonder that enthusiasts now travel from every corner of the globe to see these machines being put through their paces.

By approaching the work systematically, many of the ways of working established 100 years ago have been rediscovered. The methodology worked out by the designers, factories and their respective military arms in order to standardise production and increase efficiency is something that has impressed today's experts.

'We've built every type of B.E.2, from the early c to the late c, the d, e and f, then on to the B.E.12 and on again to the R.E.8,' Gene explained. 'You find so many common parts in the progression of the designs, and also among the suppliers. That can be the wing ribs, the profile, or simple things like the oil filler caps – they were all interchangeable. Henry Ford was definitely not the only man designing vehicles for mass production. On all sides of the conflict you can see how much thought went into the manufacturing.'

At the time of writing, TVAL was working hard on the fifth S.E.5a to be built at its premises – albeit one with a difference. Rather than a completely new-build airframe, this one can be given a genuine identity from 1918 – Austin-built E5668. A number of components were discovered in Europe and shipped back to New Zealand, enabling the team to produce the first genuine restored vintage airframe seen for more than half a century. The completed aeroplane won't fly, but will be returning to Europe to go on static display for what, one can only assume, will be a delighted owner. Fingers are now crossed that the finished product will be available for public viewing.

'It's a late Austin S.E.5a – very much like a late-build Vickers,' Gene de Marco confirmed. 'The wing sections, the ailerons and a number of other key components are original and verified. We're taking those original parts and a number of others and are rebuilding that same Austin-built aeroplane.'

Just how many more such parts of genuine provenance may be found and reassembled is a tantalising question, potentially taking the number of S.E.5s into double figures and perhaps adding to the number of other genuine aeroplanes of the period on display around the world. From TVAL's perspective, as with any company working with historic vehicles, provenance is hard to pin down.

'The debate over originality is the same with historic vehicles of every kind – cars, aeroplanes, you name it,' said Gene. 'Can you take a number of components and say that it's restoring an original? There are some small switches in the Sopwith Camel that were still in use on the Hawker Hurricane. If you build a whole new airframe around that switch, does that make it a restored Hurricane? I've got a brake assembly in the workshop from a Hawker Sea Fury. I like to tell visitors that it's my Sea Fury restoration!'

ABOVE Original wing ribs still bearing the manufacturer's mark. *(TVAL)*

LEFT The new-build fuselage is mated to the original wings of E5668 – increasing the population of restored S.E.5as by one. *(TVAL)*

67

RESTORE TO FLIGHT

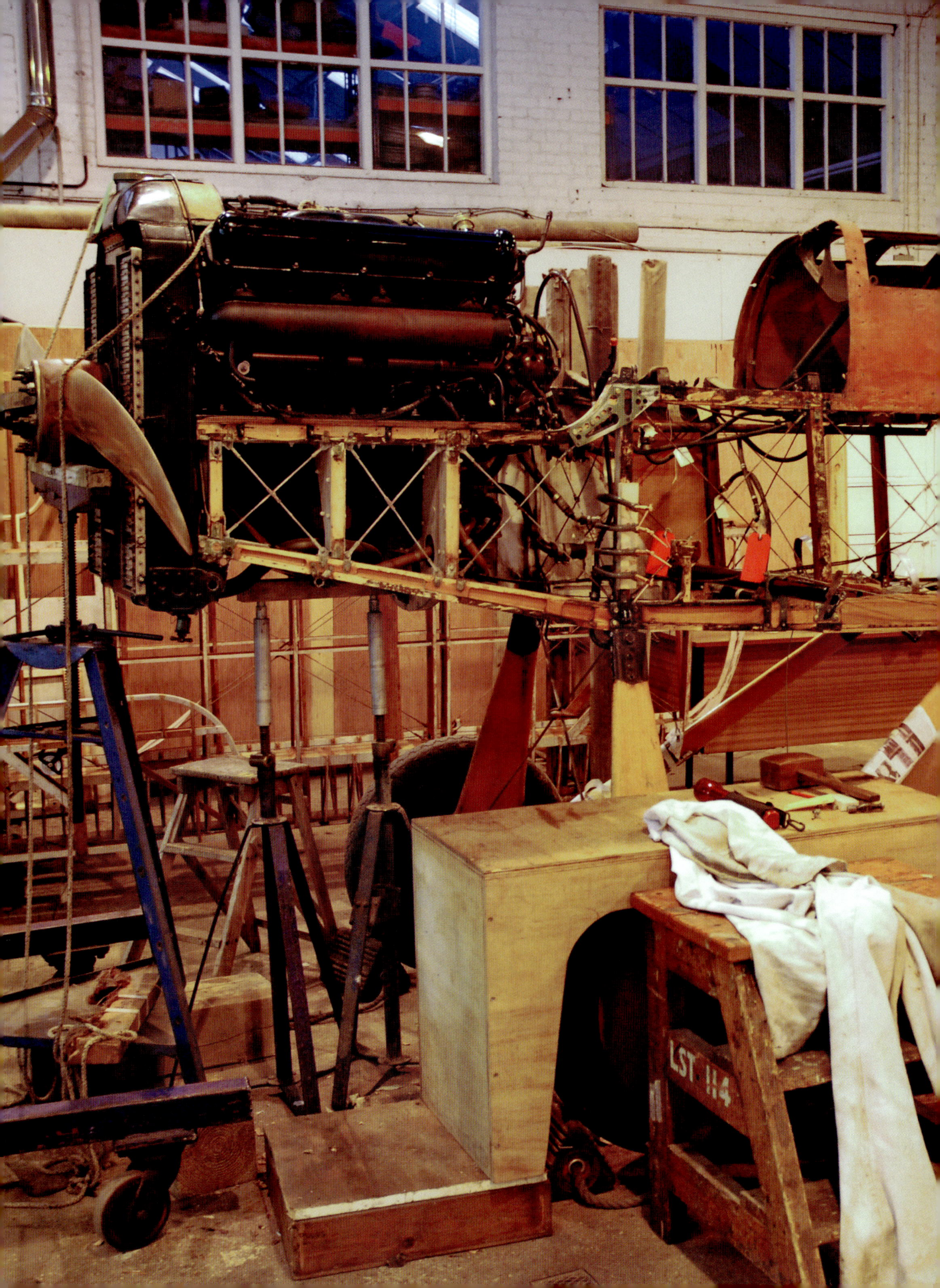
LST 114

Chapter Three

Anatomy of the S.E.5

―――――⦿―――――

The S.E.5a became the most rugged and durable of front-line fighters operated by the Royal Flying Corps and Royal Air Force in the Great War. Nevertheless, the journey from prototype form to eventual domination of the upper airspace was a long and occasionally painful journey.

OPPOSITE **The Shuttleworth Collection's F904 undressed and ready for overhaul, showing the intricacies that went in to the design and construction of these aeroplanes.** *(Darren Harbar)*

RIGHT The South African Air Force has chosen to display its S.E.5a 'half undressed' to visitors, giving a fine view of the fuselage construction. *(South African National Museum of Military History)*

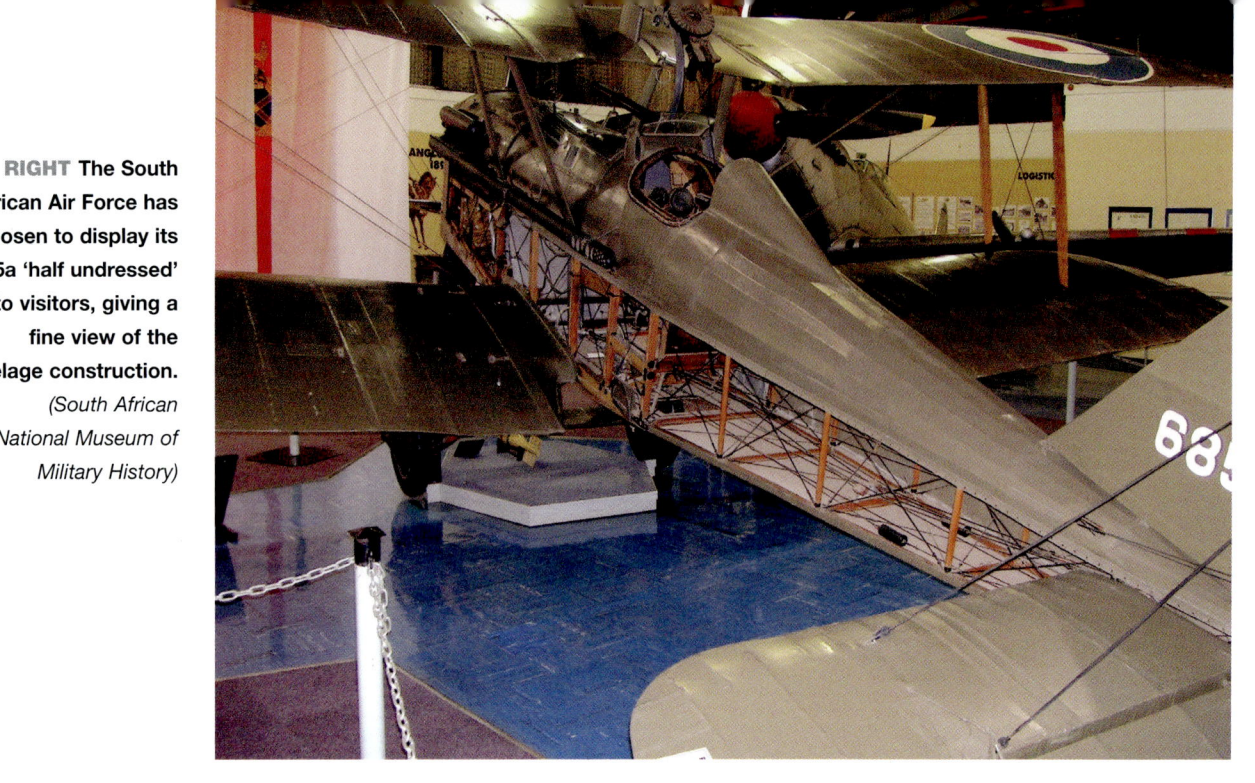

BELOW Folland's calculations were clear that mild steel offered the optimum mix of weight and strength to brace the S.E.5 structure throughout. *(Darren Harbar)*

Construction of the S.E.5

In keeping with the ethos of the Royal Aircraft Factory, there was nothing groundbreaking in the layout or construction of the S.E.5 when the first prototype, A4561, was wheeled out of the hangar at Farnborough in November 1916. Four longerons made from American spruce served as the foundation of the fuselage structure, interspersed with vertical struts and cross-members, also made of spruce.

Each of the joints within this structure was reinforced with mild steel fittings, into which mild steel tie rods were threaded diagonally across every bay to brace the structure. In the nose section, a cradle of engine bearers made of ash were supported by bulkheads made from spruce reinforced by plywood, ending with the firewall that separated the engine compartment from the rest of the aeroplane.

Buttressing the firewall and baffle plate, and attached to the top of the upper longerons using four bolts, was the 28-gallon main fuel tank. The fuel tank's capacity was somewhat restricted by the recessed hollow along its port side into which the fixed Vickers machine gun would be placed. Beneath the fuel tank the firewall baffle plate angled backwards towards the cockpit, creating space for the water pump and the oil tank, behind which sat the oil reservoir for the new and as-yet untested Constantinesco 'CC' hydraulic interrupter gear that would allow the Vickers to fire through the propeller arc.

The mounting for the Vickers gun was a tripod that was mounted to the upper longerons just ahead of the cockpit panel, straddling both the ammunition box and the empty case chute. This area was clad with plywood panels, flat along the fuselage sides and shaped to a curve over the top, supported by plywood carlins.

The plywood upper decking carried an Aldis telescopic gunsight and the windscreen which was, on the prototype, of flat-sided conical design. This would be followed by the early production 'greenhouse' half-canopy and finally a conventional aeroscreen, introduced by Albert Ball, with the Foster mount attaching to a bespoke bracket in front.

Cut into the top decking to the starboard side was a small hatch covered with Plexiglass that allowed natural light into the cockpit to illuminate the instrument panel. A similar plywood panel on the port side acted as a removable hatch for cleaning and servicing the Vickers gun.

Immediately behind this area was the cockpit, which was braced by a plywood floor that fitted directly to the lower longerons as well as a plywood stiffener that also served as a useful surface upon which the clock, altimeter and magneto switches were mounted. Beneath this shelf lay the priming pump and the tail trim wheel within reach of the pilot's left hand, while to his right sat the bomb release lever for those occasions when one was required.

The main instrument panel sat vertically at the front of the cockpit, beneath the decking, upon which were mounted the transfer air selector valve, the fuel air pressure gauge, the fuel selector switch, the airspeed indicator, the accelerometer, tachometer and the temperature and pressure gauges. Finally, on the outside of the cockpit to starboard was mounted the boost handle to be wound by the pilot, sending a spark to the magnetos prior to starting.

The original pilot's seat fitted on the prototype and the first 24 pre-production S.E.5 cockpits was a relatively complex affair, being adjustable both vertically and fore-and-aft, to ensure the comfort of pilots who came in a variety of sizes, and was armour plated. A simple wicker seat replaced it, mounted on a board. The pilots were strapped in using a single, broad webbing belt.

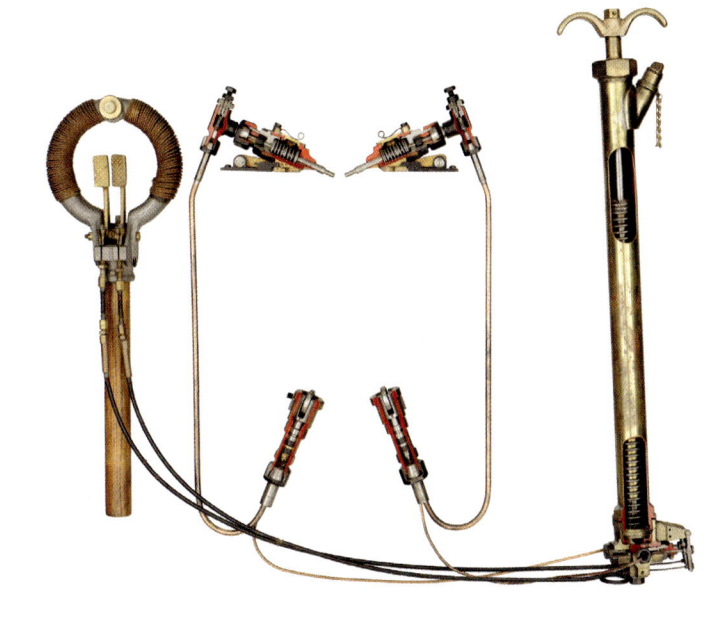

Control of the flying surfaces was achieved using an orthodox combination of column and rudder pedals, which were all-steel assemblies for strength and durability. The control column ended with a hooped metal handgrip covered in

ABOVE

Constantinesco 'CC' gear in detail: both the Vickers and Lewis guns were operated by their respective triggers on the control column (left), with the Lewis trigger feeding into the hydraulic pump (right). Actuated by the gear on the engine, it permitted a far higher rate of fire – 600 rounds per minute – than earlier mechanical gears, and remained in service into World War Two. *(Imperial War Museum)*

LEFT Plywood upper decking has a window cut into the starboard side to illuminate the instrument panel, with the Aldis mounting acting as the anchor point for the Foster mount. *(Doolittle Media)*

ABOVE The cockpit of the Shuttleworth Collection's S.E.5a, showing the floor, rudder pedals, control stick, instrument panel and plywood stiffener. *(Darren Harbar)*

BELOW Pilot's seat, control stick and CC gear reservoir sit clear of the cat's cradle of control wires, with the spring-loaded footstep in the lower left foreground. *(Darren Harbar)*

a cord binding, within which sat a thumb lever to fire the Vickers gun. The trigger mechanism was an integral part of the Constantinesco interrupter mechanism, with a motor fed via the feed block mounted on the rear butt plate of the top decking beside the Aldis sight.

The plywood upper decking reached back to the rear of the cockpit opening, where the rounded profile was continued by spruce stringers fastened to plywood formers, over which the Irish linen outer skin would be stretched. Along the flat sides of the fuselage the linen sheets were stitched along the upper longeron in order to make an effective access panel if maintenance was required on the control wires. These side panels also continued beneath the wooden decking to reach the engine cowl, with the only break in their surface being the footrest that allowed pilots to climb into the cockpit. To minimise the effect of the footrest on the aeroplane's aerodynamics, a spring-loaded metal flap closed the opening when not in use and sat flush with the outer skin of the fuselage.

Beneath the cockpit and lower wing the main undercarriage legs were attached, made from streamlined steel tube to reduce weight and drag and braced using Rafwire. The axle was enclosed within a streamlined fairing and sprung using bungee cord, with the wheels being attached at either end. These were standard 500 x 100 wire wheels, covered with fabric discs to reduce drag and fitted with Palmer Cord aero tyres.

The lower wings were attached to the fuselage by way of their main spars, which slotted into a spar carry-through tube that extended into the stub wings, which extended outside the fuselage by about 8in. The round tubes terminated in a fitting with a hinge bolted to it. On to this hinge the wing spars were fixed by vertical bolts.

The upper wing centre section was attached to the fuselage using steel tube cabane struts that were fitted with streamlined wood fairings and wrapped with linen tape. Inside these fairings, pipes fed down to the engine from the gravity fuel tank and water header tank.

Structurally the upper and lower wings mirrored each other. They were constructed from spruce with the main spars forming the

ABOVE Plywood decking reaches behind the cockpit with a small stowage area before the upper fuselage formers continue the structure. Above the undercarriage is the starboard steel spar tube to mount the lower wing. *(Darren Harbar)*

BELOW LEFT Mounting point for the lower wings. *(TVAL)*

BELOW Upper and lower wings are mirrored in dimension, layout and construction, with a sturdy main spar, compression ribs, plywood webbing and a false spar around the ailerons. *(Darren Harbar)*

S.E.5 cutaway. *(Mike Badrocke)*

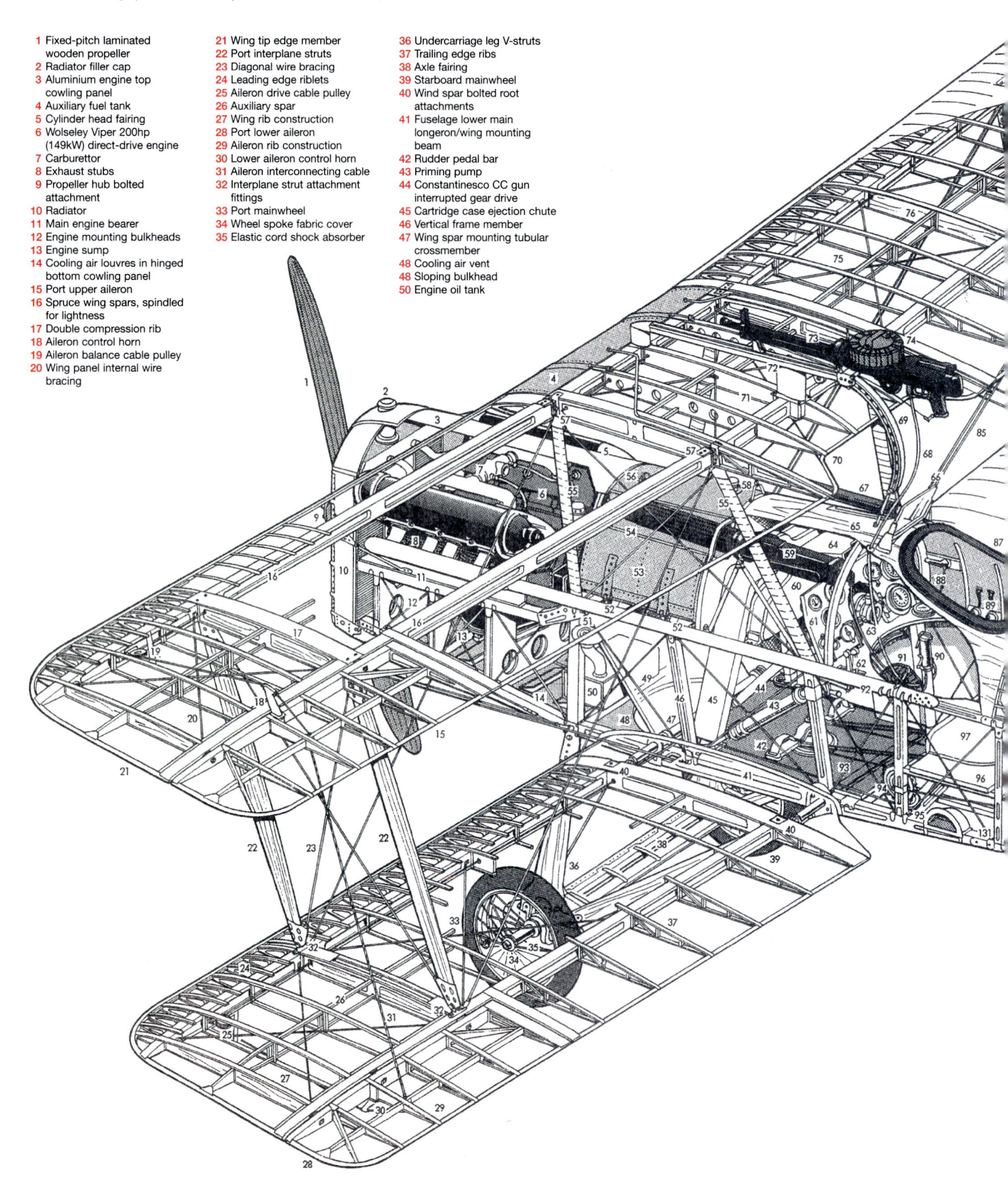

1 Fixed-pitch laminated wooden propeller
2 Radiator filler cap
3 Aluminium engine top cowling panel
4 Auxiliary fuel tank
5 Cylinder head fairing
6 Wolseley Viper 200hp (149kW) direct-drive engine
7 Carburettor
8 Exhaust stubs
9 Propeller hub bolted attachment
10 Radiator
11 Main engine bearer
12 Engine mounting bulkheads
13 Engine sump
14 Cooling air louvres in hinged bottom cowling panel
15 Port upper aileron
16 Spruce wing spars, spindled for lightness
17 Double compression rib
18 Aileron control horn
19 Aileron balance cable pulley
20 Wing panel internal wire bracing
21 Wing tip edge member
22 Port interplane struts
23 Diagonal wire bracing
24 Leading edge riblets
25 Aileron drive cable pulley
26 Auxiliary spar
27 Wing rib construction
28 Port lower aileron
29 Aileron rib construction
30 Lower aileron control horn
31 Aileron interconnecting cable
32 Interplane strut attachment fittings
33 Port mainwheel
34 Wheel spoke fabric cover
35 Elastic cord shock absorber
36 Undercarriage leg V-struts
37 Trailing edge ribs
38 Axle fairing
39 Starboard mainwheel
40 Wind spar bolted root attachments
41 Fuselage lower main longeron/wing mounting beam
42 Rudder pedal bar
43 Priming pump
44 Constantinesco CC gun interrupted gear drive
45 Cartridge case ejection chute
46 Vertical frame member
47 Wing spar mounting tubular crossmember
48 Cooling air vent
48 Sloping bulkhead
50 Engine oil tank

74

ROYAL AIRCRAFT FACTORY S.E.5 MANUAL

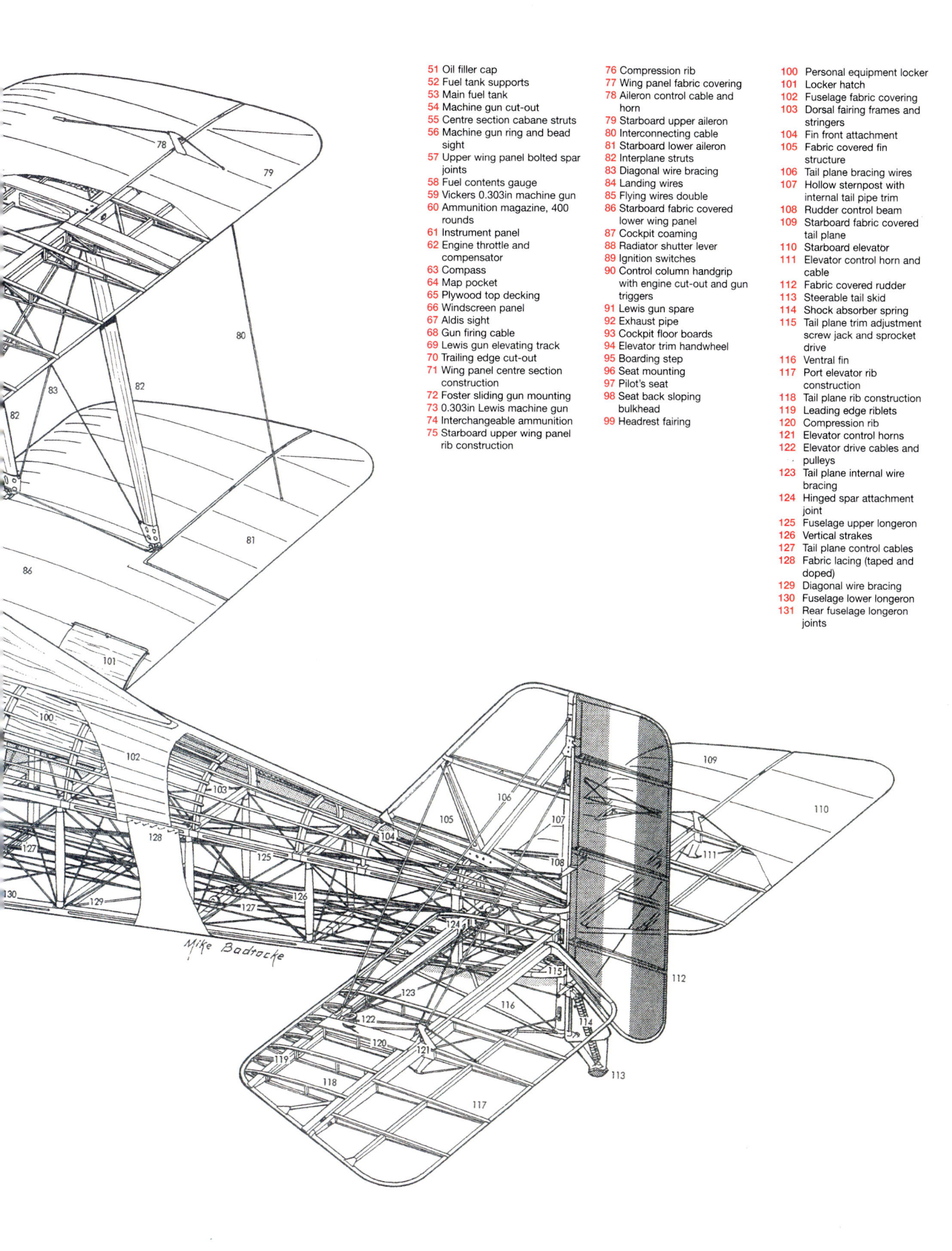

51 Oil filler cap
52 Fuel tank supports
53 Main fuel tank
54 Machine gun cut-out
55 Centre section cabane struts
56 Machine gun ring and bead sight
57 Upper wing panel bolted spar joints
58 Fuel contents gauge
59 Vickers 0.303in machine gun
60 Ammunition magazine, 400 rounds
61 Instrument panel
62 Engine throttle and compensator
63 Compass
64 Map pocket
65 Plywood top decking
66 Windscreen panel
67 Aldis sight
68 Gun firing cable
69 Lewis gun elevating track
70 Trailing edge cut-out
71 Wing panel centre section construction
72 Foster sliding gun mounting
73 0.303in Lewis machine gun
74 Interchangeable ammunition
75 Starboard upper wing panel rib construction
76 Compression rib
77 Wing panel fabric covering
78 Aileron control cable and horn
79 Starboard upper aileron
80 Interconnecting cable
81 Starboard lower aileron
82 Interplane struts
83 Diagonal wire bracing
84 Landing wires
85 Flying wires double
86 Starboard fabric covered lower wing panel
87 Cockpit coaming
88 Radiator shutter lever
89 Ignition switches
90 Control column handgrip with engine cut-out and gun triggers
91 Lewis gun spare
92 Exhaust pipe
93 Cockpit floor boards
94 Elevator trim handwheel
95 Boarding step
96 Seat mounting
97 Pilot's seat
98 Seat back sloping bulkhead
99 Headrest fairing
100 Personal equipment locker
101 Locker hatch
102 Fuselage fabric covering
103 Dorsal fairing frames and stringers
104 Fin front attachment
105 Fabric covered fin structure
106 Tail plane bracing wires
107 Hollow sternpost with internal tail pipe trim
108 Rudder control beam
109 Starboard fabric covered tail plane
110 Starboard elevator
111 Elevator control horn and cable
112 Fabric covered rudder
113 Steerable tail skid
114 Shock absorber spring
115 Tail plane trim adjustment screw jack and sprocket drive
116 Ventral fin
117 Port elevator rib construction
118 Tail plane rib construction
119 Leading edge riblets
120 Compression rib
121 Elevator control horns
122 Elevator drive cables and pulleys
123 Tail plane internal wire bracing
124 Hinged spar attachment joint
125 Fuselage upper longeron
126 Vertical strakes
127 Tail plane control cables
128 Fabric lacing (taped and doped)
129 Diagonal wire bracing
130 Fuselage lower longeron
131 Rear fuselage longeron joints

ANATOMY OF THE S.E.5

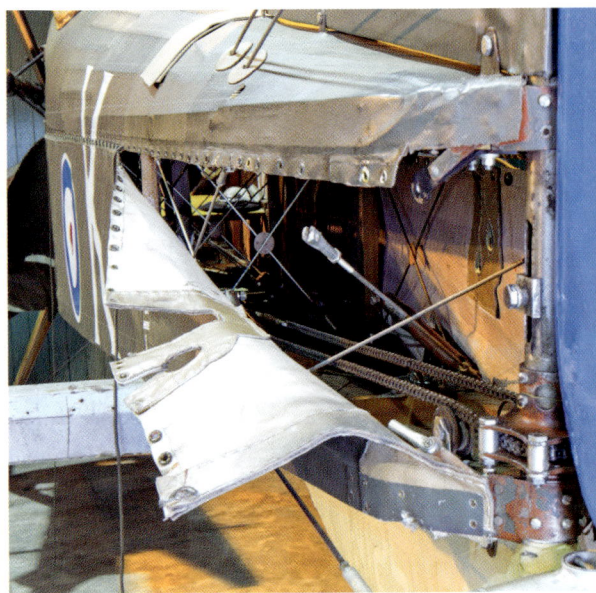

ABOVE The RAF Museum's S.E.5a F-938 shows off her rigging to full effect. *(Author)*

ABOVE RIGHT Recreation S.E.5a features all-original design, with the sternpost and elevator trim chain very much in evidence. *(Darren Harbar)*

BELOW Tail assembly shows through the virginal linen as S.E.5a F-904 goes back together after her overhaul, showing the elegant yet efficient design. *(Darren Harbar)*

structural core, to which ribs were attached – although the spacing was different on the upper and lower wings. False ribs were used to strengthen the wing leading edges and a combination of false ribs and spruce interplane struts, streamlined in finish, maintained the integrity of the structure. Bracing on the wings was considerable, with Rafwire bracing to support the struts and reinforce the spar tubes. Although not a birdcage like the B.E.2, there was considerable wiring on display outside the structure, as well as internally mounted wires.

Behind the cockpit, the fuselage tapered elegantly back to the tail, although not quite as dramatically as had been the case on the S.E.4 or the B.E.2. A degree of sturdiness was required due to the higher stresses of combat manoeuvring that were to be expected from a fighting scout. The sternpost of the fuselage was formed of hollow steel tube, which seated the main spar of the tail assembly. Folland's horizontal stabiliser made from spruce and covered in linen was attached via this spar on either side of the tail section.

There was vertical travel in the construction which allowed the angle of attack to be subtly altered by the pilot in flight using an endless chain connected to the cockpit-mounted trim wheel to adjust the balance of the machine as its load of fuel and ammunition became depleted. The trim mechanism is a work of art, using cable and a chain that operates a screw mechanism adjusting the entire tail plane at its rear attach point pivoting at the leading edge; even the rear brace wires travel up and down with the rear spar of the horizontal stabiliser.

Large elevators formed of streamlined steel tube and braced with spruce ribs were attached to the horizontal stabilisers. Their size was intended to maximise the authority of the controls and to balance the weight of the engine, fuel, pilot, machine gun and ammunition forward of the centreline.

Kenworthy's vertical tail surfaces were formed from streamlined steel tube over which the linen skin was stretched. These were fixed to the fuselage using mild steel joints and were braced to the stabilisers using Rafwire. A shock absorber for the tail skid was also housed in this section, using a pair of compression springs over telescopic dampers.

This was the form in which the first of the three S.E.5 prototypes, serial A4561, was built over a period of ten weeks as the summer of 1916 turned autumnal. Between November 1916 and April 1917 the definitive specification of the S.E.5a was reached through trial and error, through the savage loss of Frank Goodden, through 56 Squadron's experimentation in the field and, not least of all, by the preferences of Captain Albert Ball.

The S.E.5a with shortened wingspan, small aeroscreen and internally mounted gravity tank in the upper-wing centre section began arriving at the Front in May 1917, with Albert Ball making use of the first example, A8898, while his own A4850 was under repair. The next big step forward came in June 1917 with the arrival

ABOVE When she was first rebuilt by the Royal Aircraft Establishment at Farnborough, F-904 gave a pleasing view of her upper centre section, within which the gravity fuel tank and water tank are hidden in the leading edge. *(Farnborough Air Sciences Trust)*

LEFT The S.E.5 and early S.E.5a featured slender metal undercarriage legs that suffered with prolonged use, regularly collapsing and causing damage to the lower wings, propeller and engine. Solid wooden legs replaced them. *(Farnborough Air Sciences Trust)*

RIGHT Wing structure of F-904 on display when she was first restored to airworthiness. *(Farnborough Air Sciences Trust)*

of the first 200hp geared Hispano-Suiza engines in service.

With volume production under way, the first contract-built airframes from Martinsyde and Vickers were delivered to 56 Squadron in July 1917. More than 100 detail changes were made to the specification between June and December, including bracing wires on the dorsal fin to prevent it buffeting in a prolonged dive, but the most obvious of these was the request from 56 Squadron to make the undercarriage sturdier. The slender metal legs could not long survive the rough handling demanded of them in the field, with the result that a tougher design made from rosewood was brought in.

The plan was for all new S.E.5as to be fitted with the new wooden undercarriage at the factory and for existing airframes to be upgraded at their next overhaul, but the entry of the USA into the war combined with the U-boat blockade sinking so much Atlantic shipping caused a huge shortage. Eventually cypress was used instead.

Early in 1918 a new and terrifying problem confronted the pilots: wing failure on the S.E.5a upper wings during and after diving. The problem was encountered – and survived – by future ace Bill Lambert while he was performing an aerobatic display in his S.E.5a: 'I heard a sharp crack like a shot from a Vickers gun; the aeroplane lurched a little and I felt a quiver through the fuselage and into the seat of my pants. I noticed what appeared to be a slight flutter in my top wings and looking through the centre section I noticed one of the cross-bracing wires had broken.' Lambert barely got the aeroplane down in one piece from an altitude of 4,000ft, the flutter in his upper wing getting increasingly pronounced and giving both himself and the watching crowd an almighty scare.

At almost the same time in France at least two pilots were killed by upper wing failure, which accounted for Martinsyde-built B41 and C5334 built by Vickers at its Crayford factory. Clearly this was a potentially widespread problem, which was traced back to the same location as the original structural flaw: the outer section of the upper wings, where weakness and flex took its toll over time. The solution was to strengthen the upper wing around the aileron, and after that wing failures were virtually unheard of.

Finishing touches

Once the fabric skin was in place on an S.E.5 it was treated with dope to tauten and weatherproof it. After this process (see Chapter One, *Mass production*) it was painted at the factory, with the upper surfaces receiving standardised PC10 'Khaki green' as the camouflage colour (some aeroplanes were repainted in the more red-brown shade of PC12, particularly for use in the Middle East). PC stood for 'protective covering', the varnish being laid over the doped linen to complete the process of weatherproofing. With the advent of air-to-air combat a camouflage finish was achieved by mixing pigment into the varnish, giving finishes such as PC10. The undersides of the wings were treated only with clear varnish, allowing the natural ivory shade of clear-doped linen to show through.

National markings would then be painted – roundels of red, white and blue plus rudder stripes of the same colours. The allocated serial numbers and the 'Lift here' instructions on the rear fuselage would be in white. If the aeroplane had been paid for by donation or subscription this would usually be signified in white, such as 'Wanganui presented by E.R. Jackson' as recreated by Gene de Marco and TVAL on one of their examples.

Individual squadron markings were almost universally white and would be allocated by order of the wing or brigade. Usually these were simple shapes (a white horizontal bar for 74 Squadron, a white vertical bar forward of the cockpit for 24 Squadron, a white hexagon for 85 Squadron and so on). Individual identification would usually be denoted with numbers or letters.

Of all the squadrons equipped with the S.E.5/5a it was No 56 that went through the greatest variety of markings, including white tail bands, two white bars at angles and a dumbbell shape. Throughout its active service 56 used colours to denote flights (red for 'A' Flight, white and blue for 'B' Flight and Blue for 'C' Flight), which were usually carried on the wheels. Albert Ball added a red radiator housing and red on the cowlings on either side of the engine on A4850 and A8898.

Personal markings were generally frowned upon but left up to the commanding officer of each unit. Sometimes the name of a wife or girlfriend would be added, sometimes something more extravagant like 'Grid' Caldwell's chequerboard tail as CO of 74 Squadron, or his earlier red stripes and New Zealand fern leaf when flying with 60 Squadron.

In rare cases the camouflage would be enhanced, as seen with the mottled green/brown camouflage applied to Roderick Dallas' 40 Squadron machine and the blue and grey diamonds painted on to the night fighters of 61 Squadron. In general, however, S.E.5s of all kinds were to be found in PC10 over clear with white unit markings.

BELOW Classic PC10 over clear finish and the white unit marking on Shuttleworth's F-904. *(Author)*

ABOVE The engineer airman – Major J.T.B McCudden, VC. *(Author)*

JIMMY MCCUDDEN'S HIGH-FLYING BIRD

The structure of S.E.5a on active service changed little from the arrival of the first mass-produced models to the last, with the majority of updates coming to its often-troublesome engines (see below). One exception to this rule, however, was the most successful individual S.E.5a of them all, serial number B4891, which became the personal mount of the new star of 56 Squadron, James McCudden.

McCudden's life was the Army, having been 'born in barracks' as the third of six children of Sergeant-Major William McCudden, Royal Engineers, and his wife Amelia Byford. He joined the Royal Engineers aged 15 and spent 18 months in Gibraltar, where he read all that he could about his great passion: flying. In 1913 he transferred to the Royal Flying Corps as a mechanic in which role he travelled to war with 3 Squadron, but as an expert marksman he was soon spending time as an observer/gunner.

BELOW The 'maternity jacket' of Major J.T.B. McCudden, displaying medal ribbons for his Victoria Cross, Distinguished Service Order and Bar, Military Cross and Bar, Military Medal and French Croix de Guerre. *(Author)*

In 1915 McCudden officially qualified as an observer and flew throughout the second half of the year. He was accepted for pilot training in February 1916, at which he proved to be supremely adept, having already flown 100 hours as a passenger with 25 different pilots, including his older brother Bill, and 46 hours as a regular observer since November 1915, when he had seen off an attack from the first great German ace, Max Immelmann. He was also so adept at explaining the principles of aeroplane behaviour to his colleagues that he became an instructor within days of receiving his aviator's certificate.

It was in the role of instructor that his brother Bill had been killed, but McCudden proved to be inspirational in the job. Among his fledglings was another Irish Catholic 'camp rat' by the name of Edward Mannock, and the two men from such similar backgrounds enjoyed each other's company.

Once he was on the front line, McCudden flew the F.E.2b and later the D.H.2 scout, in which he made 'ace' after shooting down five enemy machines by February 1917, when he was returned to Home Establishment service. While in England McCudden flew Home Defence missions and encountered Albert Ball socially, who explained to him that the best method of attacking larger aeroplanes was from the blind spot below the tail. McCudden put theory into practice when the Gotha bombers started terrorising London, and succeeded in getting significant hits on two of the giant bombers from the helm of his tiny Sopwith Pup.

It was at this time that McCudden first encountered the men of 56 Squadron, who had been sent back from France to counter the Gotha threat. He was deeply impressed by the unit's *esprit de corps* and elected to join them as soon as possible.

He stepped into the void that was left by Albert Ball's death and, while developing 56 Squadron as a unit capable of thinking and flying in unison, he also worked hard with the unit's mechanics to minimise the losses incurred due to technical faults. Alex J. Gray, Air Mechanic First Class at 56 Squadron, remembered: 'When McCudden came to No 56 he certainly kept us on our toes to begin with. In the first few weeks he tried out just about every fitter in the flight, and none of them seemed to please him. Finally, Corporal Tom Rogers and myself were detailed as his fitters and Corporal Bert Card as the rigger, and from that day on we formed a great friendship with him.'

While building and developing 56 Squadron as a team, McCudden also flew regular and lethal individual patrols in his personal mount, Farnborough-built S.E.5a B4891, which featured the narrow chord elevators (10in as opposed to 15) fitted in an experiment to reduce the effort needed to pull out of a dive. His particular targets on these patrols were the high-flying German two-seater aeroplanes, particularly the Rumpler C.VIII, which appeared able to operate with impunity at altitudes that the S.E.5a could not reach.

ABOVE McCudden at the helm of his earlier S.E.5a, written off while he was on home leave in the autumn of 1917. *(Imperial War Museum)*

He put B4891 on a dramatic diet, hoping that reducing weight would give him altitude. Stalking the high-flying Rumplers from below and behind in their blind spot, he began to take a mounting toll upon these previously invulnerable 'eyes in the sky'. Soon he mounted a rounded spinner taken from an LVG which, McCudden claimed, gave him several more mph, and finally he smoothed out the airflow around the cockpit with a raised turret-like surround.

In January 1918 he fitted a set of high compression pistons from the new 220hp Hispano-Suiza engine that was being fitted to the latest SPAD, the S.XIII. This boosted A4891 from a standard compression of 5.3:1 to a dizzying 5.6:1 – and moreover, thanks to McCudden's mechanical abilities, it did so reliably. When testing his enhanced S.E.5a, McCudden's logbook recorded that A4891 climbed to 10,000ft in nine minutes and flew at 135mph at ground level – shaving roughly 90 seconds from the climb and adding 2–3mph, which were to prove vital.

These modifications were unique to McCudden's aeroplane and not picked up by the rest of 56 Squadron or any other unit. He alone managed to take the S.E.5a into the highest reaches which, after modifying the engine (see next colum), got to around 19,000ft. With B4891 he claimed no fewer than 32 of his eventual 57 victories, almost all of which were independently confirmed.

In the wake of Albert Ball's death the press had been denied access to pilots of the Royal Flying Corps, with the feeling that the loss of a hero would be bad for national morale. Yet such was the scale of McCudden's achievements that when he returned to Britain on leave in the spring of 1918, Lord Northcliffe's *Daily Mail* publicly shamed the War Office into being allowed to name 'Captain X' the mystery hero with nearly 60 Huns to his credit.

Once the press was given such freedom, it was inevitable that a degree of inaccuracy crept into its reports, including the myth that McCudden was flying at 22–23,000ft in his modified S.E.5a. It might have been helpful for the Germans to believe that the S.E.5a was capable of reaching such a height, but in 1953 McCudden's squadron-mate, Gerald Maxwell, pooh-poohed the claims, saying: 'McCudden had special high-compression pistons fitted to his machine and it was this that enabled it to get to about 19,000ft, but I never heard of any S.E. getting higher than that. Also, we had no oxygen and even at 19,000 it was getting pretty tricky. I used to spend a good deal of time at over 18,000ft, and it gave one pretty bad headaches.'

McCudden detested the intrusion of the press and keenly felt the resentment that his fame generated among his fellow airmen. When he tried to return early to France to escape the attention he was posted to command 85 Squadron, a fairly wild rabble of mainly colonial officers, which refused to take him, suggesting that McCudden was too low-born to command and would anyway only be interested in adding to his own score and renown. Eventually McCudden was given command of 60 Squadron.

BELOW McCudden poses with what was the most-modified S.E.5a to see front-line service, ready to tackle the high-flying German reconnaissance machines. *(Imperial War Museum)*

The Hispano-Suiza V8 and Wolseley derivatives

The very obvious development potential shown by Marc Birkigt's V8 engine upon its debut in 1915 translated into a programme that was epic in its scale and diversity. Thanks to the Allied powers agreeing to a massive build programme (at the Admiralty's insistence), a constant stream of new iterations of the Hispano emerged not only from the central factory but also from its international contractors.

The first two prototype S.E.5s were both fitted with the 150hp direct-drive Hispano-Suiza 8Aa, the standard power plant for the SPAD S.VII in 1916 and early 1917. Already work was advanced on more powerful, geared variants and from the options available it was the 200hp geared Hispano-Suiza 8B that was selected for use as the standardised power plant to be fitted to the S.E.5a in early 1917 – the same specification that was chosen for the later SPAD S.VIIs and SPAD XIII.

Supplying such a complex engine to meet such a massive volume of orders proved to be something of a challenge to the contractors. Engines arrived from different contractors with components that were not interchangeable. Mismatched parts, such as different crankcases, crankshafts and propeller bosses, varied from one factory to the next and conspired with poor-quality finish on such vital elements as the enamel coating on the aluminium components to cause endless problems with overheating and general serviceability.

The gears proved to be an even bigger hurdle for the manufacturers. Steel that was improperly hardened did not long survive under the high tooth-pressure generated, and replacements were often hard to come by – not least because factories employed their own gearing.

The knock-on effects from differently geared engines were significant. With the specified 24:41 gearing the propeller should have been turning at a peak 1,170rpm but some engines arrived with 26:39 gearing to give 1,333rpm while others had 21:28 gearing to give 1,500rpm. Such differences in performance played havoc with formations, leaving stragglers to get picked off by opportunistic enemies.

None of the problems that beset the Hispano-Suiza stemmed from its design but rather from the manufacturing processes of individual contractors. The Royal Aircraft Factory went to painstaking lengths to ensure compliance from its contractors building the airframes but Hispano-Suiza had no such system and, faced with ravenous demand, no

BELOW A direct-drive Hispano-Suiza 8Ab on display at the Royal Air Force Museum. *(Author)*

BELOW RIGHT The gearing of the 200hp Hispano-Suiza 8Ab shown off to good effect in the RAF Museum's Sopwith Dolphin. *(Author)*

opportunity to develop and implement any form of quality control.

When it came to engines for the S.E.5a, orders went out that engines from the Brasier factory in France were only to be issued as a last resort due to persistent flaws in the gearing. Wolseley's licence-built version, the Adder, was an improvement and offered increased performance over the standard Hispano by virtue of a higher compression ratio – 4.7:1 compared to the 4.8:1 of the original – but persistent crankshaft failures meant a strict rev limit of 1,750rpm.

In some desperation, Wolseley was asked to deliver a stock of 150hp direct-drive engines. Wolseley did some tinkering and found that a direct-drive variant of the Hispano, when fitted with high compression pistons, could reliably reach 200hp from a compression of 5.3:1. This new engine was called the Viper and presented a solution to one of several interlinked problems.

The Viper wasn't perfect but it was a dramatic improvement, to the point where Hispano-Suiza made its own 200hp direct-drive engine, the 8Ab. In total the Hispano-Suiza and Wolseley engines were the subject of 23 orders regarding their preparation, maintenance, modification and servicing in the relentless effort that was needed to get and keep them in serviceable condition.

All of this meant that the Engine Repair Shops (ERS) were kept extremely busy. In total the Hispano-Suiza and Wolseley engines accounted for 36% of the work undertaken, when they accounted for only 28% of the total number of engines on charge. It also took twice as long to remove, repair, refit and test an Hispano than a simpler engine. Nevertheless, the performance gains of the design as a whole were held up as being worth the effort – as the RFC Quartermaster Brigadier-General Brooke-Popham reminded his disgruntled engineers.

ABOVE Choosing the Hispano-Suiza 8B as the standard engine for the S.E.5a, as seen here, was counter-productive thanks to manufacturing issues. *(Farnborough Air Sciences Trust)*

ABOVE The S.E.5a and Bristol Fighter were an effective team in 1918 and fly together today at the Shuttleworth Collection.
(Darren Harbar)

Brooke-Popham, together with generals Sir David Henderson, Sefton Brancker and 'Boom' Trenchard, felt that they had a mixed bag of designs available at the start of 1918. Of the three new fighters debuted in 1917, the Bristol F2 was upgraded to F2B specification with the 275hp Rolls-Royce Falcon III and flown aggressively with better tactics, becoming a huge success. The S.E.5a was also improved but it had weaknesses, and senior figures in the RFC simply didn't trust it – perhaps a legacy of Albert Ball's criticisms. Its major flaw, in the generals' opinion, was that it was fitted with the same engine as the SPAD yet it was slower and couldn't climb as fast or as high. Nevertheless, it would have to do for the time being.

The third new type to arrive was the Sopwith Camel and that was an even greater disappointment. It was slow and its inherent instability was killing inexperienced pilots. Its inability to operate at more than 10–12,000ft was killing more of them because the Germans had free rein to dive down on Camel formations, and while the pilots who had mastered it could usually escape, the vast majority of its pilots weren't aces, and more airmen died in the Camel than any other type – even the cumbersome two-seaters.

Sopwith had meanwhile developed a new product, the 5F1 Dolphin, which was fitted with the Hispano engine. It showed enormous potential – more so than either the S.E.5a or the SPAD – but Hispano engines were in short enough supply. The War Office had bulk-bought Le Clerget engines to power the Sopwith Camel and these would have to be used up, requiring Sopwith and its contractors such as Ruston Proctor, Beardmore, and Clayton & Shuttleworth to press on with Camel construction.

By fitting the Viper as the standard engine for the S.E.5a the hope remained that a suitable stock of gear-driven Hispanos could then be available for large-scale production of the Dolphin. In this way the Camel could be phased out sooner rather than later, leaving the British with a fleet formed of big Bristols, reliable S.E.5s and the impressive Dolphin.

In the shorter term, switching across to the Wolseley Viper made big inroads into the lack of S.E.5s available for squadron service. In early 1918 stocks showed that half of the S.E.5a airframes finished to date were in storage awaiting engines. Five squadrons of Camels had been brought into the line by July 1917 but only 56 Squadron flew the S.E.5.

By November 1917 there were five

LEFT The enduring fame of the Sopwith Camel would not have been anticipated by Brigadier-General Brooke-Popham 100 years ago. *(Author)*

squadrons operating the S.E.5, and in total 22 British and Australian squadrons would be operating the type by the Armistice, plus one American unit. The Viper was the major factor in achieving this level of delivery and also maintaining acceptable levels of serviceability – provided that its inherent faults were managed effectively.

For all the virtues of the Viper, it managed to claim at least one high-profile victim through a fault: Jimmy McCudden. Having taken off from Hounslow in C1126, a new Viper-engined S.E.5a, he flew to RAF Headquarters at Hesdin before heading for his ultimate destination, Boffles airfield, home of 60 Squadron. It was getting late and the weather was closing in and McCudden called in at the airfield of Auxi-le-Château, some five miles short, to ask for directions.

Leaving Auxi-le-Château, McCudden took off and then dropped the nose to gain speed before hauling the S.E.5a into a steep climbing turn. The engine cut out and he crashed into woodland beyond the airfield perimeter, where McCudden was found alongside the wreckage. He had suffered a basilar skull fracture and would not survive for long. Because McCudden was his star man, Trenchard sent Hubert Charles, formerly the chief engineer at 56 Squadron, to personally investigate the crash.

Charles concluded that the Viper's carburettor had flooded as a result of the manoeuvre that McCudden had pulled after take-off, stating that unless the standard metering and altitude control systems were redesigned and then re-machined to watchmaker tolerances, the outcome would always be a flooded carburettor. It was a preposterous way for McCudden to have been lost.

BELOW Windscreen from James McCudden's crashed S.E.5a C1126 on display at the Imperial War Museum. *(Author)*

85

ANATOMY OF THE S.E.5

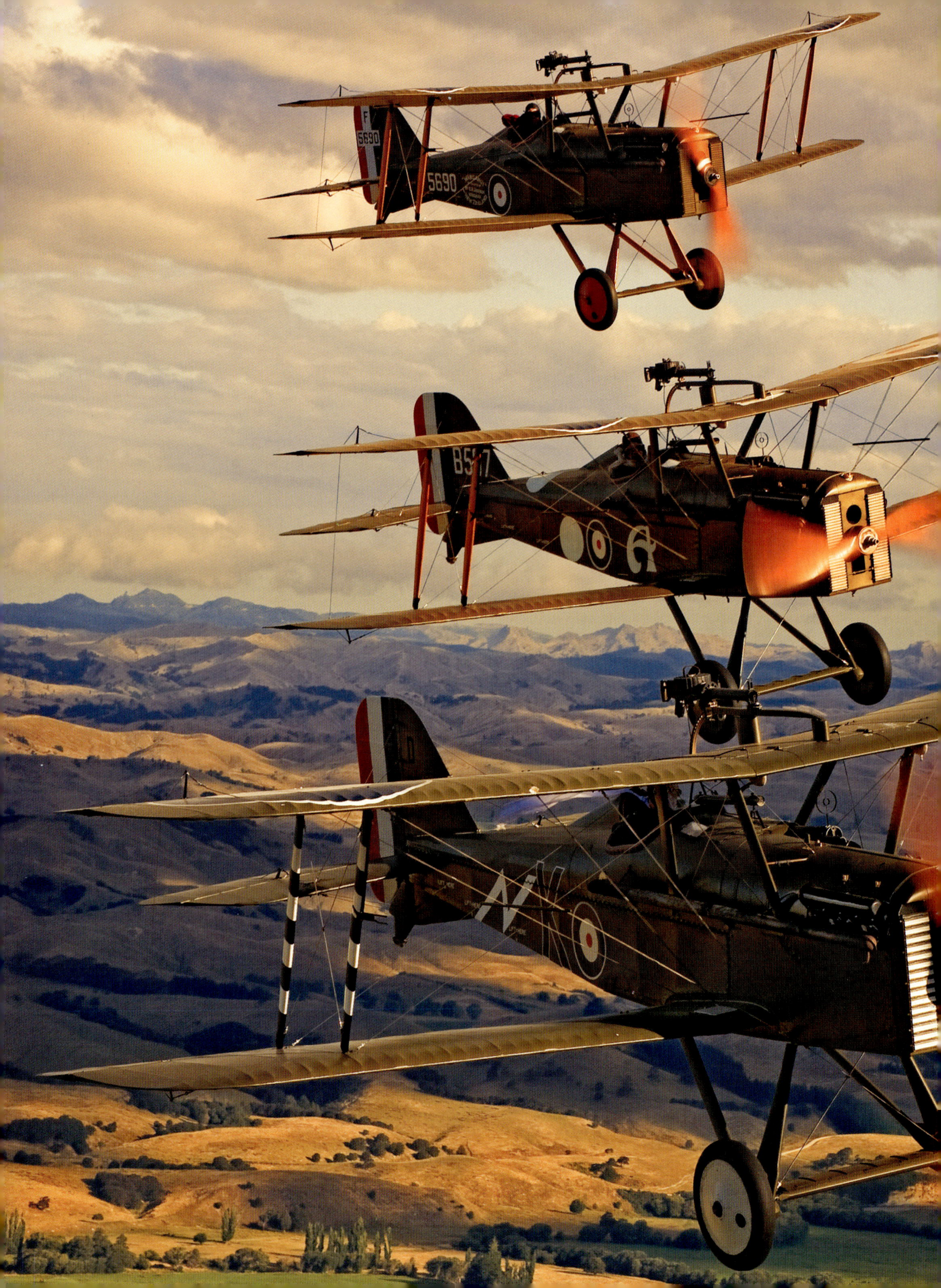
F
5690
5690

Chapter Four

The pilot's view

Flying an S.E.5a is a rare privilege in the 21st century. The number of truly authentic recreations is minuscule and only two airframes with provenance still fly. Yet thousands of pilots benefited from its handling qualities in war and peace and it remains one of the most sought-after entries in any present-day pilot's logbook.

OPPOSITE TVAL's trio of authentic reproduction S.E.5as in echelon over the splendour of a New Zealand sunset. *(Phil Makanna/Ghost)*

ABOVE The 10–15 hours' total flying time of many novice pilots, mostly trained in a Farman 'Rumpty' like this, was poor preparation for combat flying, and contributed to huge losses. *(Shutterstock)*

BELOW Pilot training was comprehensively reorganised during 1917 thanks to Robert Smith-Barry devising the 'Gosport System' and phasing in the Avro 504 as the primary training machine. *(Author)*

Pilot training in 1917–18

Many hard lessons were learned from 'Bloody April', not the least of them being that British pilot training was woefully inadequate. Cecil Lewis, who would make his name after flying S.E.5s with 56 Squadron, was typical of newly qualified pilots when he first arrived in France during 1915 with just 13 hours of solo flying to his name.

The problem was that demand was outstripping supply. The vicious circle of inexperienced pilots being sent out too early and being killed required more new pilots to take over from them with equally little seat-time to that point. One of the reasons for keeping the hours down among trainee pilots was that many of them were being killed before earning their 'wings'.

On the eve of the Battle of Arras, a review of current pilot training was carried out in anticipation of significant losses in the weeks ahead. The report stated that, out of the 6,000 recruits then in training, 1,200 could be expected to be killed before reaching a front-line squadron. In total half of the casualties among British airmen in 1914–18 came from training accidents. Of the 10,000 British and colonial airmen to be killed during the Great War, 4,000 died in training and a further 2,000 died between being handed their 'wings' and arriving on active duty, whether through mechanical failure, by being caught out by weather conditions or simply by showing off too near the ground.

In December 1916 Captain Robert Smith-Barry, the commanding officer of 60 Squadron, had written in dismay to his superiors about the woeful inadequacy of pilot training. He was most vexed about pilots being unable to get their aeroplanes out of a spin, which often induced panic even in many experienced airmen. Indeed, Smith-Barry had only recently learned that it was possible to control a spin, after Captain R. Balcombe-Brown, a New Zealand pilot, landed at 60 Squadron's airfield and demonstrated how to start and stop a spin at will. Such was his determination that Smith-Barry was transferred almost immediately to No 1 Reserve Squadron at Gosport in order to lay the groundwork for more effective pilot training.

Smith-Barry effected wholesale changes to the way in which pilots were educated – introducing what became known ultimately as the 'Gosport System', which forms the basis of pilot tuition to this day. He cast out all the unsuitable instructors – those who were either raw novices themselves or, worse, the war-weary veterans who felt ashamed of no longer being at the Front and therefore bellowed insults at their terrified pupils.

Encouragement and comradeship were vital in Smith-Barry's eyes – and so too was the equipment that the instructors had to call upon.

ABOVE **The cockpit of an S.E.5a was a user-friendly place to be that allowed fledgling aces to master their craft.** *(Darren Harbar)*

He invented a simple intercom system – the Gosport Tube – that allowed instructions to be spoken rather than shouted. Step by step he eradicated the pre-war Caudron and Maurice Farman box kites from the flight line and instead got pupils into the Avro 504J and 504K as soon as possible – modern aeroplanes that were forgiving of learners' faux pas but could also give a decent indication of what flying a Sopwith, S.E.5 or D.H.4 might be like.

Learning how to enter and hold a tight turn was of paramount importance and so too was spinning. Many other manoeuvres were introduced at Gosport, including the sideslip landing, which, when it was first demonstrated in France by Gosport-trained pilots, was misinterpreted by even seasoned veterans as a narrow escape from death!

The Gosport System wasn't foolproof and it took time to roll it out across all the pilot-training facilities in Britain and elsewhere. Among the other enhancements to overall flying training was the secondment of front-line types to the programme, with the first S.E.5a arriving at the Central Flying School as early as June 1917, in line with the first deliveries at the Front.

From a total of 10–15 hours' flying time that novice pilots took to the Front in 1916–17, this increased to four hours' dual before being allowed to fly solo, whereupon they would have to amass a further 25 hours, including cross-country and altitude flights as well as time logged in front-line equipment such as the S.E.5a, before a week's gunnery training.

For 18-victory 'ace' Bill Lambert, his relationship with the S.E.5a was one of love at first sight. American Lambert, who was working in Canada during early 1917 and volunteered to join the Royal Flying Corps, first saw an S.E.5a on the ground during his advanced training at Chattis Hill airfield in Hampshire. He asked for permission to take it up, which was granted, and with minimal instruction he took off.

'It could roll, spin, loop, climb, loop and dive at the least touch of the stick and rudder bar and was under perfect control at all times,' he remembered. 'I flew with my right hand on the stick and my left hand on the throttle. The two of us were as one: what the machine did I did, what I did the machine did.'

Not all pilots enjoyed Lambert's natural gift for handling a high-performance aeroplane, however, and as a result the first fatality was recorded on 27 August, when A8927 spun in shortly after take-off, killing Second Lieutenant F.M. Wood. The solution was to convert several airframes into two-seaters by removing the Vickers gun and synchronising gear and fitting a small 12-gallon fuel tank. It was then possible to squeeze in a second cockpit between the rear cabane struts, the first of these conversions taking place on S.E.5a B18 during March 1918.

The relatively benevolent handling of the S.E.5a and the opportunity that its design gave

The S.E.5a in action

The soubriquet 'mount of aces' has been given to the S.E.5a because the vast majority of high-scoring pilots from Britain and her Empire flew the type. It could also very well be given the name 'mount of survivors'.

With so many parameters to be considered, accurately comparing almost any two aeroplane designs is all but impossible, but a general impression can be formed when looking at the S.E.5a and its famous stablemate, the Sopwith Camel. Among the variables, the Camel was often used as a ground-attack aircraft, dropping bombs and strafing German positions on the ground and thereby being exposed to intense ground fire as well as presenting an easier target to enemy fighters. The S.E.5a was far less suited to ground attack and this would have given aircrew a much better chance of survival.

Losses among Sopwith Camel pilots up to 11 November 1918 stood at 831 dead, with 424 pilots being killed in action and 407 killed in accidents. A further 324 pilots were wounded or made POWs, giving a total of 748 Camel pilots taken out of the war. These figures look fairly grim in contrast to those of the S.E.5/5a, which show 286 pilots killed, with 207 lost in action and 79 in accidents. A further 170 S.E.5/5a pilots were wounded or made POWs.

Camel pilots claimed a total of 3,318 victories in air combat, while S.E.5/5a pilots claimed 2,704 victories. In pure data terms, therefore, this means that Camels accounted for 4.4 enemy aeroplanes claimed for every pilot killed, wounded or captured, while the S.E.5/5a accounted for 5.9 enemy aeroplanes claimed for every pilot killed, wounded or captured. But pure data is only ever half the story at best. To paraphrase one envious Camel pilot, in an S.E.5 you could sit in warmth and comfort, point it towards Germany and be confident of fighting on your own terms. In a Camel it was a case of fighting all the way to where you were going then fighting all the way home again.

ABOVE The S.E.5 lent itself to two-seater trainer conversions far better than many front-line fighters, allowing trainees vital experience before joining active squadrons. *(Imperial War Museum)*

to such conversions paid enormous dividends. Only 2.5% of losses sustained in training during 1917–18 were among pilots flying the S.E.5a, compared to almost 15% flying the tricky Sopwith Camel. Pilots fortunate enough to have gone through this training were invariably posted to S.E.5a squadrons on active duty, where they would hopefully master the art of formation flying and unified attacks that had been developed since 'Bloody April'.

LEFT Politicians and newspapers spoke of a gallant 'cavalry of the clouds', but the reality was setting fire to your enemy before he set fire to you. *(Alamy)*

One very clear barometer is the 'scorecard' of 80 victories attributed to Manfred von Richthofen. After extensive research, he is credited with shooting down nine Camels but only three S.E.5as, the first of which he managed to 'bounce' while it was strafing German Army positions on the ground on 30 November 1917. Richthofen's fame and his unsurpassed total of victories came from his tactical efficiency and his ability to effectively stage-manage every attack. By no means a brilliant pilot, the 'Red Baron' struck hard and fast with greater weight of numbers and would always choose to get cleanly away rather than be drawn into a dogfight. Life became increasingly difficult for Richthofen when the forces he was up against were not only wise to his tactics but were well able to parry them.

James McCudden may have been successful on his high-altitude solo flights, but he remained a focal point of 56 Squadron's successes as a whole. He said: 'I consider it a patrol leader's work to pay more attention to the main points of the fight than to do all the fighting himself. The main points are: (1) arrival of more EA [enemy aircraft] who have tactical advantage, i.e. height; (2) patrol drifting too far east; (3) patrol getting below bulk of enemy formation. As soon as any of these circumstances occur, it is time to take advantage of the SE's superior speed over EA scouts and break off the fight, rally behind leader and climb west of EA until you are above them before attacking them again.'

This was all well and good, but fortunes often conspired against the pilots. Fighting for one's life against experienced and determined enemies ensured that any minor issue was magnified many times, and Cecil Lewis, for one, found the S.E.5's frequent need for attention to the Vickers gun and its troublesome Constantinesco 'CC' gear, and the Lewis gun with its requirement to replace ammunition drums, to be the cause of enormous peril.

'Those guns could jam and very often did jam,' he explained in footage held by the BBC. 'And when they did jam in the middle of a fight a pilot was in a very precarious position as you can understand. The un-jamming of a gun when you're flying at 100mph plus with icy hands at 15,000ft was a very difficult thing because you

ABOVE Richthofen's 'Flying Circus' received the excellent Fokker Dr.I triplane by early 1918 but found itself facing an enemy that had adapted to counter its tactics. *(Brian Harmer)*

LEFT The cockpit of an S.E.5a could be terrifying in a dogfight when either the Lewis gun jammed or a pilot needed to change its ammunition drum. *(Darren Harbar)*

91
THE PILOT'S VIEW

had to put your hand out round the windscreen, round into the wind and try and get hold on the handle of the gun and try and jerk it over in order to clear the belt, which was a collapsible belt, which used to get jammed in the breech. That was one sort of jam.

'Or, if you'd had a good go at a Hun and possibly got rid of all your Lewis gun ammunition you used to have to change drums. Now, changing drums on the S.E.5 was a terrific job because the gun was up on the top plane clear of the top of the propeller and it was sort of a brass quadrant down which it slid when you caught hold of the back of it to release the catch; the gun came down into your hand and then it was firing vertically upwards or pointing vertically upwards. The drum was quite a heavy thing and when the wind was blowing past it at 100mph or so, as soon as you unclipped it it flew back, you see, and you had an awful job to get it down into the cockpit.

'Then you had to get the full drum up, again

S.E.5/S.E.5A SQUADRONS ON THE WESTERN FRONT

Squadron	Date formed	Date converted to S.E.5/5a	Date disbanded	Notable pilots
No 1 RFC/RAF	May 1912	January 1918	January 1920	31 ranking aces including future Air Vice Marshal Quintin Brand
No 24 RFC/RAF	September 1915	December 1917	February 1919	33 ranking aces including Bill Lambert and George McElroy
No 32 RFC/RAF	January 1916	March 1918	December 1919	16 ranking aces including Arthur Claydon
No 40 RFC/RAF	February 1916	October 1917	July 1919	Ranking aces included George McElroy, Edward Mannock, Indra Lal Roy, Gwilym Lewis
No 41 RFC/RAF	April 1916	November 1917	December 1919	17 ranking aces including William Claxton
No 56 RFC/RAF	June 1916	March 1917	January 1920	Ranking aces included Albert Ball, James McCudden, Gerald Maxwell, Arthur Rhys Davids
No 60 RFC/RAF	April 1916	July 1917	January 1920	26 ranking aces including 'Billy' Bishop, Keith Caldwell
No 64 RFC/RAF	August 1916	March 1918	December 1919	11 ranking aces including James Anderson Slater
No 68 RFC/RAF No 2 AFC	January 1917	January 1918	May 1919	18 ranking aces including Roy Philipps and Frank Alberry
No 74 RFC/RAF	July 1917	July 1917	July 1919	17 ranking aces including Edward Mannock, Ira Jones, Keith Caldwell
No 84 RFC/RAF	January 1917	September 1917	January 1920	Aces included Andrew Beauchamp-Proctor
No 85 RFC/RAF	August 1917	May 1918	July 1919	Aces included Edward Mannock, Billy Bishop, Elliott White Springs
No 92 RFC/RAF	July 1917	June 1918	August 1919	8 ranking aces including Oren Rose, James Robb
25th Aero Squadron, USAAS	May 1917	October 1918	June 1919	RFC ace Joseph Boudwin

S.E.5 SQUADRONS IN OTHER THEATRES

Squadron	Date formed	Date converted to S.E.5/5a	Date disbanded	Theatre of operations
No 61 RFC/RAF				Home Defence
No 72 RFC/RAF	June 1917	September 1918	September 1919	Mesopotamia
No 111 RFC/RAF	August 1917	January 1918	August 1919	Palestine
No 143 RAF	February 1918	May 1918	October 1919	Home Defence
No 145 RAF	May 1918	September 1918	August 1919	Palestine
No 150 RAF	April 1918	April 1918	August 1919	Greece/Balkans

out into the wind, and then push it on to the gun and then you had to push the whole gun up on to the top plane and then lock it into position. So you can see this was quite a thing to do with your right hand, flying with your left hand, Huns about, chaps coming down on you in the middle of it. It was not a situation to be caught in.'

Eventually the problems endured by Lewis with his Vickers gun were resolved. The Constantinesco gear was made reliable in the summer of 1918 when the hydraulic fluid was changed from pure oil to a mixture of 90% paraffin and 10% oil, which proved far less susceptible to the disturbance of combat flying and the changes in temperature and air pressure to which life on an S.E.5a subjected it.

In total 12 squadrons of the British, Australian and American air services would go to war on the Western Front flying the S.E.5 and S.E.5a. Six further British squadrons would be equipped with the type for Home Defence or overseas duties.

Life on the airfield

As has been seen in the previous chapters, to be the pilot of an S.E.5a in 1917 to 1918 was to be given every possible advantage that could be achieved within the parameters of available supplies and technology. It was a compromise but in general the balance was weighted in the pilot's favour. The cockpit of an S.E.5a was therefore a relatively happy place to be, when viewed against its predecessors or many of the alternatives.

It was sobering indeed for any airman who visited the trenches – whether by accident or design – and this could often lead to a sense of guilt about the conditions in which they lived. Cecil Lewis reflected upon the 'great divide' between the life and culture of the trenches and the airfield when speaking to the BBC in the 1960s: 'You see, you were 15 or 20 miles behind the lines, you had a comfortable bed, you had sheets, you had even electric light or something like that. You didn't have this terrible strain that could occur if you never could get

ABOVE Changing the Lewis drum: no mean feat at 15,000ft in a 120mph gale, even if you weren't being shot at. *(Aviation Images)*

BELOW The S.E.5s of 40 Squadron at rest in 1918, with the distinctive two-tone camouflage applied to the S.E.5a of 40-victory ace Roderick Dallas in the foreground. *(Aviation Images)*

ABOVE 32 Squadron kept a fox cub as one of its mascots – animals were popular additions to any squadron.
(Imperial War Museum)

BELOW Pilots of 1 Squadron stage a last-minute briefing for the cameraman.
(Imperial War Museum)

out of gunfire. You never could get out of the possibility that you might get hit even if you were asleep.'

One airman, Stuart Wortley, went to take a tour of the nearest sector to better understand his job and that of the men that the Royal Flying Corps was duty-bound to assist. He came away somewhat in awe of his guide: 'Suddenly I felt we two were poles apart. We were both fighting the same enemy – he on the ground and I a few hundred feet above his head. But those few hundred feet constituted an abyss almost unbridgeable. We had not the remotest notion of each other's feelings. I wish it could be arranged that infantry officers should be attached to RFC units and vice-versa.'

The use of the term 'infantry officers' is telling. The overwhelming majority of airmen were officers, many with a public school education that informed the entire culture of their squadrons. In the air they were 'playing the game', as though representing their house at rugger or fives, and when not in the air many of their preoccupations came straight from the school dormitory – such as getting 'de-bagged' during a drunken night in the mess. This was the sort of behaviour that Jimmy McCudden could never understand, from his relatively low-class beginnings, and which he felt to be unprofessional in the extreme.

For those new non-commissioned airmen in a squadron, as McCudden had been for so long, life was infinitely tougher. It was not the disparity in pay (10 shillings per day and an additional 8 shillings per day flying pay for an officer, half of those sums for an NCO), that affected them so much as the absolute solitude of their existence.

With no means of communicating with the outside world from the cockpit, beyond signalling via hand gestures, firing flares or rocking the wings, each man was left to confront the stresses of combat flying alone, which in turn magnified the importance of the boisterous behaviour and camaraderie on the ground. Seldom was there ever more than one NCO in a squadron, who was shut out of the officers' affairs by his rank and shut out of the world of the mechanics and batmen by the wings upon his chest.

Cecil Lewis in particular felt the strain that came with the intense isolation of flying when compared with the men in the trenches or on board ship, saying: 'You had nobody at your side, nobody who was cheering with you, nobody who would look after you if you were hit. You were alone, you know, and you fought alone and died alone. But those who died weren't there when we came back.'

Among a pilot's creature comforts, the importance of a batman to young officers in a Royal Flying Corps squadron is hard to overstate. Most would have been entirely familiar and at ease with domestic staff and,

ABOVE 1 Squadron heads out on patrol from Saint Omer, 1918. *(Imperial War Museum)*

conversely, whether they were a former butler or valet, or perhaps a former soldier doing what they could behind the lines, the batmen themselves had few qualms about acting as the keeper and conscience of young men in peril. One batman in particular is worth saluting for his Jeeves-like enquiry when unpacking a newly arrived pilot's bag and discovering, at the bottom, his much-loved woollen golliwog. With great reverence, he asked the embarrassed lieutenant: 'And where will you have this, sir?'

A greater proportion of pilots were of private means than almost any other branch of the armed forces, but even so, as we have seen, a second lieutenant was being paid a relatively enjoyable sum of 18 shillings per day including flying pay. This is why so many pilots had the use of private cars and motorcycles, and how the level of alcohol consumption that typified a front-line fighter squadron could be riotous in the extreme.

Former pilot Vernon Yeates also stated that 'no flying man could live in France and remain sober', going so far as to recount in his autobiographical novel *Winged Victory* an occasion when the lead character climbs into the cockpit for a morning patrol and realises that he is not even hung-over but in fact still intoxicated. This was not a rare occurrence. 'We lived, as it were, always in the stretch or the sag of nerves,' Cecil Lewis recalled. 'We were either in deadly danger or we were in no danger at all. And this conflict between something which was really more or less just like being at home and being really in quite a tight position had a great effect on us all, it produced a certain strain probably because of the change.'

The sense of camaraderie was intense between men confined within this isolated world. It did not equate to any other relationships that these men had ever enjoyed, be it family, friends, school or university peers. Yet Sopwith Camel pilot Arthur Gould Lee spoke for all airmen when he said: 'We seldom talk to each other about our private affairs. You seldom get to know much about a fellow's background … the only thing that counts is whether a chap has guts and can shoot straight. You share the same risks every day. Some get shot down the other side, and that's the last you hear of them. Some go home, and that's probably the last you hear of them, too. Yet, here in France, we're sort of a brotherhood. It's a rum life.'

That 'rum life' was all-consuming. Even when not flying, therefore, there was a sense of duty to be present whenever members of the squadron were aloft, as Cecil Lewis recalled: 'During the day there were other

ABOVE 1 Squadron flight leader returns to Saint Omer with his streamers fluttering in the evening sun. *(Imperial War Museum)*

patrols up besides our own, and very often our best friends were up on these patrols, so naturally we were up on the airfield waiting for them to come down, waiting to see how they fared. Waiting for them to come back, indeed. Sometimes they didn't. Then when they came down there was always the gossip of how they'd done, had they met anybody, had they had a kill and all that sort of thing. And the damage to their machines, perhaps they'd been in a dogfight and got shot up and they might have holes through their rudder, holes through their engines, we wanted to see what had gone on in fact.

'Then the pilot had to go into the Orderly Room and make out his Combat Report. Then he was free to do as he liked. And the messes, you see, were right out in the country. We were living usually on the outskirts of quiet villages. So when we wanted to whoop it up we usually went into town.'

The image of young men getting steaming drunk together and playing destructive games while singing popular songs of the day has become established as part of the airman's myth. It was almost uniquely a British trait – the Germans and French could let rip with the best of them, but it was never considered to be fundamental to their existence in the same way as the British boys went about their off-duty antics.

Alcohol and young women ('horizontal refreshment', as these brief liaisons were often referred to) were in ready supply in the villages and towns near the British airfields. It was easy to spot the men who were suffering the strain of their daily lives because they would be the ones who turned increasingly serious or morose as the evening went on. Vernon Yeates recounted a conversation in which one colleague grew quietly angry at the arrival of American forces in France. He put forth what is known today as a conspiracy theory, based on his belief in darker powers beyond the governance of kings or politicians:

'You see, this war is being financed for the Allies by an international gang that works in London, Paris and New York. It was getting hold of Berlin as well … As financiers widen their influence it is the ever-lessening group of nations to which they are fastening tentacles that bear the ever-increasing brunt. … But the side on which America has been brought in is the side of international finance. Enormous sums of money have been invested in this war, and an Allied victory is essential to preserve them as capital.'

FAR LEFT The 'Sidcot' suit was popularised throughout the last year of the war, replacing the random assortment of knitwear and furs in which airmen had dressed to that point. It would continue through to World War Two. *(Author)*

LEFT A suitably youthful re-enactor waits pensively in the Ready Room at Stow Maries Great War Aerodrome. *(Author)*

Such talk was not uncommon among airmen who became embittered in the belief that each flight was taking them closer to their doom. Even as they gained experience and craft, the vast majority of pilots held fading hopes of surviving to see the return of peace. This feeling was compounded when, in the last year of the war, virtually all of the high-scoring aces flew out to their deaths. For the hard-trying and hard-pressed men who looked up to the high scorers, it offered a bleak view of their own future.

'The fate of a pilot is a foregone conclusion,' said Edgar Taylor. 'Some of the most brilliant flyers who have ever come to the front and shot a score of Huns down went home for a rest only to "do it" at a training camp. Of course nothing can be perfect in this world so why worry. You cannot afford to waste time thinking of tomorrow when today is so important. I am afraid we are in for a long and deadly war. We must all buckle to, and so do our bit until we take "the longest flight of all".'

In the case of 56 Squadron – the 'squadron of aces' that gave the S.E.5 its combat debut after Cecil Lewis led the squadron out to France – it was easy to see how this sort of belief could be established. Of the 14 pilots who left London Colney for France on 7 April 1917, four were killed, four were seriously wounded and three, including Lewis, were sent back to lighter duties after physically or mentally cracking under the pressure. Later, during the German Spring Offensive of 1918, the officers of 56 Squadron suffered a proportionally higher rate of attrition than those in the infantry, with 41% killed (compared to 21% cent in the infantry), 15% wounded and 28% made prisoners of war.

The intensity of living within the bubble of a squadron meant that time away from the front was something of a trial to the vast majority of pilots. Those who had served sufficient time, or were adjudged to be close to breaking under the strain, would be sent to Home Establishment duties – instructing, Home Defence or test piloting. Yet for them the battle was then to try and get back to France, despite knowing full well the likely outcome.

Even periods of home leave – the longed-for passes for a few days in 'Blighty' – turned out to be something of a trial for many pilots. They were returning to loved ones and friends who existed as ideals to the pilots of all that they were fighting for while they were away, yet infuriated them in person with their domestic concerns and complete lack of understanding of squadron

RIGHT Home away from home: the Royal Flying Corps Club (later the RAF Club) at 13 Bruton Street in London allowed men on leave to enjoy the comradeship that they knew in France. *(Author)*

FAR RIGHT The Royal Automobile Club in Pall Mall was where pilots would find their mail and, if they were lucky, an affordable lodging for the duration of their home leave. *(Author)*

BELOW London offered excitement and entertainment to men on leave, and a means to escape the well-meaning but often irritating presence of loved ones. *(Getty)*

life. For pilots on leave, therefore, life on home leave tended to revolve around the RFC Club in London's Bruton Street, where they were free to continue their rowdiness and shop talk with fellow fliers and revel in their shared experience.

The London base for most pilots home from France was the Royal Automobile Club on Pall Mall, to where RFC officers' mail was directed for the duration of their leave. Many pilots also stayed there, although if it was full they would take rooms at the Strand Palace or Regent Palace hotels. The next priorities were alcohol and other refreshments, which American volunteer Bill Lambert and his party discovered in abundance at the Café Royal in Soho in the summer of 1918, where they discovered a social whirl like no other:

'When we entered those doors a blast of heat, smoke and odours of alcohol and human bodies almost knocked us off our feet … That place was packed with bodies, both male and female. The males were in the minority. Wild women, tame women, meek women, ferocious women and beautiful women. Amazons all. And out to conquer the male … I rolled into the Strand Palace at about 9.00am and slept until mid-afternoon.'

Such was a fairly standard start to a spell of home leave, which almost invariably focused around London, and the pleasures of going to the theatre (the perennial favourite being musical comedy *Chu Chin Chow*) or the cinema were light relief from hedonism. Then there were the tea dances and the chance to relive the pre-war craze for exotic steps like the Hesitation Waltz, Argentine Tango, Maxixe Polka or the Foxtrot.

Before heading back to their squadron, pilots would go in search of the latest records of ragtime and show tunes to take back for the mess gramophone, perhaps some sheet music of the latest hits for the piano or some goodies from Harrods. Finally they would head for the railway station, then towards the docks and onward, back to the life of the squadron.

Laddie's war

Like a great many young officers who flew the S.E.5a, one particular ranking 'ace' was born to an affluent middle-class family, went to public school and was being lined up for Oxford by proud parents who were looking forward to the day when their son would enter the diplomatic service. What made him unique was that he was Indian.

Indra Lal Roy was born in Calcutta in 1898, the second son of barrister Piera Lal Roy, the Director of Public Prosecutions for the city, and his wife Lolita. This was a well-heeled and well-connected Indian family, and Lolita's father, Dr Surya Kumar Goodeve Chakraborty, had been one of the first Indian doctors to be trained in Western medicine. Amongst the family, Indra was known as 'Laddie'.

In 1901 Lolita and her six children moved to England for their education, moving in to 77 Brook Green, West London. The boys – Paresh Lal, Indra Lal and Lolit Kumar – all appear to have been educated at Colet Court Preparatory School prior to attending St Paul's College, Kensington. By 1914 Lolita had moved the family to 15 Glazbury Road before moving on again in October 1915 to 67 Fitz-George Avenue in Kensington.

Laddie was a strong athlete like his brothers, captaining the swimming team and playing in the St Paul's first XV at rugby. In 1917 Laddie left the school but his parents' hoped-for career in diplomacy was set aside in favour of joining the Royal Flying Corps and flying into battle over the Western Front.

It would take months of wrangling with the authorities to take any great strides towards this ambition. No matter how anglicised the family may have been in its ambitions and outlook, Laddie was an Indian, and neither the Army nor Navy would take him on for pilot training. When pressed for a reason for rejecting him, it was claimed to be on the grounds of defective eyesight – although he was offered a place as a junior ground engineer.

In response, Laddie sold the motorbike that he used to get around London and paid a leading eye specialist to give a second opinion. No defect was found, and finally a significant backer was found in the form of Brigadier-General Sefton Brancker, the Director of Air Organisation, whereupon Laddie's application was finally accepted on 4 April 1917. He was commissioned as a second lieutenant on 5 July, given pilot and gunnery training and finally posted to join 56 Squadron on 30 October.

As a member of 'A' Flight, commanded by

LEFT Ace of India: Indra Lal Roy wrote a unique chapter in history during his time in 40 Squadron. *(Author)*

BELOW A factory-fresh S.E.5a powered by the geared 200hp Hispano-Suiza, as flown throughout 'Laddie' Lal Roy's front-line service. *(Farnborough Air Sciences Trust)*

RIGHT Among the many myths about Indra Lal Roy was that his grave was inscribed in Bengali saying: 'A valiant warrior's grave; respect it, do not touch it'. It has, however, always read: 'He died for the ideals he loved'. *(Author)*

Captain Richard Maybery, Laddie seems to have had a fairly uneventful war until he crashed while flying S.E.5a serial B567 on 6 December 1917. Lying unconscious in the wreckage, he was taken for dead and laid out in a morgue at nearby Étaples. After coming to his senses, Laddie kept banging on the morgue door but the terrified attendant dared not open up for some considerable time for fear of what might be awakening in the darkness beyond.

The records of the resulting Medical Board show that Laddie was declared unfit to resume flying for five months. He contested this opinion as strongly as possible while in recuperation, otherwise occupying himself by sketching aeroplanes – many of these drawings have survived to this day – before he was passed fit for a return to the Armament School at Uxbridge. In April 1918 he was posted to 40 Squadron in France, but for some reason was soon readmitted to hospital and sent back to Britain. He finally rejoined 40 Squadron on 14 June, where his flight commander was George McElroy, who was famously tutored by his great friend and mentor 'Mick' Mannock.

Evidently, McElroy's tutelage was every bit the equal of Mannock's, and on 6 July Laddie was credited with his first victory in combat – and in the space of 13 days he would be credited with nine more, whether individual or shared victories. On the morning of 22 July, however, the brief but vigorous war of Indra Lal Roy came to an end. His flight of eight S.E.5as encountered four Fokker D.VIIs from *Jasta* 29 at 16,000ft over Carvin, of which two were shot down. Yet from this melee one of the British aeroplanes also fell away burning brightly, carrying Laddie to his death.

India's first and only ranking air ace was gone. Confirmation of his death was only received in September 1918, when his posthumous Distinguished Flying Cross was gazetted.

Flight magazine carried a telling obituary to Laddie, which might best be described as an accomplished act of spin-doctoring when it stated: 'He was one of a band of young Indians staying here who, precluded until recently from any chance of obtaining commissions in the Army, found scope for striking a blow for the Empire in the new arm of our forces.'

'Mick' Mannock: Ace of Aces

No book on the S.E.5 would be complete without mention of its greatest exponent, 'Mick' Mannock. So much about this man

RIGHT The small terraced house in Wellingborough where the greatest British pilot of the Great War lodged before the conflict and which he regarded as home throughout the rest of his life. *(Author)*

100

ROYAL AIRCRAFT FACTORY S.E.5 MANUAL

has become enshrined in myth that he makes 'Laddie' Lal Roy appear like a straightforward character. It is impossible to verify more than half of the legends around Mannock, but what remains still holds unparalleled resonance.

Like his great friend James McCudden, Mannock was 'born in barracks' into the family of an Irish Catholic non-commissioned officer in the British Army, one Patrick Mannock. Unlike McCudden, Mannock never really knew stability or security because he moved between England, Ireland and India before his father deserted the family and was never seen again. The young Mannock eventually took work with the National Telephone Company and moved to Wellingborough, where he found lodgings with the leading light of the local Independent Labour Party, Jim Eyles and his wife.

In 1914 Mannock took a lucrative offer to work in Turkey. At the outbreak of the war, however, Turkey sided with Germany, and Mannock was among the British nationals held captive, suffering severe privation until the US embassy negotiated his release. Upon his return to Britain, Mannock almost immediately volunteered for the Royal Army Medical Corps and then transferred to the Royal Flying Corps for pilot training.

After gaining his 'wings', Mannock went for advanced training at Joyce Green aerodrome near Dartford, which was a bleak place run like a penal colony by instructors who hadn't set foot in France and resented those who were about to. A ray of light was the arrival of a new instructor, McCudden, who managed to impose himself and to find some latent talent in the highly strung recruit.

Their friendship literally saved Mannock's life – and, as a result, those of many others – when he accidentally got his DH2 into a spin on finals and narrowly avoided crashing into the munitions factory on the other side of the Thames. The colossal explosion that would have resulted can scarcely be imagined, yet despite regaining control and landing safely it took some sharp diplomacy to keep Mannock from official censure as the factory owners demanded that a stern example was made of him.

Instead of being sent to the trenches in disgrace, Mannock ended up at 40 Squadron in the spring of 1917, flying Nieuports throughout the killing season of 'Bloody April' when the Germans wrought such havoc upon their opposite numbers. He was not initially popular, being outspoken and boorish on the ground while many of his comrades felt that he was holding back in the air, with whispers of cowardice being uttered until he finally began to show skill at bringing down the enemy.

Mannock was afraid, and desperately so. His letters and diary made passing reference to the state of his nerves but his confidantes knew that he was a man on the edge of the abyss, nauseous before every flight and over-compensating for his fears with a surfeit of bravado on the ground. Yet he refused to be beaten by his fears, and thanks in no small part to a burning sense of injustice at his treatment in Turkey he used his maturity – at 30 years of age, a decade clear of most airmen – to study air combat from the cockpit and develop tactics that would reap enormous rewards for him personally – scoring 21 victories with 40 Squadron and for the many pilots his leadership would inspire.

One outlet for Mannock's nerves was an intense dislike for the S.E.5a when 40 Squadron was first equipped with it, in the autumn of 1917. The Constantinesco gear on these Hispano-engined aeroplanes was deemed to have been from a bad batch turned out by a factory lacking the required tolerances to produce such a piece of precision engineering. When General Trenchard made one of his visits, Mannock left him in little doubt about the shortcomings of the new fighter as he saw

ABOVE **The airfield at Joyce Green is as bleak now as it was a century ago.** *(Author)*

ABOVE **The S.E.5as of 74 Squadron at rest, the unit with which Mannock peaked as a leader.** *(Aviation Images)*

them, and would regularly rant about the S.E. while insisting that pilots spend more time at the gun butts and load their own ammunition in order to weed out any poorly made rounds that would exacerbate the problems.

By coincidence, Mannock was soon back in England on Home Establishment duties, although from the outset he was pushing to return to the front line. In desperation he met with Brigadier-General Sir David Henderson at the RFC Club and demanded that he be sent back, lest he climb into one of the aeroplanes on his station at Biggin Hill and fly there himself. Henderson told Mannock that he would be shot for desertion, to which Mannock replied: 'Better death than dishonour, sir!'

Soon he was posted to the unit with which he became most closely associated, 74 Squadron, which was then at London Colney in the process of readying itself for front-line service, as 56 Squadron had been a year earlier when Albert Ball arrived. Mannock and 74 were a match made in heaven, not least thanks to the encouragement of its commanding officer, New Zealand veteran Keith 'Grid' Caldwell.

Mannock and Caldwell were a double act: the former full of wild excesses on the ground while targeting his attacks in the air with precision and ferocity, while the senior man was a solid commander whose wild-eyed leadership in the air almost decimated the squadron on occasion. Both inspired the men, who were all subject to a relentless stream of consciousness from Mannock on tactical awareness and self-preservation.

'Gentlemen: always above, seldom on the same level, never underneath.' It was a mantra that began and ended every pep talk. Mannock insisted that the men load their own guns and pay attention to the rigging and servicing of their aeroplanes. After every flight Mannock would give a thorough assessment of every man's performance, even when he had scored or the sky had been full of whirling fighters – so much for the legend of Mannock being blind in one eye.

He would roar hatred towards Huns and give wild-eyed descriptions of them trapped in burning aeroplanes. 'Frying tonight!' and 'Sizzle, sizzle wonk!' became clarion calls around the airfield. Meanwhile he would snap off a volley of 'what if' questions over the breakfast table. When the neighbouring unit, 4 Squadron of the Australian Flying Corps, was proving less than adept in combat, Mannock was seconded to give the men a talking-to. 'Mannock took upon himself the task of making all the pilots around him keen and aggressive,' remembered future ace Arthur Cobby. 'Several talks of his to the Australian pilots there were responsible for some fine aggressive shows against the enemy, and numerous combined affairs were successfully carried out.'

Mannock's own victories were also piling up and he was not averse to softening up a suitable target in order for a promising or hesitant newcomer to issue the *coup de grâce*. What he would not tolerate under any circumstances was shirking, and if he felt that anyone in his flight was looking for a way up and out he would fire his Lewis gun across their bows.

That determination was born of his own fear of the job in hand, which became an ever-increasing issue no matter how experienced he became or how many victories he amassed. The loss of his star pupil Henry Dolan came as a bitter blow and Mannock was clearly on the verge of breaking down. His remaining confidante was Ira 'Taffy' Jones, to whom one morning he solemnly asked: 'Are you ready to die for your country, Taffy? Will you have it in flames or in pieces?'

In June 1918 he went back to England on leave, where he returned to the Eyles family home in Wellingborough and promptly broke down. 'He was ashamed to let me see him in this condition but could not help it,' Jim Eyles later recalled. But on 5 July he was back in France, taking up command of 85 Squadron at Saint Omer, having said his goodbyes to England.

It was 85 Squadron that had turned down Jimmy McCudden for the CO's position because of his low birth, and also because they feared he was selfish about claiming victories. Mannock, however, in many ways lower-born than McCudden, galvanised the men and set about drilling them with his many dicta through a furious three weeks in charge.

The fury within Mannock was enflamed still further when news reached the squadron of McCudden's death on 10 July. It would not be long before Mannock also fell, having brought down a German two-seater that had been troubling the British trenches. He was flying low over the German trenches at Pacault Wood when his S.E.5a, serial E1295, was hit by ground fire and began to burn. It described a lazy figure of eight as the flames consumed it before crashing behind the German trenches next to Butter Lane.

The Germans found his body some distance from the S.E., removed his identification and personal items and buried him. They noted in detail where he lay. In 1920 the Commonwealth War Graves found the remains of an unidentified airman buried near Butter Lane and interred them at Laventie Military Cemetery in Block F, Row 12, Grave 3, with the inscription 'Known unto God'. Jim Eyles spent the remaining 40 years of his life trying to prove that it was Mannock, in efforts to grant his friend a last resting place.

Investigation has followed investigation, and in the 1980s Major T.A. Edwin Gibson MBE, chief records officer for the Commonwealth War Graves Committee, wrote an internal report stating that all evidence did indeed point to Mannock being the 'unknown airman' in Laventie. Since then technology has been

ABOVE 74 Squadron waiting on the flight line in France. *(Aviation Images)*

BELOW Not the recommended position for changing the Lewis drum on a 74 Squadron mount. *(Aviation Images)*

RIGHT Major Edward Mannock, VC, DSO & two bars, MC & bar.
(Imperial War Museum)

BELOW To fly an S.E.5a is to join one of the most exclusive clubs in modern aviation.
(Darren Harbar)

perfected that could even identify King Richard III though he had lain under a council car park in Leicester for nearly 550 years. It is time to take that technology to France.

'Mick' Mannock was not only a phenomenal fighter pilot but he also did his best to ensure that the men who served alongside him stood the best possible chance of survival. Moreover, his achievements were made in the face of crippling self-doubt and by confronting his basest fears each time he took off. He was and remains a hero, and it is a national disgrace that the bravest airman to rank as an 'ace', and one of only 19 airmen to be recognised with the Victoria Cross, has still not had his name restored to him.

Flying the S.E.5a today

Pilots are precise in pretty well every aspect of their lives, so when a pilot says casually that they've flown 'about 27 different types', they mean 27 exactly. And they can remember, with about the same ease that they can tell you their children's birthdays, exactly where, when and for how long they flew each one.

A pilot's logbook is his or her most valued possession, and the number and type of aeroplanes logged are of immense personal value. That is why, if you were to offer pretty well any active pilot in the world the opportunity to fly an S.E.5, they would be at the airfield gates in a heartbeat.

'I did about 15 hours on it,' said Henry Labouchere of his time flying the Eberhart SE-5E G-BLXT in the early 1990s. 'I didn't aerobat it. I suppose the best description would be that it's like quite a nice Tiger Moth. Of course, that sounds like a conflict of interests as there's no such thing!' Labouchere, an airman renowned for his abilities with vintage machinery, is a world authority on the Tiger Moth and other 1930s designs, and for him it was the comparative abundance of power that made the SE-5E stand out. 'It's a very low-revving engine. It was flat out straight and level at 1,700rpm. I recall it needed about 1,450 on take-off. It wasn't in any way demanding from that perspective.'

The first flight that Henry Labouchere made in G-BLXT was probably its longest for more than half a century, when he carried the colours of James McCudden to the 80th anniversary of the founding of the Royal Flying Corps. 'We got it going at Rendcomb and I flew alongside my brother-in-law in a Westland Scout helicopter, who did radio work. We flew it to Netheravon and then onwards from Netheravon to Norfolk via Old Warden.'

Almost a quarter of a century on and G-BLXT is back in the air. 'It's a delightful aeroplane,' Richard Grace confirmed, having made his first flight in it after restoration. 'It certainly leaps off the ground a lot more quickly than I thought it would – I'm more accustomed to the Stampe, where you have time to get the tail up and pootle along a bit before it takes off, whereas the S.E.5 was leaping off the ground in a three-point attitude after 50 yards in nil wind, which is quite something.'

To any pilot making their first flight in an S.E.5 the lustiness of an on-song V8 is a pleasant surprise. 'As they say with these things, it's a 150hp Wright-Hispano – which it would be, being an 'E' – but it's 150 shire horses!' Richard Grace added. 'I hadn't quite appreciated how strong these shire horses were going to be. I didn't push the rate of climb on the first flight; I was getting a feel for the controls and checking temperatures and pressures and then flew around for five minutes before coming in to land. The landing is – well, it lands like an aeroplane, really. It's quite a draggy machine and if you got behind the drag curve you'd end up thumping it in, but as long as you don't get behind the drag curve it just kind of lands, really. I did read that people said it's incredibly speed-critical, but as I didn't have an airspeed indicator I couldn't really worry about that. My view looking out of the windows told me that it lands just like an aeroplane! You couldn't really ask for too much more.'

One of the most experienced S.E.5 pilots active today is Rob Millinship of the Shuttleworth Collection, whose pilots are often former test pilots and who are all committed to preserving the fleet of priceless machinery for posterity. 'It's a military aeroplane with all the complexity of any military machine,' Rob said. 'And if you look at the fuel system, particularly in the S.E.5, you need to know what you're doing in order to operate it properly. It's not a Cessna: it's a fighter – admittedly an early one.'

The fuel system as fitted to the S.E.5 is probably the greatest mystery to unravel for a new convert. Gene de Marco's first outing came after he and the craftsmen of the Vintage Aviator Limited had already built three examples – and fortunately proved to be a rewarding experience!

BELOW The cockpit of an S.E.5 is rewarding and user-friendly for prospective pilots. *(Darren Harbar)*

ABOVE Take-off for TVAL's S.E.5a takes pilots back to basics in a thoroughbred 'B'507'. *(Brian Harmer)*

BELOW The rugged terrain of New Zealand holds no fears for Gene de Marco. *(Phil Makanna/Ghost)*

'Admittedly the S.E.5a was never a favourite of mine,' said Gene, who had flown a host of designs from the same period, most notably with Cole Palen's operation at Old Rhinebeck Aerodrome in New York State. 'It looked difficult to build and not particularly attractive – after all, it has a nose that looks more like a doghouse than a streamlined flying machine.'

Fortunately for all concerned, Gene discovered the virtues of the S.E.5 that lie beneath its functional exterior. And in so doing he discovered that managing the flow of fuel was the most taxing part of operating the type: 'Located in the leading edge of the centre section is the expansion tank for the cooling system. If the engine runs hot and begins to overheat, the small drain tube that extends over the centre section and ends at the trailing edge will be spewing coolant. In the same centre section leading edge is the emergency fuel tank. There's no filler cap for this tank. Fuel must be forced into it from the main tank using the engine-driven air pump or the hand air pump to pressurise the main fuel tank, and then selecting a position on the fuel selector which allows the fuel to flow uphill to the emergency tank. When it's full another overflow tube that extends from the tank to the trailing edge will alert you.

'During flight the fuel system is straightforward, but one must be aware of several different settings. There's a fuel selector position that allows fuel to gravity-feed from the centre section tank in an emergency. This provides about 15 minutes of flying time.

There's also a setting for the "source", to allow you to switch from engine-driven pump to the hand-operated air pump, in case the engine-driven pump fails.'

The reliability of 100-year-old engines is a vexed question, but Gene de Marco is unequivocal that a well-prepared Hispano-Suiza is a trustworthy power plant. He has flown over the 14-mile Cook Strait in an S.E.5a between the two islands of New Zealand and would do the same again tomorrow. 'When you look at the Cook Strait it doesn't perhaps look like much, but if you know the geography of the North Island and the South Island there's actually about 60 miles where you can't set an aeroplane down. And I was entirely confident in flying that with the Hispano,' he said.

Converting from modern aeroplanes to a 100-year-old design might be a daunting prospect in theory, but all the pilots agree that it's less of a leap into the unknown with the S.E.5 than it would be with a rotary-engined machine with the very different engine management and dynamics that would be required. In fact, the S.E.5 feels relatively modern – or 'conventional' – making it a type that's well suited to converting from less exotic machinery.

For Rob Millinship and the pilots at the Shuttleworth Collection, the path towards mastering each type is smoothed by experience. 'If you come to the S.E.5a via the Shuttleworth Collection, you've built up experience on relevant technology because the Collection has been subdivided into groups of aeroplanes. Those groups are designed to teach you what to look at for the next one in the group each time: it's a very structured route. From memory the S.E.5 is in the same group as the Bristol Fighter and the Hawker Hind because they're all liquid-cooled V8 to V12, from direct to reduction gears and from un-supercharged to supercharged. With a group like that you'd probably go from S.E.5 (V8 un-supercharged direct-drive) to the Bristol V12 geared engine and then the Hind V12 geared supercharged.

'In my case I flew the Bristol first because they needed somebody to fly the aeroplane for a film and I was available midweek, so I got fast-tracked on to the Bristol Fighter – but I'd got experience on all the Collection Moths and Magisters and so on, and had a lot of experience on Don Cashmore's Hawker Signet, which is very similar to the Bristol in some respects, in that it's got massive adverse yaw. And I'd flown that for probably 70 or 80 hours before I flew the Bristol Fighter, which gave me a unique "heads-up" on flying that type of aeroplane.'

As the most recent convert to flying the S.E.5, Richard Grace climbed into the cockpit without the extensive support of the Shuttleworth Collection to call upon, but instead his extensive experience of all manner of different historic types. 'I obviously wasn't dumb enough to not talk to Tony Bianchi (who restored it in 1985), and Henry Labouchere and see what I could glean from them, but all I really gleaned from them was that it flies quite a lot like an aeroplane, so I should get in it and get on with it! That's exactly what I did,' Richard said.

Given that many types of the 1920s and 1930s that might be close to the S.E.5 in terms of handling are no less rare or cherished than a fighter from 1917, it is generally agreed that the relatively humble Stampe SV4 is the best-suited machine for a prospective S.E.5 pilot to get to grips with. Rob Millinship certainly feels that the S.E.5 is not an aeroplane that should cause new pilots to fret unduly.

'If you take your average Tiger Moth pilot, they'll fly it very nicely,' he said. 'Take-off and flying won't be a problem. Coming in to land they'll have a lot of stuff to keep an eye on, temperatures and the fuel system and adjusting tanks in order to keep flying. But the actual

ABOVE A flying dynasty: Richard Grace restored and flies the Seafire Mk III, while his father Nick restored the two-seat Spitfire Mk IX now flown by mum Carolyn. *(Alamy)*

RIGHT The Stampe SV-4C is agreed to be a good training ground for prospective S.E.5 pilots today. *(Alamy)*

BELOW Checking the flying wires is essential before every flight. *(Darren Harbar)*

BOTTOM The glamorous life of a pilot! S.E.5s reward minute inspection. *(Darren Harbar)*

flying of the aeroplane is quite Stampe-like in a lot of ways.'

The Stampe was certainly Richard Grace's main point of reference before flying the SE-5E: 'I would say that the Tiger Moth wouldn't stand you in good stead to fly the S.E.5. I've got a lot of time in a Stampe and that's far more like the S.E.5 in that it handles very similarly, whereas the old Tiger is a bit sluggish in comparison. The S.E.5 is very sensitive to fly. Obviously, this is speaking from my vast ten-minute experience!'

Before climbing into any aeroplane the onus is on the pilot to ensure that it's in good working order. Preflight checks on a wood-and-canvas biplane are, by their nature, more extensive than those of a modern metal monoplane, and require considerable care and attention. 'Preflight of the S.E.5a consists of the usual walk-around inspection, checking for abnormalities and defects as well as a few specific items,' said Gene de Marco. 'The two lower aileron control horns are susceptible to damage and must be carefully checked. The entire tail skid assembly is complex and also requires a close look, and finally the main fuel tank and engine are checked.

'As you lower yourself into the cockpit of the S.E.5a, it just feels right. Visibility is adequate, the controls are in the right place, the cockpit isn't too large or too tight, and as you take to the air you realise it isn't all that noisy or even that windy.'

Rob Millinship is quick to point out that the S.E.5 requires focus and that getting up and down are the important elements of the job. 'At the end of the day it's an aeroplane,' he said. 'If it comes apart in the air it will kill you, so there's no point in being overawed by it. You can't sit in it thinking, "This is an actual S.E.5 from World War One and on the day before the Armistice it shot another aeroplane down." If you start on that game you'd never fly it!

'You need to be cold-hearted and say it's an aeroplane with all the same potential failings as any other. Your preflight checks must be good, although Shuttleworth engineers operate in a military fashion and complete a comprehensive set of preflight checks for you, but as the pilot the onus is on you to complete those checks and confirm that you're confident to fly the aeroplane. It's no different whether it's a Jumbo or an S.E.5 – you need to go around it and have a look. And from my point of view, because I spend a lot of time flying biplanes, I'm not just looking for obvious loose things. I personally tend to look at all of the flying wires and all of the flying wire pickups.'

Getting in to the S.E.5 reveals a snug working environment. Edwardians were generally smaller than most people in today's world – in photos 'Mick' Mannock appears to tower over his companions, but he was 5ft 10in tall according to his medical papers. Just like a classic racing car, therefore, a compact build is the best start to getting comfortable.

'The SE5 fits me perfectly, and I'm 5ft 7in,' Rob Millinship said. 'I don't need a cushion – my view through the Aldis gunsight is perfect. All of the cables go directly under the seat, so you can't lower that if you're taller. My shoulders, or just below my shoulders, touch the sides of the cockpit. We don't have the leather coaming on the cockpit – a lot of front-line aircraft didn't, and we decided not to. Some I've seen are a bit padded and look a bit Mickey Mouse. I like ours as it is, and it fits me perfectly. If you say to a six-foot-six pilot, "Do you want to fly the world's last operational World War One aeroplane?", they'll shoe-horn their way into it even if it's the most uncomfortable thing in the world! It's a monster privilege to be able to fly these things.'

The pilot is an active participant in the starting procedure. Whether fitted with a Hispano-Suiza or Wolseley Viper engine, there's plenty to do before the propeller starts to spin. 'First thing to do is make sure both magneto switches are in the "Off" position,' said Gene de Marco, 'then pressurise the fuel system by selecting the hand pump instead of the engine-driven pump and start pumping. If the tank is full it'll only require a dozen or so pumps to reach the necessary pressure (1.5psi). At this point an engineer would be preparing to prime the engine with raw fuel through small brass priming cups located on the intake manifold. Once the engine is primed and pulled through several revolutions with the switches off it's ready to start.'

Once started and idling smoothly, the pilot will be maintaining a watching brief on the temperatures, allowing the coolant to warm up and the fuel pressure to stabilise while checking

BELOW Bracing wires on the tail were insurance for high-speed dives – not a regular manoeuvre in 2017, but it's reassuring to have the support. *(Darren Harbar)*

BOTTOM Climbing aboard the S.E.5 is to enter a functional environment where there are many pleasures to be found. *(Darren Harbar)*

ABOVE With an airframe that is less than a decade old, Gene de Marco can throw his 'Hisso'-engined S.E.5a around with glee. *(TVAL)*

the magnetos – and ensuring that they're both in the 'On' position. 'It's really silly little things like the mag switches that can trip up the unwary,' said Rob Millinship. 'To have both mags the switch needs to be in the middle. It would be very easy for most pilots to get airborne on one mag.'

Once those hundred-year-old shire horses have pulled the S.E.5a into the sky it's time to get a feel for its handling qualities. Anyone expecting a docile little old lady of the skies is in for a rude awakening, according to Millinship, who has flown the S.E.5 for almost 25 years. 'It's a gun platform,' he said flatly. 'Unlike the other stuff of that era, particularly the rotary engine machines, you just point it. It's a point-and-shoot machine and it's very stable. You can aim it beautifully.

'The S.E.5 flies conventionally and we used to aerobat it, which was good fun. We're not allowed to fly it like that any more because of its age and importance, but it was a very nice aerobatic aeroplane.'

For a recently built airframe, like the three S.E.5as built by TVAL in New Zealand, there can be a little more fizz in the pilot's handling. An S.E.5 that doesn't yet need to be preserved for posterity is an opportunity to sample some of the manoeuvres that were regular daily occurrences in combat flying.

'To get a better feel for what this airplane can do, steep turns, lazy eights and wingovers are attempted, all easily carried out but an excessive amount of adverse yaw is experienced,' said Gene de Marco. 'I'm still amazed that it's so easy to fly and feels so stable. Turns in either direction are simple as long as they're coordinated with the rudder. Climb performance is a respectable 750ft per minute or so. The controls feel good at low speed and there's plenty of warning before the stall. The S.E.5a isn't overly agile but it can be thrown around with a little effort and has the ability to dive away and pick up speed rather quickly. The engine speed is easily regulated and only occasional glimpses of the temperature gauge are needed to regulate the radiator shutters and keep the engine cool.'

For a newcomer to the type, like Richard Grace, the exploratory process of the first flights in an S.E.5a are a thoroughly enjoyable learning curve. Details of the design over which Henry Folland and John Kenworthy laboured so intensely, and which were honed by the flying skills of men like Frank Goodden and Roderick Hill, still leap out to the modern pilot no matter how great his experience.

'It's very sensitive in all planes, especially in yaw,' Richard said. 'The rudder doesn't need to be moved too far to create quite a surprising effect. Obviously that's compounded by the fact that the cockpit sides are very low so as soon as you use the rudder you feel it on your shoulder in terms of airflow. Which is quite handy, really, because this particular aeroplane doesn't actually have a slip ball in it, and never has had one either, so you're flying around without a slip ball in an aeroplane that needs a lot of rudder. It keeps you on your toes! I kind of like the challenge. I think with all of these sorts of antiquated aeroplanes, they've all got their idiosyncrasies. If you find yourself flying one of the two or three – certainly no more – original S.E.5s in the world you shouldn't really need a slip ball. In fact no instruments at all would probably be for the best. My airspeed indicator didn't work, so you really shouldn't rely on any instruments to be able to fly it. Taste, smell and that feeling in your arse should get you by.'

Comparing the handling qualities of various hundred-year-old designs is a luxury afforded to few airmen. Thanks to his experience around the world, Gene de Marco is well qualified to comment – and he believes that the S.E.5a is about the optimum single-seat fighter of its era.

'Of the three main Hispano types – the SPAD, the Sopwith Dolphin and the S.E.5 – the SPAD is really strong and really fast but it's not manoeuvrable at all,' he said. 'The Dolphin flies nicely but one thing stands out about it – the pilot. If anything goes wrong on the ground and it goes over there's no way that the pilot is going to walk away from that … you can't crouch down because the centrifuge is lifting you.

'The wings of the S.E.5 aren't as strong as the SPAD. If you go into a vertical dive and then pull out, you have to be gentle, or the wings will fail at some point. The SPAD had double-rigged two-bay wings, and it wasn't going to fail when you pulled out from a dive, but it simply couldn't turn anything like as well. So you dive on your target, it's stable, you've got time to aim and take your shot. But dogfighting was best avoided in the SPAD – fortunately you could just put the nose down to get away, and you know that any German aeroplane is going to lose its wings trying to chase you.'

As for the other single-engined types, most notably the Sopwith Camel, again the S.E.5a strikes the best compromise between agility and safe handling for pilots of all levels of ability. 'If you're a pilot with six or maybe ten hours total before you first get into a front-line aeroplane, it would be very easy to kill yourself in a Camel,' said Gene. 'The statistics bear that out. You can say, with hindsight, that perhaps they weren't flying it right, or that there are better ways to handle it than were being taught at the time. But you simply can't apply what we know today to the situation as it was. Young guys with very little experience were getting thrown into these machines and it was sink or swim. In the Camel they had to fly an extremely difficult machine while working out the fuel and engine settings as they went – the pilot was basically the carburettor. In the S.E.5 there were so many luxuries, so many problems engineered out of it, that it was and remains a very modern, pleasant aeroplane to fly.'

LEFT The start of a new partnership: Richard Grace takes the restored SE-5E on its first flight after restoration, 21 October 2016. *(Air Leasing)*

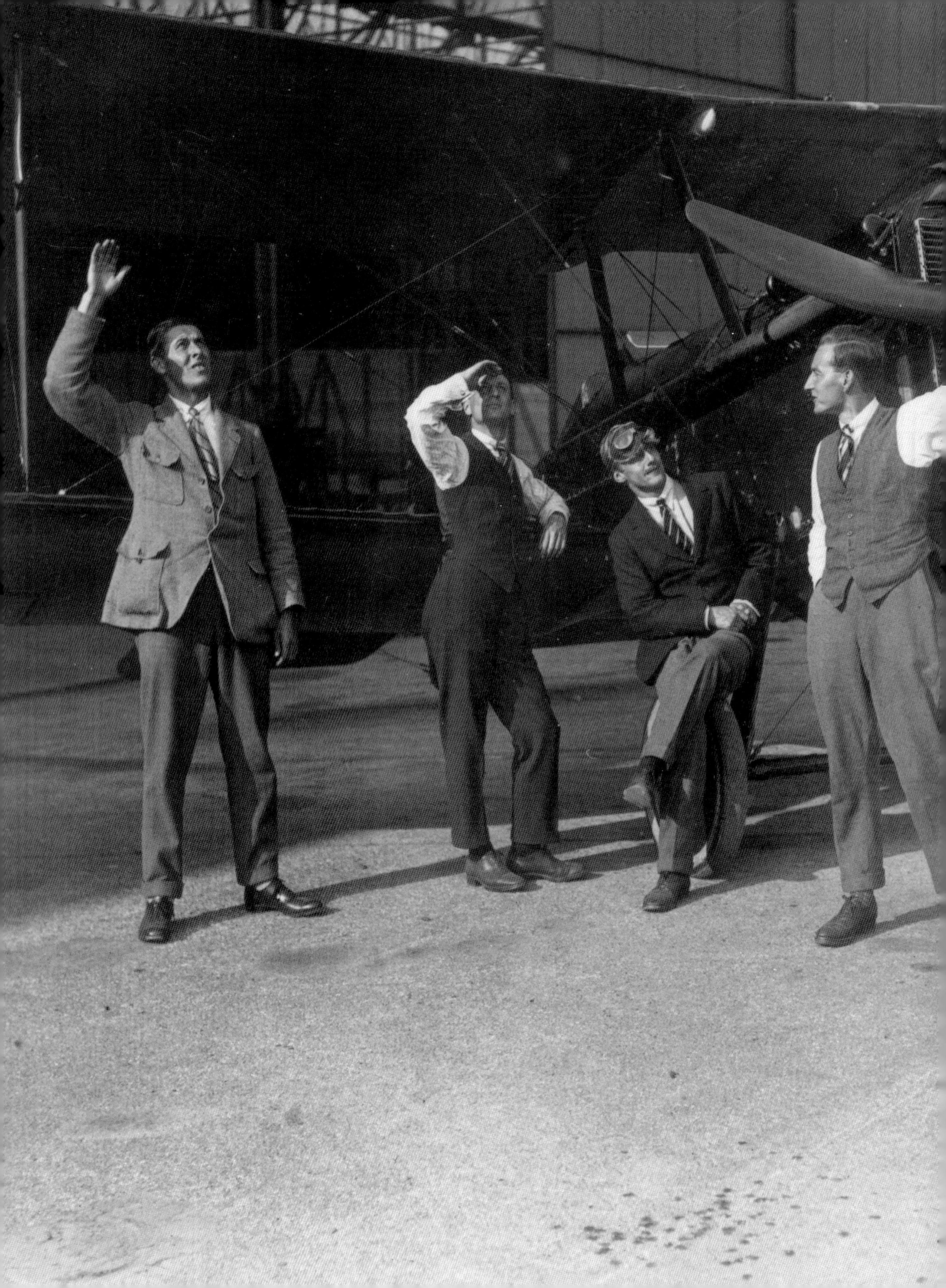

Chapter Five

The owner's view

The S.E.5a was already out of favour as a front-line fighter by the end of the Great War, having been surpassed by the performance of the Sopwith Dolphin and Snipe. In the months that followed the Armistice, the 'peacetime' Royal Air Force sought many and varied ways to disperse its unwanted aeroplanes and recoup some of the staggering costs that had been incurred in order to meet the challenge posed by Germany's illustrious *Jagdstaffeln*.

OPPOSITE Preparations for the first and only University Air Race of 1921, when teams of dashing young blades from Oxford and Cambridge performed a lap of London and the south-east. *(Getty/Topical Press)*

ABOVE In total 20 S.E.5s were sent to Poland, where they were flown in Polish colours against the Bolsheviks. Two were believed to have been captured, with one being operated by the Red Air Force. *(Aviation Images)*

Post-war and civilian aircraft

Although the politicians – and to an extent the public – pronounced the Armistice of 1918 to be the end of the 'war to end all wars', there was still plenty of conflict in the world through 1919 and 1920, where S.E.5s could be dispatched. One of the first military recipients of the type was Poland, which had a fighting force drawn from her own nationals and dispossessed White Russian servicemen loyal to the Tsar who waged a short and bitter war against the new post-revolutionary Soviet Russia.

The Imperial Gift scheme saw S.E.5s distributed among the dominions, and further airframes were sold to the governments of America, Argentina, Chile, the Netherlands and Japan. None of this put much of a dent in the thousands of spare aeroplanes left gathering dust as, one by one, the wartime squadrons were wound down and disbanded. Many of these were sold off through officially appointed disposal companies.

The first civilian registration to be given to an S.E.5a was G-EATE, applied to a 200hp Hispano-Suiza-engined S.E.5a (formerly F9022) in 1920, and which was subsequently offered for sale at £700. This was significantly less than the construction cost but also a colossal amount of money for a civilian to have available. Prices came down, then down further, until finally they were priced to be attractive to a ready market in the form of recently demobbed airmen.

One former Bristol Fighter pilot, Philip Townsend, went to Hendon where a huge clearance sale of former Royal Air Force equipment was on display. He went in company with another former combat pilot, and while they marvelled at the prices the pair of them decided that the opportunity of buying an S.E.5a for £5 was too good to miss.

'We agreed the price, he bought one, I bought one. We had them filled up with petrol and oil, tested them there and then for engine efficiency, then took them up and flew around Hendon for about half an hour. We landed

RIGHT G-EBPA was owned by Mrs Eliott Lynn and regularly competed in air races. *(Aviation Images)*

within five minutes of each other, stopped our props, climbed out and shouted for joy at having such a wonderful flight. At the time, the S.E.5a was the "honey" machine of the war. We discussed things, reckoned up how much it would cost us – neither of us had a job to go to. I was 20, he was 21, and we were told that it would cost us £10 more to have the certificate of airworthiness … So we talked to the mechanics and they agreed to buy them back for £4 10s. It took us, I should think, half an hour in silent tears to walk away from Hendon aerodrome…'

Although young Townsend and his companion were thwarted in their dreams of S.E.5 ownership, plenty of other young men were not. Well-trained, experienced and wealthy former service pilots were thick on the ground, and ten S.E.5as were registered to private owners through the 1920s. The first to find a new owner was G-EAZT, owned by Dr Whitehead-Read of Canterbury. He wrote the aeroplane off in a landing accident in 1923 but replaced it with another example, G-EBCA, which was fitted with a 90hp Renault engine and a new cowling.

Most S.E.5s in private ownership took part in air races, which were enormously popular with participants, public and media alike. A total of ten S.E.5s were seen in competition, including regular air-race competitors G-EBOG (owned by Dudley Watt), G-EBPA (Mrs Eliott Lynn), G-EBQK (K. Hunter), G-EBQM (A. Wheeler), G-EBPD (H. Waghorn) and G-EBQQ, also owned by K. Hunter, which was kept at Brooklands until it was crashed on take-off, cartwheeling on to the Byfleet Banking and killing the pilot, Lieutenant Gwynne Maddocks.

The first appearance of S.E.5s in air racing came as early as 1921, when, in an effort to restore some former glories, an Oxford student and erstwhile test pilot, A.R. Boeree, decided to organise a University Air Race to rival the long-standing Boat Race as an outlet for the rivalry between the dark blue scholars of Oxford and their pale blue counterparts at Cambridge.

To join either of the teams the requirement was to have more than 1,000 hours logged as a pilot. In total six pilots from each university signed up to take part, of whom three would race and three would be held in reserve. Meanwhile the Varsity Air Race was incorporated within the programme of the 1921 Aerial Derby at Hendon, with the Royal Aero Club providing the students with sufficient funds to hire eight decommissioned S.E.5a fighters for the event.

Although they were only hired, the university colours were applied to the aircraft – dark blue for Oxford and pale blue for Cambridge. A prize fund of £400 was also established thanks to an entrepreneurial event promoter by the name

LEFT G-EBQQ was written off in this accident on take-off at Brooklands, killing Lieutenant Gwynne Maddocks. *(Brooklands Museum)*

ABOVE THe Shuttleworth Collection's G-EBIA shown in her skywriting pomp during the 1930s.
(Alamy)

of Jack Savage, more of whom shall be seen anon. Most of the funding came from Shell, which also provided the fuel. A shortened version of the main Aerial Derby course was chosen, measuring around 43 miles and running in a triangle from Hendon to Epping and Hertford and back. Three laps of the course was the decided length of the event.

Race day was Saturday 16 June and it delivered scorching hot conditions and a near-cloudless sky. The six competing aircraft were lined up at 2:30pm with Oxford represented by Boeree (Oriel College), Pring (New) and Hurley (Keeble), while Cambridge had Francis (Caius), Philcox (Caius) and Muir (St Catherine's).

The Oxford trio took an early lead by thundering off at tree-top height, while the Cambridge contingent climbed as hard as they could to find cooler air where the 220hp Wolseley Viper engines would produce more get-up-and-go. The early running was made by Pring's machine for Oxford, but soon Cambridge's tactic of going for height paid off and Philcox took the lead halfway round the second lap.

On the final lap Pring's Wolseley Viper began to struggle and he was eventually forced to find a suitable field near Epping after the fault with his ignition proved terminal. The result was 1-2-3 for Cambridge, with Hurley fourth and Boeree, whose idea the race was, coming home last.

It was widely hoped that the University Air Race would become an annual event, to rival the Boat Race as a social fixture for the two great universities. Sadly, Oxford was never as keen as Cambridge on aviation in the first place and, with Boeree departing, the idea was shelved. All of the S.E.5s were later scrapped.

Far and away the biggest customer of the surplus S.E.5 sales was none other than Jack Savage, whose inventiveness and business acumen saw that salvation was granted for a total of 33 S.E.5s from the military stock sales. Savage's flying circus would soon become a transatlantic hit.

Major Savage's skywriting aeroplanes

In the days immediately before World War One an accidental discovery was made: if low viscosity oil inadvertently found its way into a hot exhaust it would vaporise, creating a vast and dense cloud of white smoke without any real detriment to the aeroplane. In these early days of flight, any such discovery was investigated for its possible usefulness in war – in this case smoke signals to ground troops or a defensive 'fog' to confuse attackers.

An aspiring aviation engineer at the time was one John Savage, born in 1891 and apprenticed to Claude Grahame-White in 1909. Savage had a flair for the theatrical and broke off his engineering career in order to become manager and agent to B.C. Hucks, the first Englishman to loop the loop.

During the war, Savage served as a lieutenant in the wartime Royal Naval Air Service, rising to become a major in the new Royal Air Force, but with the onset of peace he was wondering what to do with his future. He tried his hand at being a journalist, writing for *Flight* magazine under the nom de plume of Oiseau Bleu, but that did not quench his entrepreneurial spirit.

By 1921, 'Mad Jack' Savage had revisited the idea of producing smoke, and experimented with making first shapes and then letters in the air … and the art of skywriting was born. Enlisting former delivery pilot Cyril Turner to help develop the pre-war idea, Savage spent a year perfecting the technology and experimenting with different colour smoke until he was ready to reveal the fruits of his labour.

With the support of Lord Northcliffe, Savage's skywriting exploits received a very public debut at the 1922 Epsom Derby. A bumper crowd for one of the biggest racing weekends of the year was enthralled as the silver speck 10,000ft above them spelt out 'DAILY MAIL' in vast white letters which, the newspaper later claimed, was 'the greatest single development in outdoor advertising' and that 'everyone within an area of a hundred square miles – and there were millions – gazed spellbound at this fascinating sight'. Among those in the VIP enclosure at Epsom was none other than the leading novelist of the day, Virginia Woolf, who used the occasion as the opening segment in her next book, *Mrs Dalloway*.

Flushed with this success, Major Jack Savage shipped one of his aircraft to the USA with Cyril Turner, who carefully wrote 'HELLO USA' in the sky above New York. The following day the silver speck reappeared, writing: 'CALL VANDERBILT 7100'. The number put potential advertisers through to the hotel where Savage was staying – and the demand for his $1,000 service was insatiable.

Savage's business thrived on both sides of the Atlantic. His 33 fighter aircraft were equipped with air-to-ground radio in order for

ABOVE One of the many S.E.5as purchased by John Clifford Savage that would become famous for air racing and skywriting. *(Aviation Images)*

LEFT The elongated, asbestos-lagged exhaust pipe of a skywriting S.E.5a is shown clearly. The two pipes merged in a 'Y'-shape tail pipe, the rudder being trimmed to accommodate it. *(Aviation Images)*

ABOVE Under a different flag: Persil skywriter visits its homeland in the mid-1930s. Photographed at Croydon Airport, the swastika appeared on all German-registered aeroplanes at the time. *(Alamy)*

BELOW G-EBIA/F-904, the last airworthy Great War fighter, on display at the Shuttleworth Collection. *(Author)*

him to give personal instructions to the men at the controls. The biggest European success for Savage's skywriters came in 1928 when he was employed by German pharmaceutical company Henkel to promote its Persil brand of detergents. A German subsidiary was established and several of Savage's aeroplanes were re-registered with German identities, being painted brilliant green to match Persil's advertising. In the mid-1930s the Persil campaign was still going strong, although all of the aircraft involved were required to add a red stripe on the tail carrying the new national flag of National Socialist Germany. To this day, a cloudless blue sky is known as a 'Persil sky' in many parts of Germany.

By 1934 Savage's own skywriting operation at Hendon had been closed down and he had sold his Düsseldorf company to the Henkel organisation. Gradually his fleet was broken up – in most cases literally, having performed more than a decade of hard labour. Three of his aeroplanes survived the cull, however, with G-EBIA going into storage at the Armstrong-Whitworth factory, G-EBIB being donated to the Science Museum in 1939 and G-EBIC being sold to the Nash Collection of landmark aeroplanes, held in storage at Brooklands (later moved in 1940 to spare the collection from Luftwaffe bombers). Today these three aeroplanes stand as the longest-serving examples of the S.E.5 in the public eye. G-EBIA was winkled out of its long-term home in the rafters of the Armstrong-Whitworth factory by Air Commodore Allen Wheeler, a trustee of the Shuttleworth Collection, who negotiated its retrieval and restoration by the Royal Aircraft Establishment in 1957–59 and piloted the aeroplane on its first flight for 20 years (see Chapter Two).

The identities of G-EBIB and G-EBIC are thought to be somewhat confused, but two complete S.E.5as remain, in the Science Museum and the RAF Museum respectively. G-EBIB hung for many years from the Science Museum roof in her Savage skywriting apparel, but in 1961 she was taken down and given a makeover, being restored to her wartime livery of PC10 upper surfaces and clear varnished linen with the serial F-939. As a finishing touch her paddock number '6' was painted on, as worn when performing at the 1937 Hendon Air Day, and in this form she would remain for more than three decades. In 1992 she was taken down and restored again, with the opportunity being taken to return her to full Savage skywriting specification – requiring 30 gallons of dope, 60 square yards of Irish linen and 800ft of replica asbestos tape – as a unique tribute to the interwar era.

G-EBIC meanwhile joined the Nash Collection of historic aeroplanes, which was passed on to the Royal Aeronautical Society in 1953. She was rebuilt, alongside the rest of the collection, in 1959–60 at Heathrow Airport by volunteers from the engineering staff at British European Airways as the first step towards founding the Royal Air Force Museum, travelling

RIGHT G-EBIB has been part of the Science Museum inventory since 1939. In 1992 she was restored to skywriting configuration as flown with Major Jack Savage's troupe. *(Author)*

CENTRE F-938/G-EBIC went to the Nash Collection, which formed the basis for the RAF Museum. Restored in 1960, she has resided at Hendon almost ever since. *(Author)*

to various events for static display until her permanent home in Hendon became available.

In 1992 the Ministry of Defence purchased the Nash aeroplanes, ensuring that they would remain at Hendon. In 1968 some further cosmetic work saw the restoration of G-EBIC's original serial F-938. In 2003 the museum transferred the original Grahame-White aeroplane factory brick-by-brick to its premises and moved the S.E.5a, together with her peers from 1914–18, into their new permanent home shortly afterwards in what is the most evocative display area in the entire museum.

Were it not for the foresight of men like Jack Savage and Allen Wheeler, it is highly unlikely that any original S.E.5as would have remained in existence. Thanks to their efforts these aeroplanes remain the most visible reminder of the men and machines that served in the second half of the Great War.

Wingnuts take flight: Sir Peter Jackson

The establishment of TVAL a decade ago came as the brainchild of one of New Zealand's greatest ambassadors, the movie director Sir Peter Jackson. He rose to prominence as the darling of the arthouse movie world thanks to his hilariously twisted horror-comedies such as *Braindead* and *Meet the Feebles* before bringing his quirky vision and attention to detail to mainstream cinema.

RIGHT Sir Peter Jackson's day job: as director and anchor of some of Hollywood's finest output in recent years – adaptations of J.R.R. Tolkien's novels *The Lord of the Rings* and *The Hobbit*. *(Alamy)*

ABOVE Helldivers and a great ape in Sir Peter Jackson's 2005 movie *King Kong* – with not a Sopwith Camel in sight. *(Alamy)*

Thanks to his stunning adaptations of J.R.R. Tolkien's *The Hobbit* and *The Lord of the Rings*, he has entered Hollywood legend for turning out blockbusters that are rich in depth and detail – a novelty in the 21st century. He is also passionate about the history of the Great War in New Zealand and around the globe as well as an aviation enthusiast par excellence. With all of these ingredients, therefore, Sir Peter has done more than most to revitalise interest in the conflict and, most importantly, the human stories within it. He has created an exhibition about the war which not only features movie-quality visual effects and a trove of genuine artefacts, but also an array of odours including dead bodies, rats, trench cooking, gun oil and latrines.

And then there are the aeroplanes…

When Sir Peter first planned his remake of the classic *King Kong* some 20 years ago, the draft story involved a former Great War pilot, which would have allowed Jackson the opportunity to bring one of his greatest passions to life on screen: dogfighting biplanes above the trenches.

'I found a rotary-powered Sopwith Camel replica which was for sale and grabbed it for the movie,' Sir Peter recounted. 'Unfortunately the movie was cancelled the very same day

RIGHT Sir Peter Jackson shows the Duke and Duchess of Cambridge around his Manfred von Richthofen display at the Omaka Aviation Heritage Centre. *(Alamy)*

ROYAL AIRCRAFT FACTORY S.E.5 MANUAL

ABOVE Working in collaboration with TVAL, the Wingnut Wings range of subjects has revitalised model kit making worldwide. (Andrew Eaton)

that the Camel arrived in New Zealand. As I had an aircraft and no movie, I made it available for airshows. The crowd reaction really inspired me to find more First World War types. Now we have a museum at Omaka Airfield, in the north of the South Island, and workshops at Hood Aerodrome at Masterton, North Island.'

Eventually Sir Peter did get to make his update of *King Kong*, in which the star aircraft were CGI recreations of the 1930s Curtiss Helldiver biplanes seen in the original movie – with not a Sopwith Camel in sight. His own collection of artefacts has grown over time, and now includes genuine pieces of Manfred von Richthofen's Fokker Dr.I and several of the silver cups that he ordered to commemorate early victories, as well as Eddie Rickenbacker's US Army Air Service uniform. Meanwhile work was under way to create a fully fledged aircraft factory from which an ever-increasing array of Great War aircraft would soon start emerging: the Vintage Aviator Limited.

For those of us mortals who will never have the chance to own either a genuine Great War aeroplane or an authentic reproduction, Sir Peter has also come to the rescue. As a keen model maker – recreating Tolkien's Middle Earth would have been impossible were it not for his model maker's eye – he wanted to utilise the expertise and data being generated at TVAL and turn it into something for the hobbyist to enjoy at home.

Bringing together experienced 3D model makers and the best that computer technology can bring to the quality of finish and design, the 'Wingnut Wings' range of 1914–18 model kits has turned the hobby on its head over the past decade. Thanks to the wonders of the Internet, the model making community can share tips and builds from every corner of the globe, and Wingnut Wings has gone down a storm – prompting people who never would have modelled an aeroplane, still less a Great War subject, to try their hand.

In underutilised 1/32 scale the models are big enough to be detailed and to give even less experienced fingers something to grab on to. The simplest and earliest kits included the S.E.5a and Albatros D.V, but have gone on to embrace even the gigantic Gotha G.IV bombers that terrorised London – offering their own terrors in miniature, like where to put a model with a 3ft wingspan!

Wingnut Wings kits are by no means the only models available of aeroplanes like the S.E.5 – see Appendix 5 for full details of all available models – but they offer a unique experience that has forced traditional manufacturers to reassess and improve their own products, ensuring that the entire hobby has gained as a result.

Whether it's through putting long-extinct aeroplanes back in the air, creating extraordinary museums for the public, producing watchmaker-quality model kits or – we can but hope – the first decent World War One flying movie in decades, it appears that the sky appears to be the limit for Sir Peter and his Great War projects.

RIGHT Built as C1916, then transferred to the Australian Flying Corps in 1919 and restored as C9539, this fine example remains in the Australian War Memorial. *(Clive Boyce)*

BELOW Built from the remnants of Imperial Gift airframes F7781 and F7783, this S.E.5a holds pride of place in Johannesburg. *(Shutterstock)*

Other surviving S.E.5s

Four other genuine S.E.5s are available to view around the world, with two other airframes known to be in existence. The focal point for two of these aeroplanes is Point Cook in Australia, where a pair of original Imperial Gift S.E.5as lingered in component form for decades after their retirement in the late 1920s.

Of this pair A2-4, which was originally C9539, was brought back to the UK by AJD engineering – now Hawker Restorations – with the intention of trying to restore it for static display in the Royal Australian Air Force Museum, now housed at Point Cook. Ultimately it was felt that discretion was the better part of valour and AJD built a perfect static replica aeroplane which stands in the museum, while quietly working away at building up more parts in order to return the original S.E.5 to the skies (see Chapter Two).

Still in storage at Point Cook are components from A2-11, serial D8474. It must be assumed that these were the less promising components, and as such some considerable distance further back down the path towards restoration than their stablemate. Nevertheless, the prospect of sufficient parts to revive another priceless airframe is a tantalising one, and if sufficient public interest – and value – can be generated from such a restoration then perhaps it may come to pass.

For Australians seeking an original S.E.5a in the meanwhile there remains another Imperial Gift machine on permanent display in the Australian War Memorial in Canberra. This is C1916, restored to the colours of S.E.5a C9539, flown by the Australian ace Captain H.G. Forrest DFC of No 2 Squadron, Australian Flying Corps, in which he shot down three German aircraft in two separate engagements.

The final S.E.5a on display around the world

LEFT Originally built by Austin, then modified and reassembled by the Eberhart company in the United States, A.S.22-325 is a fine example of the post-war SE-5E. *(National Museum of the US Air Force)*

is another Imperial Gift machine, this time standing proudly in the National Museum of Military History in Johannesburg. This aeroplane was beautifully conjured out of the remains of two original airframes, F7781 and F7783, and wears a generic Royal Flying Corps scheme with the serial number 6856 in memory of the South African airmen who flew the type in war and peace, most notably the most successful S.E.5 'ace', Anthony Beauchamp-Proctor.

Rounding off the opportunities to see genuine airframes around the world are the two Eberhart SE-5E machines, originally built at the Austin factory in Longbridge but dispatched to America, where they were rebuilt and modified by the Eberhart Company, becoming SE-5Es. In full 5E trim, with plywood fuselage sides, redesigned cockpit and 150hp Wright-Hispano engine is A.S.22-325, which now hangs from the rafters of the National Museum of the US Air Force in Dayton, Ohio. This aeroplane was purchased from the estate of a late S.E.5a ace, American

LEFT SE-5E G-BLXT has been flown by Charles Lindberg and Chuck Yeager. She returns to the skies in 2017. *(Air Leasing)*

volunteer Bill Lambert DFC, whose love affair with the type proved to be an enduring one.

The second SE-5E remaining is the celebrated G-BLXT, which was a star performer in Howard Hughes' movie *Hell's Angels* and enjoyed an illustrious flying career before being placed in a museum. She was purchased by British collector the Hon Patrick Lindsay in 1985 and rebuilt to 'semi-S.E.5a' specification and, after Lindsay's death in 1986, spent several years in the hands of Henry Labouchere, the late Mark Hanna and the late Doug Arnold before going back to America. After a 23-year hiatus she has emerged from storage in the UK and been restored to airworthiness by Richard Grace in time for the 2017 display season.

Operating the S.E.5 today

Everyone involved in flying and operating the S.E.5 today has the same goals: to share in the enthusiasm and passion for the original warbirds, to educate and inform new generations and to enjoy the raw, unadulterated experience that they offer. Equally rewarding for engineers and airmen, they are to be treasured – although there are many ways to skin a cat.

'We don't fly the aeroplanes frivolously, so it might only fly half a dozen to a dozen times a year at the most – making each flight is fairly precious,' said Shuttleworth Collection display pilot Rob Millinship. 'The thing is that at the moment the First World War is very popular because of the centenary, so there's been a lot of emphasis on that and on those aeroplanes. I don't know if it will continue after 2018, but these aeroplanes have had such a following over the years that we can be fairly sure people will still come.'

Flying these priceless machines comes with the knowledge that some significant expenditure is going to be required to keep them going. Although they use significantly less fuel than, say, a P-51 Mustang or a Spitfire, replacement parts are thin on the ground, and their servicing is all the more critical. This means that every flight must count as the sands of the big, invisible egg-timer run towards the next major overhaul.

'Hopefully we'll fly more this week just to complete the testing programme, and then it'll probably go away for the winter,' said Richard Grace after the maiden flight of SE-5E G-BLXT following restoration. 'It would also be nice to make a few more short flights when the weather is good enough. Then it's going to be up to me negotiating with the owner regarding what they would like to do with the aeroplane. That's about it really. It'll come down to whether the

BELOW Building up to showtime: TVAL's recreation S.E.5a awaits her turn at Omaka. *(Shutterstock)*

phone rings for bookings, then the financial aspect of those bookings. If you're going to risk an aeroplane that Charles Lindberg has had a pole in then it's got to be worthwhile!

'Personally I'd like to see it do a minimum of ten hours a year across the summer – not all at once, but who knows. It might get a full permit and fly once a year, but that's not up to me, sadly. If it *was* up to me I'd be flying it every day. It's a novelty to fly it, as well as being a nice thing to fly. You can't sit in something like that which is so original and not think of the others who've sat in it.'

Working out a display routine for a 100-year-old aeroplane is a surprisingly straightforward process. An original airframe can't be thrown around with the same abandon as it was 20 years ago, or even as vigorously as a World War Two design. For a truly mind-boggling display it's best to head towards Omaka in New Zealand, where Gene de Marco and the Vintage Aviator anchor a genuine step back in time with all the associated pyrotechnics and tight-turning dogfights that could be hoped for with their reproduction machines. For the originals, life is a little more sedate but no less popular.

'We don't know what we're going to do until the brief because very often the World War One aeroplanes are flown as a group in one slot,' Rob Millinship explained of Shuttleworth's display planning. 'It doesn't necessarily mean that we're going to fly four aeroplanes all together, but what it does mean is that to use the slot you get the first aeroplane airborne, then after five minutes get the second aeroplane airborne, fly together for a couple of passes and then the first aeroplane lands. As soon as he's down the next aeroplane gets airborne, does a two-ship and then the second aeroplane lands. As the second aeroplane lands the last aeroplane goes up. We've never really got more than two aeroplanes up at once, but all four aeroplanes have taken up the same slot.'

ABOVE Engine maintenance and spare parts create the main limitations on flying time. *(Author)*

BELOW With recently built S.E.5s, displays can be more ambitious for the team in New Zealand, with many types dogfighting over pyrotechnic displays. *(Brian Harmer)*

Shuttleworth's G-EBIA/F-904 is only ever seen in the skies over Old Warden these days, on those occasions when the airshow gods are smiling and the weather is sufficiently calm. The 2016 season has been relatively quiet, thanks to some inclement weekends – which is all part and parcel of operating these aeroplanes today, even if it results in disappointment for visitors. Even if conditions appear perfect, there may still be gremlins awaiting, as Rob Millinship explained:

'We're under strict, strict instructions to take care of the engine, and that's the most important thing, and there are a lot of issues with it being a liquid-cooled engine. It's critical when you actually start it because you need to have it warm before you fly, but it's like a lot of early liquid-cooled engines and you can get a temperature runaway where the temperature starts to increase. You open the radiator shutters, but if you're slow opening them the temperature will continue to rise regardless of whether they're open or not. And then if it gets to critical temperature you've got to shut it down, whether you've flown or not. If that happens then you feel very sorry for the airshow public, but that aeroplane gets shut down.'

The unique benefits of putting on displays at Old Warden and Omaka is that the majority of aeroplanes are based on site or within easy reach. Venturing further afield is an undertaking that has its supporters as well as those who simply wouldn't trust the technology to be able to sustain regular cross-country or over-water flying. Richard Grace is very firmly in the latter camp, and is looking forward to ferrying G-BLXT to a variety of locations: 'It's just an aeroplane with a V8 engine that you're never going to be asking too much of,' he said. 'It was originally conceived to be a very flyable machine and there's no reason why it shouldn't be a very flyable machine. Display flying these aeroplanes is just as dangerous as transiting them. It's up to the owner but I think the plan will be to get out to a few shows with it next year.'

Richard's approach of going to where the shows are is one that Gene de Marco fully endorses. 'If I had any doubts about the reliability of the Hispano-Suiza engine, I wouldn't fly the S.E.5a across the Cook Strait to attend the Classic Fighters Airshow each year,' he stated. 'It's comfortable, manoeuvrable yet stable, fast and easy to fly. The cockpit is warm, not too windy, and the visibility is very good even for a biplane. Best of all, the engine inspires confidence. It develops a tremendous amount of power, responds well and is extremely smooth.'

Venturing too far from the runway no longer features in the Shuttleworth Collection's plans for the S.E.5a, although the Bristol Fighter does make selected trips out each season. For the Shuttleworth Trust and its pilots discretion is the

RIGHT Very little can beat an afternoon of biplanes in the sky, a sight preserved at the Shuttleworth Collection. *(Alamy)*

ABOVE Set pieces with dogfights between formations set new standards at Omaka. *(Alamy)*

better part of valour as they continue to ensure that these aeroplanes remain airworthy for the longest possible time.

'Whirring along cross-country on old aeroplanes is prohibitively expensive because you're wearing out a very expensive engine with very limited lifespan before it needs complete overhaul,' said Rob Millinship. 'If you've got a priceless aeroplane with a maximum of 30 hours between major engine overhauls then you wouldn't want to waste it trundling around. There's also serious risk to the pilot, because when the engine cuts out you have to land immediately. There's too much drag to glide far, and you don't know the condition of the field you might drop into. The S.E.5 is relatively stable but it's not like the Avro 504 or even the Bristol Fighter, which have a long tail to keep you upright, and even a ski under the nose that's quite robust on the Avro.

'You don't want to tip it over because most hundred-year-old designs wouldn't fare well. In a lot of cases the cabane structure would probably collapse and trap you in the cockpit, and none of the aeroplanes of that age have got fuel systems that'll stop fuel tiddling out when it's on its back. I don't want to burn to death in a World War One aeroplane. And I'm not going to put myself in a position where that can happen!'

There is no right or wrong answer to the question of how best to enjoy and display an aeroplane like the S.E.5. Nobody who currently flies one is anything other than a vastly experienced and highly qualified expert, with thousands of hours logged and their own way to approach doing the same thing: ensuring that these remarkable aeroplanes stay in the sky to be enjoyed by those on the ground and those in the cockpit alike.

None of the potential pitfalls of operating an S.E.5 really hampers owners, pilots or enthusiasts from attending air displays and enjoying the opportunity to witness the sights and sounds of a century ago. They are too special for that, and will remain so for many years to come.

Chapter Six

The engineer's view

From the outset the S.E.5 required intensive labour to maintain it, and little has changed in the course of a century, bar the diminishing availability of spares. While the design may be straightforward and the hangar space required minimal, an awful lot of work goes into keeping an S.E.5 in good health.

OPPOSITE Erecting the airframe is a labour-intensive process requiring absolute precision. *(Darren Harbar)*

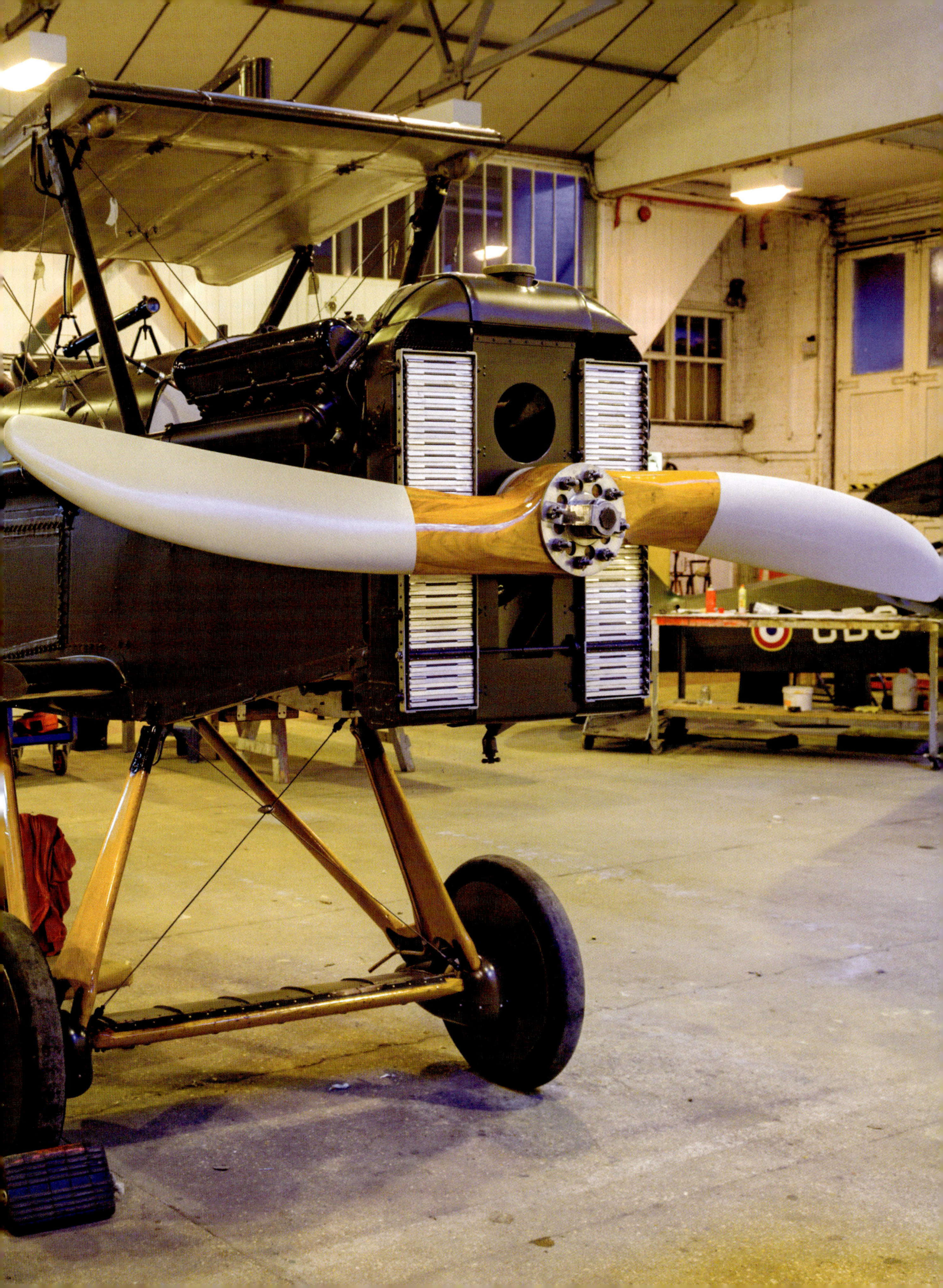

ABOVE Ground crew fought their own war against the laws of demand and supply. *(Aviation Images)*

BELOW Field canteen for the NCOs and mechanics in France. *(Getty/Universal)*

The size of a front-line squadron in France doubled in 1917–18, from 12 aircraft to as many as 24. Logistically this put a lot of pressure on the commanding officers and their complement of fitters, riggers, mechanics and armourers to ensure that serviceability remained acceptable.

Depictions of Great War airfields are of breezy places dotted at random behind the lines, with perhaps an old farmhouse sitting moodily behind a row of canvas Bessoneau hangars and very little in the way of infrastructure. This is a false image of what was one of the most technically rigorous theatres of operations ever seen in the combat zone to that point in time. Everything had a place and there was a place for everything – and the location of each airfield was decided by how easily it could be resupplied with parts, munitions and above all fuel.

Each squadron was divided into three flights, 'A', 'B' and 'C', each of which had its own flight sergeant overseeing the maintenance and management of its aircraft through his team of 35 mechanics. Their main servicing roles were patching up holes in the fuselage and wings, engine repairs and ensuring that the rigging was in peak condition, although spares allocations included two full sets of wings and two engines per flight. In addition there was a fourth group of engineers in the headquarters flight, which took responsibility when an aircraft needed to come out of the line for more than simple servicing or field repairs.

Each flight's allocation of spares was managed by the equipment officer, who was also responsible for the tools and facilities on site. These included one equipment truck per flight, which would be parked up and the hangar built around it. Sitting plum in the middle of the hangar, the truck's engine would be used as a generator that turned out 110V and housed the larger tools, such as the lathe and grinder.

The equipment officer would make requests for parts and send updates on stores to the wing headquarters responsible for his squadron. Stores were all held at the nearest army air park and both regular allocations and emergency orders were fulfilled by truck from these larger depots.

Until late 1917 the army air parks were also responsible for receiving, assembling, storing and dispatching replacement aeroplanes to the front-line squadrons. When deliveries reached 400–500 new machines per month the workload demanded that new aircraft be siphoned off into new aeroplane supply depots (ASDs) for assembly and distribution – only a tiny minority of aircraft were being flown across the Channel, with the remainder being crated up and moved en masse by ship.

Once a new airframe or engine had been built, its journey towards the front began with the Aeronautical Inspection Department, with whose approval it could then progress to the Air Acceptance Park and be prepared for transporting to an aeroplane supply depot in France. When an aeroplane was lost, destroyed or severely damaged its squadron's equipment officer would request a replacement (by post at all times when it wasn't in the battle zone, by telegram if its aircraft were in daily combat). The ASD would then assess what was available and whether it would be flown out by one of its delivery pilots or whether a pilot from the receiving squadron should be dispatched.

Fuelling victory

In the aftermath of the Great War, Lord Curzon declared that the Allies had 'floated to victory on a wave of oil'. In the case of British airmen, that usually meant Shell, whose unique supply of lighter and more potent fuels, rich in the required toluenes, xylenes and benzenes, heralded from the Dutch East Indies. These properties were essential both for high-octane fuel and for the production of explosives, guaranteeing Shell a complete monopoly upon some of the most significant properties in the world until the Americans arrived in force. Indeed, not only did Shell have a monopoly on the right grade of oil to be refined into aviation spirit, but it also held more than 50% of the world's tanker fleet, enabling the raw products to be shipped back to Britain and the refined fuel onward to France, Macedonia, Palestine, Egypt, East Africa, Arabia and Aden.

Two grades of aviation spirit were used by front-line squadrons – Shell A, from Sumatra, and Shell B, from Borneo. Shell chemists and research scientists provided the armed forces with technical advice, including any carburettor adjustments required in the field, thanks to the highly classified work conducted by Harry Ricardo at Shoreham in identifying and applying a measuring system – octane – to grade the properties of the fuels.

In general the aviation spirit used by air forces up to 1917 was 60-octane, the highest available at that time. Ricardo soon worked out that if he were to add common-or-garden benzol (processed from coal production) into the fuel blend, he could reduce pre-ignition ('knocking' or 'detonation') and allow the aircraft engines to run at a higher compression and thereby deliver increased performance. Shell, however, wasn't keen on the 'purity' of its product being so besmirched, fearing that it would damage its reputation for light, clean and potent fuel, so Ricardo's work was quietly shunted on to a siding. As a result some high-compression engines that had been developed on Ricardo's blend, such as the Wolseley Viper, had to be pulled back from peak compression of 5.68:1 to a sustainable 5.3:1 to eliminate knocking.

Official pressure was brought to bear upon Shell which was resisted until it became apparent that its subsidiary, the Romanian fuel company Astra, was cheerfully supplying the German air forces with a benzol-enhanced high-octane fuel! At that point, in the late summer of 1917, Shell relented and Ricardo's higher-octane fuels became the standard issue.

The arrival in force of the Americans meant that an alternative supply of high-octane fuels was readily available – not as high as Ricardo's modified aviation spirit (a secret that Shell preferred not to divulge to the likes of Standard Oil), but sufficient not to affect engine performance too greatly. In addition to abundant fuel reserves, the Americans also brought additional infrastructure, including the first automatic refuelling pumps to be installed at airfields. Until 1917 aviation spirit was distributed in two-gallon tin cans that had to be physically emptied into the often less than accessible openings of each aircraft's fuel tank, with the S.E.5a requiring 15 cans to be hauled around at each refuelling.

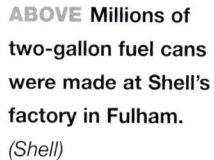

ABOVE **Millions of two-gallon fuel cans were made at Shell's factory in Fulham.** *(Shell)*

LEFT **Original fuel cans form part of the *mise en scène* at Stow Maries Great War Aerodrome.** *(Author)*

ABOVE When she was overhauled in the mid-1970s, F-904 was rigged in exactly the manner laid out by the Air Board. *(Farnborough Air Sciences Trust)*

Increasingly, therefore, the location of an airfield depended upon its proximity to a railway line along which fuel could be transported in sufficient bulk. Once the automatic pumps were in place, large fuel tanks were positioned at the point on the field closest to the line and replenished directly from the train, cutting down significantly on the requirement for wrestling two-litre tins around the field and reducing refuelling times accordingly.

How to build an S.E.5

Ease of maintenance and turning around brand new, crated airframes and battle-damaged aeroplanes to get them flying quickly was of paramount importance in the front line. That is why the Air Board, together with the manufacturers, produced comprehensive manuals to guide the men responsible for maintaining aeroplanes at home and abroad.

In this Air Board document, the mysteries of rigging a biplane are revealed with elegant simplicity:

Manufacturers' order of erection for the S.E.5a 200hp Hispano-Suiza

1. Fuselage assembled and trued up.
2. Undercarriage fitted with fuselage in inverted position.
3. Lower centre section planes fitted.
4. Rear fairing of fuselage fitted and fixed: front fairing fitted but not fixed.
5. Seat fitted.
6. Flying wire lugs fitted to fuselage.
7. Oil tank fitted.
8. Holes drilled for carburettor countershaft bracket and the latter fitted.
9. Engine mounted.
10. Constantinesco gear fitted.
11. Radiator fitted.
12. Oil and water pipes fitted.
13. Vickers gun mount and ammunition box fitted.
14. Controls fitted.
15. Tail plane actuating gear fitted.
16. Footsteps fitted.
17. Main petrol tank fitted.
18. Front fairing fixed.
19. Instrument board fitted.
20. Air and petrol pipes connected up.
21. Water and emergency petrol tanks fitted to upper centre section plane before the latter is fitted to machine; also the Foster gun mount for Lewis gun.
22. Upper centre section plane fitted with machine in flying position.
23. Leads to water and emergency petrol tanks connected up.
24. Lower centre section planes covered and doped.

25 Hinge jaws fitted to upper and lower centre section plane spars.
26 Main planes attached.
27 Tail plane fitted and locking washers hammered over.
28 Top cover at rear of fuselage attached.
29 Upper fin attached.
30 Rudder fitted.
31 Elevators fitted.
32 Controls connected up and adjusted.
33 Bottom cover at rear of fuselage attached.
34 Lower fin fitted.
35 Tail skid fitted.
36 Engine cowl fitted.

Truing up the fuselage

- Support the fuselage so that the rear transverse steel tube is level transversely, and the engine bearers are level longitudinally, as far as possible.
- By means of side bracing wires between front and rear transverse steel tubes which form attachments for spars of lower main planes, adjust until the tubes are parallel.
- Check by holding two straightedges, one each side, longitudinally across corresponding points on front and rear transverse steel tubes. The *upper* edges of the straightedges should be in line.
- Mark the mid points of all cross struts, top and bottom.
- Insert a steel tube to fit without play into the finpost.
- Stretch a centre line below the fuselage from the *axis* of the finpost to the *mid* point of the rear transverse steel tube.
- Stretch another centre line above the fuselage from the *axis* of the finpost to the *mid* point of the front cross strut tube.
- Work from front to rear and true up the bottom cross strut bracing wires until all mid points of bottom cross struts are in line.
- Check by try square at each marked point. The base of the try square should be along the strut and the marked point on one edge of the blade. The bottom stretched line should just touch the same edge of the blade.
- Check for bottom of fuselage being square with rear transverse steel tube by taking measurements from axis of finpost to lateral extremities of the tube. Corresponding measurements should be the same on both sides.
- Proceed in an exactly similar manner for the top of the fuselage.
- Mark points on side struts at equal vertical distances – 5" is a convenient distance – below the *top* face of the top longerons.
- True up the side bracing wires on one side until all marked points on side struts on that side are in line.
- Check by levelling from marked point to marked point on adjacent struts. Proceed in exactly the same way for the other side.
- Check for their [sic] being no wind in the fuselage as follows:–
- Place a straightedge transversely across the top longerons above the front transverse steel tube. Place another straightedge transversely across the top longerons at any other point about 2½" from struts sockets.
- The upper edge of the second straightedge should be in line with the upper edge of the first straightedge.
- Check by sighting and repeat for other points. Finally tension the internal cross bracing wires.
- A plumb line dropped from the mid point of a top cross strut should strike the mid point of the corresponding bottom cross strut.

Note: – It is very important that all tie rods be cut accurately to length; otherwise it will be impossible to get the fuselage true.

Truing up the undercarriage

Adjust front cross bracing wires making corresponding diagonals equal and check by trammel.

LEFT Undercarriage rigging on the RAF Museum's F938. *(Author)*

Placing machine in flying position

- Before truing up the upper centre section plane and attaching and truing up the main planes it is necessary to get the machine in flying position. To do this, block the machine up on a trestle placed under the engine bearers and support the tail on another trestle.
- The machine is in flying position when the engine bearers are level longitudinally and the front and rear transverse steel tubes which form attachments for spars of lower main planes are level transversely.
- When this is the case the incidence of the lower centre section planes should be 5°.
- Level transversely by spirit level over rear transverse steel tube and make any adjustments by packing blocks under the front trestle. Level longitudinally by spirit level over the engine bearers and make any adjustments by raising or lowering tail.

Truing up the centre section

Note: – Before fitting the fairing for the centre section struts (steel tubes) it is necessary to fit the water pipe to the water tank and pitot tubes in the fairing for the starboard front centre section strut and the petrol pipe (for the emergency tank) in the fairing for the port front centre section strut. The tanks and the Foster gun mount for Lewis gun should be fitted to the upper centre section plane before the latter is fitted to the machine.

RIGHT Centre section coming together on the restoration of E5886 in New Zealand. *(TVAL)*

Note: – When fitting the tanks it is important to ensure that all split pins are in position, and that the tanks are completely covered and doped.

- The *stagger* of the upper centre section plane is adjusted by the side bracing wires and should be 18".
- Check by dropping plumb lines from the centres of lateral extremities of upper centre section front spar.
- The horizontal *fore* and *aft* distance between the centres of the lateral extremities of front spar of lower section planes and the plumb lines should be 18".
- Adjust the upper centre section plane to be symmetrical about the vertical line of machine by front and rear cross bracing wires.
- Check for symmetry by measuring the horizontal transverse distance between the plumb lines dropped from the lateral extremities of front spar and upper centre section plane, and the edges of straightedges placed longitudinally across corresponding points on one side of the front and rear transverse steel tubes which form attachments for spars of lower main planes.
- Corresponding measurements should be the same on both sides.

Attaching the main planes

- The hinge jaws must be removed from the main planes and fitted to both upper and lower centre section spars by the hinge pins as the main planes cannot be assembled with the hinge jaws bolted to the spars.
- The lower main planes are bolted in position and the landing wires loosely connected.
- The upper main planes are then lifted and bolted in position, the interplane struts fitted into their sockets and the flying, deflection and incidence wires loosely connected.

Truing up the main planes

- The *dihedral* is 5° for both upper and lower main planes.
- Check by straightedge along the front spars and Abney level.
- A line stretched from the *tops* of the front outer struts should be 7.55" vertically above the upper centre plane; check at lateral extremities of latter.

- The stagger is 18" throughout.
- Check by measuring the horizontal fore and aft distance between the leading edge of the lower main planes and plumb lines dropped from the leading edge of the upper main planes. These measurements should be 18" at each point checked.
- The *incidence* is 5° throughout for both upper and lower main planes. Check by Abney level and straightedge placing the latter from leading edge to trailing edge at ribs.
- Check for leading edge being parallel by placing straightedges across the leading edge of the upper and lower main planes.
- Any two of these straightedges should be in line.
- The leading edges of upper and lower main planes should be symmetrical about the centre line of machine.
- Check by taking measurements from top and bottom sockets of rear outer struts to axis of finpost. Corresponding measurements should be the same on both sides.
- Check also by taking measurements from top and bottom sockets of front outer struts to front centre of engine shaft.
- Corresponding measurements should be the same on both sides.

Fixing the empennage
- Fit and bolt the tail plane in position, not forgetting to hammer over the locking washers.
- Fit and bolt the upper fin in position.
- Hinge the rudder in position.
- Hinge the elevators in position.
- Fit and bolt the lower fin in position.
- Fit the tail skid in position.
- Take care to insert all split pins and lock up all turnbuckles on control cables which are covered by rear fuselage covering of fuselage.
- The tail plane must be square with machine. Check by taking measurements from bottom sockets of rear outer struts to lateral extremities of rear spar of tail plane. Corresponding measurements should be the same on both sides.
- The fins should point directly fore and aft and be square with machine.

LEFT Streamlined, flattened Rafwire is used throughout the S.E.5's external rigging. *(Author)*

LEFT Universal wire ends allow the rigging to be adjusted and set. *(Author)*

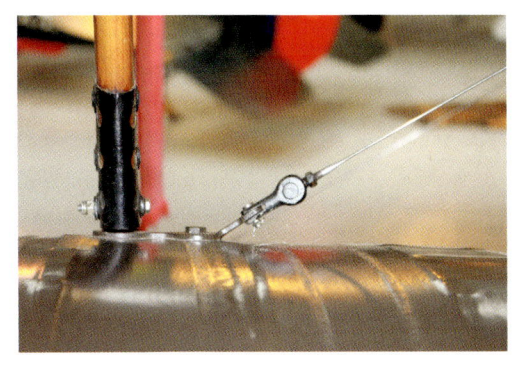

LEFT Suitably sturdy anchor points are held next to the strut on the upper wings. *(Author)*

BELOW Bracing and control wires are laid out cleanly on the tail of F-904. *(Author)*

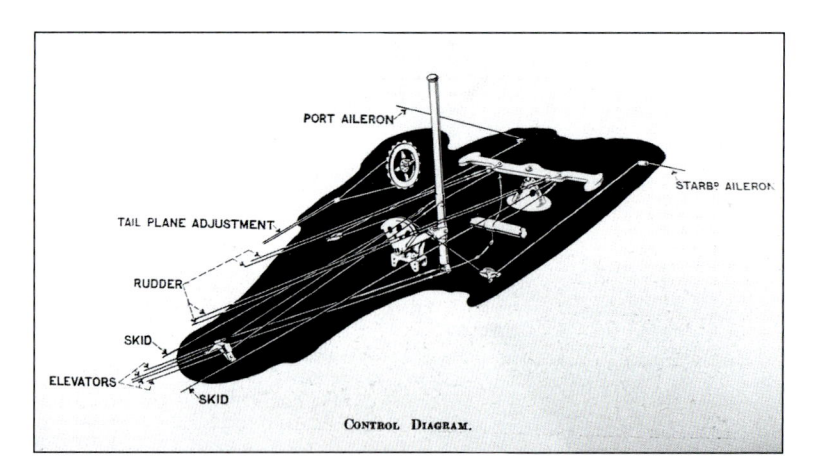

ABOVE Diagram clarifying the cat's cradle of control wires upon which the pilot depended. *(Farnborough Air Sciences Trust)*

Controls

- With the pilot's control stick central the ailerons should droop ¾" approximately.
- With knob of hand wheel, for tail plane actuating gear, opposite the word 'Normal' on strut the central line of tail plane should be at an *incidence* of 5°.
- With the rear end of tail plane in extreme top position the tail plane should have a negative *incidence* of 2°.
- With elevators horizontal, the pilot's control stick should lean forward 10° from vertical.
- With rudder bar square on fuselage, the rudder and tail skid should point directly *fore* and *aft* to be square with machine.

BELOW At the corner of each wing and on the horizontal stabilisers, viewing windows allowed mechanics to note the condition of internally mounted control wires and make any adjustments needed. *(Author)*

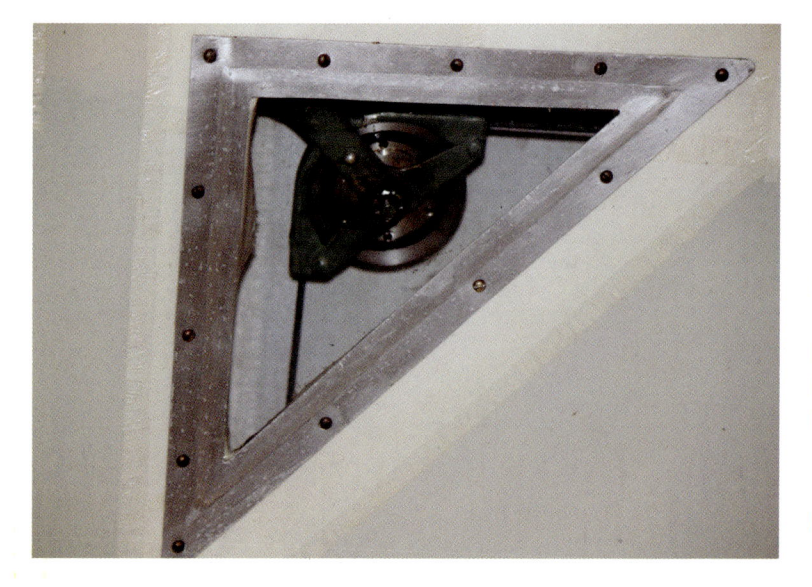

List of principal dimensions

Span of upper main planes	26' 7½"
Span of lower main planes	26' 7½"
Chord of upper main planes	5' 0"
Chord of lower main planes	5' 0"
Incidence of upper main planes	5°
Chord of lower main planes	5°
Gap	4' 7"
Stagger	18"
Dihedral	5°
Overall length	20' 11"
Height	9' 6"
Droop of ailerons	¾"
Incidence of centre line tail plane with knob on hand wheel opposite the word 'Normal' on strut	5°
With pilot's control stick leaning forward 10° from the vertical elevators are horizontal.	

Points to observe when overhauling machine

- See that leading edges of main planes are symmetrical about the centre line of machine.
- Examine the bracing wires for length and tautness in the centre section and see that all split pins are in position and that all lock nuts are tight.
- Check the dihedral.
- Check the stagger.
- Check the incidence.
- Examine all main plane bracing wires for length and tautness, and see that all split pins are in position and that all lock nuts are tight.
- Examine all control pulleys and cables and see that they work freely and that all turnbuckles on cables are locked.
- Examine tail plane and see that it is set correctly and is square with machine and that all bracing wires are correct both as to tautness and length and that all lock nuts are tight.
- See that the tail plane actuating gear works freely.
- Examine rudder and fins and see that they are set straight and square with machine.
- Examine the setting of ailerons and elevator.
- Examine undercarriage and skid.
- Examine tank mountings, engine controls and engine accessories and see that pins through control arms and levers are not worn.
- See that security bolts for gun and mount are tight.

RIGHT **A variable pitch propeller arrangement was trialled on S.E.5a C1091 in 1920.** *(Farnborough Air Sciences Trust)*

Variants and experiments

Whether it was in order to confirm that the existing components were the best design available, to trial-run future technologies or to find a potentially winning advantage, the Royal Aircraft Factory continued to modify the S.E.5 throughout its production life and for years after the Armistice.

As early as June 1917 one of the first production runs of 50 airframes was held back and fitted with a balanced rudder, 10in chord ailerons (instead of the standard 15in), and narrow-chord elevators, intended to try and induce snappier lateral control. The balanced rudder was not persisted with, but narrow chord elevators and ailerons were fitted to some front-line aeroplanes, in particular B4891 with which 56 Squadron ace Jimmy McCudden scored several victories.

Another of the early production run, A8943, was fitted with the narrow chord elevators and then subsequently rebuilt in the spring of 1918 into the S.E.5b. This was the most significantly modified S.E.5 of all, with a sesquiplane layout featuring an upper wing of 6ft chord and a span of just over 30ft. This was paired with a lower wing of just 4ft 3in chord and a span of 26ft.

The fuselage, tail section and undercarriage were retained as standard but a streamlined cowling was fitted around the 200hp Hispano-Suiza engine, with the propeller carrying a large streamlined spinner that faired into this new nose section. The radiator was moved to beneath the chin and was retracted to sit flush with the fuselage in flight to cut drag, and a longer, smoother headrest fairing was fitted.

The elegant-looking S.E.5b offered no significant performance advantage over its

RIGHT **The S.E.5b was the most stylish of all the S.E.5 types by far, and attempted to improve speed and manoeuvrability with a structurally sound sesquiplane layout. It gave no advantage over the S.E.5a and was abandoned.** *(Farnborough Air Sciences Trust)*

ABOVE **D7020 was retained at Farnborough, where it served until 1926 performing innumerable test flights.** *(Farnborough Air Sciences Trust)*

RIGHT A twin-boom tail was tried, with miniature rudders mounted at each end of the horizontal stabiliser. This was not a success!
(Farnborough Air Sciences Trust)

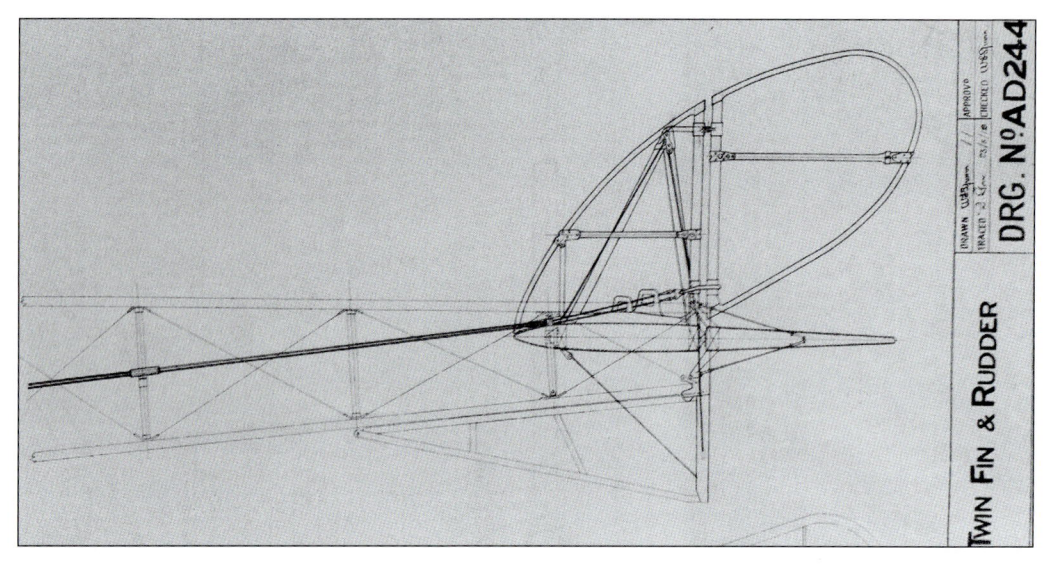

predecessors, as the drag of the large upper wing negated any gains made elsewhere. Before long A8943 was returned to standard S.E.5a specification.

Although the rudder authority and the performance of the tail section was never singled out for criticism, numerous variations were tried in case any additional advantage could be gained over John Kenworthy's original angular unit. Curved and oval shapes similar to those of Sopwith were trialled, as was a remarkable twin tail fin and twin rudder arrangement. None of these remarkable designs offered any improvement upon the handling of the S.E.5a and often worked to its detriment.

After the Armistice a number of modifications were tried on what was an abundance of available airframes. Of most interest to many pilots was the fitting of a parachute within the largely redundant pilot's stowage area behind the cockpit. Many pilots felt cheated by the 'brass' who declined to provide them with parachutes during the war – and commencing field trials with equipment just months after the Armistice would have been seen as a grave insult in some quarters.

Fear of fire was the driving force behind the experiments of Major G.H. Norman in 1920–21, who designed the first onboard extinguisher system. On the ground he would repeatedly set fire to E5927 and smother the flames with the extinguisher. After multiple tests – and presumably multiple repairs to the airframe – he elected to take the aircraft up for a 'live' trial.

Onlookers were greatly relieved when the extinguisher did its job and the flames were effectively snuffed out. Norman suffered greatly from the effects of both smoke and the contents of the extinguisher, however, and crashed, suffering injuries to which he later succumbed. Remarkably, the aeroplane

MAJOR EXPERIMENTS CONDUCTED WITH THE S.E.5A AT FARNBOROUGH

Aircraft	Date	Experiment
A8938	June 1917	Balanced rudder, narrow chord ailerons and elevators.
A8947	August 1917	Narrow chord elevators.
B4893	November 1917	6ft chord wing.
C1063	February 1918	Reduced dihedral tests.
A8947	March 1918	Converted to S.E.5b.
D203	March–August 1918	Sopwith-type rudder and fin, reduced dihedral tests.
C1134	September 1918	Variable pitch propeller.
D203	October 1918	Rounded balanced rudder, twin tail fins and rudders.
D7007	December 1918	Palethorpe landing skid.
D203	January 1919	Spinning tests (aircraft on strength until May 1922).
D7012	February 1919	Palethorpe landing skid.
C1148	February 1919	Variable pitch propeller.
C1063	September 1919	Gravity ground indicator.
E5923	Early 1920	Experimental triangular tail section.
C1091	April 1920	Variable pitch propeller.
E5927	October 1920	Onboard fire extinguisher ground tests.
E5927	Summer 1921	Onboard fire extinguisher airborne test.
E5927	October 1925	Exhaust-driven cockpit heater.
E5927	February 1926	Thermostat-controlled radiator shutters.

was salvaged and continued to be used at Farnborough until 1926.

In its peacetime role as the Farnborough workhorse, the S.E.5a was also fitted variously with a variable-pitch propeller system allowing greater engine efficiency at different altitudes, which would become a standard fitting to most performance aircraft. In addition, the fitting of thermostat-controlled radiator shutters and a cockpit heating system that worked off the exhaust were trialled, but before long the level of technology had accelerated far beyond the capabilities of the S.E.5 and it gradually faded away into obsolescence.

German report on the Hispano-Suiza V8

In 1959, when the Royal Aircraft Establishment undertook rebuilding work on the 200hp Hispano-Suiza engine that was then fitted to F-904 (G-EBIA), it discovered that the most comprehensive information available was in fact to be found in two German reports made on captured engines in 1917 and 1918.

The independent publication *Zeitschrift für Flugtechnik und Motorluftshiffahrt* contained a full investigation into Marc Birkigt's masterpiece that holds within its text a thorough admiration for the design untempered by the fact that this was enemy technology! Such an admirable commitment to journalistic integrity would be hard to imagine in most circumstances.

The even-handed treatment with which the German experts handled every element of the engine's design, construction and performance gave the RAE the best possible start it could hope for in uncovering the secrets of what was, even then, 50-year-old machinery that had long-since been forgotten about. For men whose day-job was spent at the cutting edge of jet propulsion it was doubtless an enjoyable process, and the report's text makes an enjoyable read that is reproduced here in abridged form.

1 General description

The Hispano-Suiza is constructed as an eight-cylinder V-type engine. Each set of four cylinders is contained in a single block. The two blocks are at an angle of 90° to each other.

This angle has, among other things, the major advantage that ignition with two magnetos is sufficient for the eight cylinders.

In order to obtain the highest possible concentration of the total power system, the radiator is situated between the plane of rotation of the propeller and the front face on the cylinder block: the engine is [therefore] striking with its streamlined design, apparent simple construction and the encasing of all moving parts. All means have been aimed at extracting maximum power with minimum weight.

The design originates from the Spanish Hispano-Suiza Automobile factory in Barcelona. The firm had already obtained the first prize in 1910 in the 'Coupe de Voiturettes' [automobile race] with a very light high-speed four-cylinder

ABOVE The post-war Eberhart SE-5E was powered by the direct-drive 180bhp engine that is still giving reliable service after 100 years. *(Air Leasing)*

BELOW Inspecting the original installation of the 200hp Hispano-Suiza at the RAE, 1959. *(Farnborough Air Sciences Trust)*

ABOVE Inside the cylinder block of the Hispano-Suiza 8B. *(Author)*

engine (normal rpm 2,300) of 65mm bore and 200mm stroke with an effective output of 45 metric horsepower (Cheval Vapeur). This car was driven by Zucarelli.

The eight-cylinder aero engine manufactured by this firm was built under licence by the majority of engine firms in Allied countries. Hitherto only engines built under licence by the English firms of Vickers Sons and Maxim Ltd (Wolseley Airship Engine Factory, Birmingham) have been captured.

2 General power data

The engine has an average output of 160 metric horsepower (Cheval Vapeur) at 1,700rpm with a bore of 120mm and a stroke of 130mm. On the engine casing there is a data plate with the inscription 'normal setting: 1600, maximum setting: 1700'. The rpm of maximum setting must only be used in climbing, in no case may it be exceeded in order to reduce the possibility of engine failure. Danger of failure at 1,750rpm. Meanwhile investigations have shown that the drive mechanism of the engine can endure much higher rpm than 1,750 without damage. It is noteworthy that the falling off in power first arises at very high revolutions (about 2,600rpm).

This property, coupled with the extremely high lift-weight drive mechanism, makes this engine very suitable for use at high speed. The total weight of the engine in operational condition (but excluding propeller and hub, oil, radiator and water) is approximately 181 kg. Consequently its structural weight for an output of 160 horsepower (Cheval Vapeur) is about 1.3 kg/metric Ch.V.

The compression ratio is 4.65. The specific power output is 13.5 Ch.V./litre. The fuel consumption for an output of 160 Ch.V. is about 0.25 5kg/Ch.V./hour, using a normal petrol with a specific gravity of 0.745. The mean thrust, based on the rpm and output quoted above, is about 7.2 kg/cm^2.

3 Description of components and layout

Cylinder blocks

The four cylinders are screwed into an aluminium cooling block. Since the block possesses in itself a high rigidity, the individual cylinders are turned off a quite thin wall of about 2 mm. The cylinders are constructed from a high-grade steel having 62 kg/mm^2 tensile strength at 23% elongation. The cylinders are screwed into the aluminium block by means of a fine thread (63 internal threads for a 95mm length of cylinder).

The two spark plugs in each cylinder are fitted into threaded sleeves screwed for a short distance into the aluminium block and packed out against the cylinder wall by a pressed copper bushing. The threaded sleeves do not contact the cooling water at any point so that a leak, or any entry of cooling water into the interior of the cylinder, is quite impossible. In order to control any core displacement of the cooling water cavity and the unequal wall thickness of the aluminium casting caused by this, the outer cooling jacket is bored through in several places and aluminium plugs provided with threads are then screwed through the bore holes.

The aluminium alloy of the cylinder blocks is shown to be an aluminium-copper alloy with 7.61% of copper and 0.07% of silicon. The varying amounts of silicon found in analysis can be assumed to be impurities. A technically very pure aluminium is used in the production of the aluminium alloy used in the Hispano-Suiza engine. The tensile strength of the aluminium alloy of the cylinder block is approximately 15 kg/mm^2 at 1.14% elongation.

The specific weight of the alloy is 2.84 at 15°C. The total weight of a four-cylinder block (machined and assembled, with cylinder fitted, taper sleeves for the spark plugs, supporting bolts for fixing the induction and exhaust manifolds, water tubes and valve guides minus the valves themselves) is about 30 kg.

It should be noted that the cylinder head and working surfaces are machined in one piece from a solid block. The cylinder head and the corresponding contact surface of the aluminium casting are carefully turned and pressed together in order to attain a good heat transfer from the cylinder to the aluminium of the block. The conical valve seats are machined in the head of the steel cylinder.

Piston

The material used for the pistons in the Hispano-Suiza engine is an aluminium-copper alloy with a copper content of 12.05%. The unusual level of technical purity seen in this aluminium is noteworthy. The weight of the piston without gudgeon pins and piston rings is about 1.020 kg; the complete assembly weighs 1.440 kg.

Two piston gas ring grooves are machined into the piston. In each piston ring groove there are two rings with an individual radial pressure of about 2 kg. An oil control ring groove is provided under the gudgeon pin.

Investigations showed that the surface parts of the gudgeon pin housings had exactly the same structural composition as the other parts of the piston. The aluminium-copper alloy consists of a heterogeneous mixture of homogenous mixed crystals of aluminium-copper (with 2.4% copper) and a eutectic mixture (saturated with 32.5% copper) consisting of the crystals and the $CuAl_2$ compound. The structural composition occurs in the same way in all parts of the piston material, even in the bearing surface and the edges of the bearing parts. The equilibrium point was almost completely reached, since annealing the alloy at the temperature of the eutectic horizontal (550°C) for four hours in the absence of air produced no change in the structural composition.

The alloys are then cast (in sand); all parts with uniform solidification and not quenched. The tensile strength of the piston material was 17.65 kg/m^2 for 1% elongation. The specific weight was 2.92 at 15°C. These investigations were carried out in the Institute for Metallurgy and Electrometallurgy of the Royal Technical Institute, Aachen.

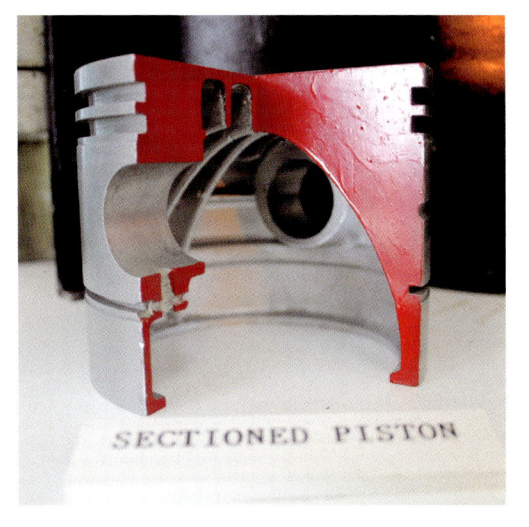

The piston bearing surfaces are lubricated by centrifuged oil which is collected by an oil groove cut half-way around the circumference of the piston on the induction side. Part of the lubricating oil collected by this groove is fed to the gudgeon pin through oil holes provided.

Camshaft

The camshafts each have triple bearings, and are bolted down to the cylinder block by means of studs and nuts. The shafts and cams are

LEFT Hispano-Suiza piston opened up. *(Author)*

LEFT Piston, valve and camshaft arrangement of the Hispano-Suiza. *(Author)*

machined from a solid piece, the cams are case hardened. The cams acting directly on the valve spring retainer are lubricated by a separate oil line placed at the front of the engine cylinder block leading from the crankcase, through which the oil is forced to the foremost bearing block of the camshaft and thus flows, through holes provided in the bearing and the shaft, into the inside of the camshaft.

In the centre of the cam there are fine oil holes through which the lubricating oil is forced on to the valve spring retainers immediately before the contact of the cam on the valve retainer.

Connecting rods

The connecting rods are centrally fitted on the crankshaft in the usual manner for automobile engine construction. An outer rod is split and forked around the bearing of the other. Connecting rods of round section were chosen. The length of the connecting rods from centre to centre is 225 mm.

Crankshaft and transmission

As has already been noted, the Hispano engine is used by the enemy in two designs, one with reduction gear and the other without. It should be noted here that recently captured engines (with the reduction gear fitted) have higher performance figures than those quoted here. The increase in performance is a result of further developments in construction. Three engines captured within a very short time showed three different reduction gear ratios.

The design and construction of the reduction gear gives a ratio of 21/28 = 3/4. The tooth width is 6.0 mm. The pitch is 5.25$^{\varnothing}$ corresponding to a circular pitch of 16.49 and a diametrical pitch of 5.3 mm. The gear is formed as helical teeth in order to attain quiet running with the small pitch of about 8½°. This corresponds to a 'jump' of about half a division. The centre distance of the gears is 130 mm. For a normal engine rotation speed of 2,000 rpm the propeller rotation speed is 1,500 rpm.

The mounting of the pinion to the crankshaft requires the substitution of the front white-metal bearing by a ball bearing. In general, the whole transmission is supported by ball bearings. The lubrication of the transmission takes place through a nozzle. A considerable amount of oil is sprayed under pressure between the gears.

The extremely efficient lubrication and cooling of the gears should be noted. The oil is sprayed under pressure in a wide jet through a wide nozzle of 4.5 mm inside diameter with a slit shape lateral opening directly between the gears. Due to the slit-shaped cross-section the maximum possible evenness of distribution of the lubricant over the whole of the tooth-width is attained. As fitted to the test engine, the reduction gear showed no traces of wear on the gears after 26 hours of running.

Carburettor and fuel supply

The engines captured until now were fitted with Zenith and Claudel carburettors. The action of the Zenith carburettor may be assumed to be known. A special feature of this system for use as an aircraft carburettor is the device for altitude mixture regulation. This consists of a channel joining the nozzle chamber with the float chamber. The internal width of this channel is controlled by a hand-operated valve. The larger the free diameter, the more the pressure of the venture manifold, transmitted to the flat chamber.

In this way the fuel delivery through the main nozzle can be reduced in accordance with the air density and the smaller cut-off. The earlier engines, as already noted, were designed to run at a rotational speed of 1,400 rpm; for the more recent engines this value has been raised to 2,000 rpm.

Due to the increased rotational speed from a normal 1,400 rpm to 2,000 rpm, the feed lines and the diameter of the carburettor venture have increased. The diameter of the nozzle chambers was increased from 27 mm to 42.4 mm *ie* by about 50%. This makes it possible for the decrease in mean pressure which is attributed mainly to the inlet valve, not to begin at 1,400 rpm but instead at 1,900 rpm.

The valve velocity of the engine tested here is about 60 m/sec at 2,000 rpm and the compression ratio of more recently captured engines shows a continual increase. The carburettors of early and later Hispano-Suiza models are of a different design as well as a different size. The throttle valves are replaced by a common throttle gate valve with two adjacent apertures. Moreover a connection is provided between the closed float chamber and

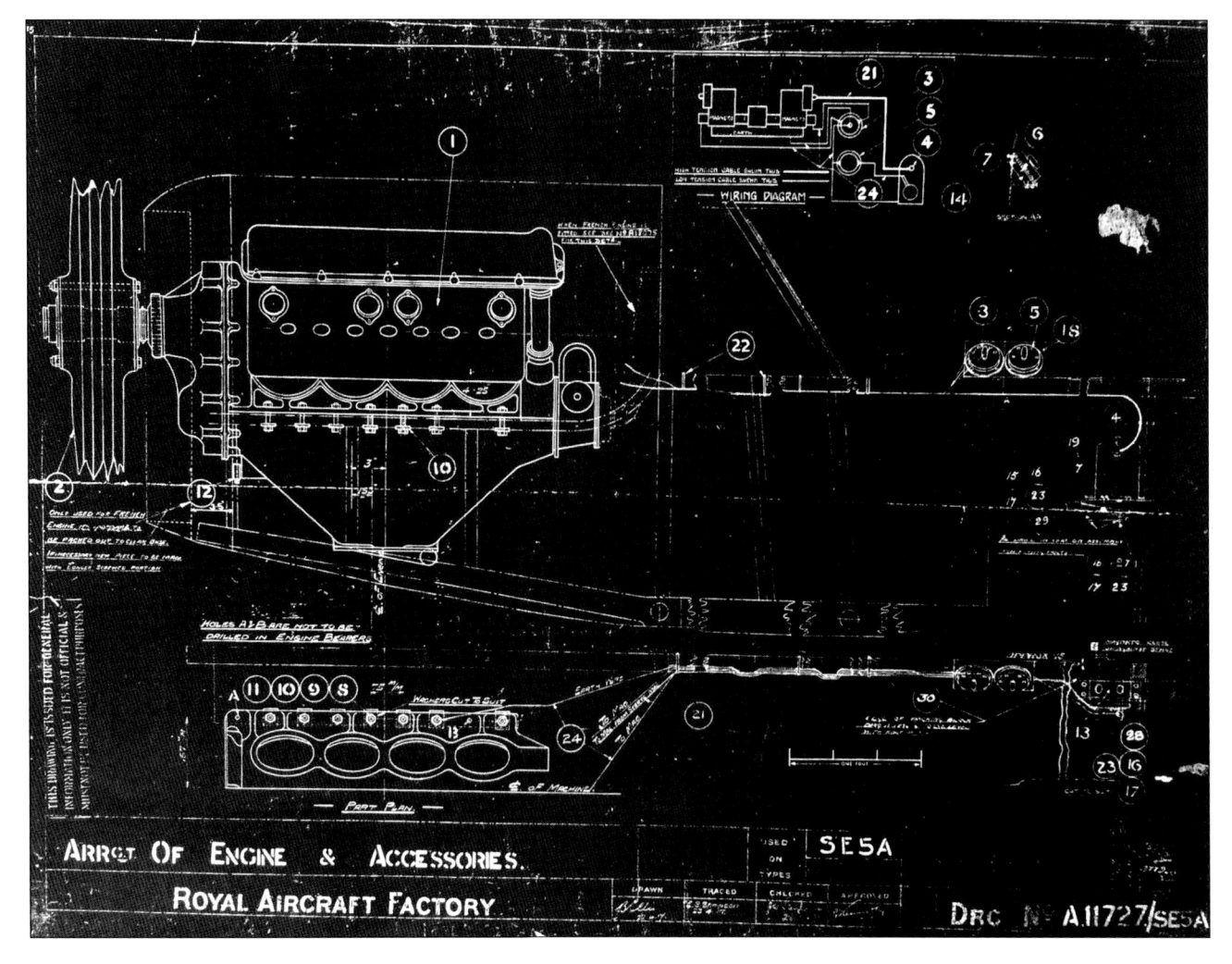

ABOVE Design blueprint for the arrangement of the Hispano in the S.E.5a. *(Farnborough Air Sciences Trust)*

the nozzle chamber, this connection can be adjusted by a valve.

By this it is aimed to produce a lower pressure in the float chamber and thus reduce the fuel flow to the nozzles. The valve now lies between the throttle gate valve and the float chamber. The fuel consumption of an engine with a higher compression ratio is 240–250 g/Ch.V./hour.

In spite of the increased mean effective pressure or compression ratio, the fuel consumption is high in comparison with German engines. For obvious reasons it is not suitable to publish here further results of investigations on the carburettor construction, the mean effective pressure and the fuel consumption.

Ignition

The ignition is carried out with two eight-cylinder SEV magnetos. A special feature of these magnetos is that the armature is fixed while a flux distributor casing rotates around the armature, producing four sparks per revolution. The contact-breaker and condenser are also fixed.

The cam plate, a gear wheel with eight lobes, rotates at half the speed of the conducting sleeve and operates the contact breaker arm. The latter conveys the primary current through a special cable from the armature. The contact breaker and condenser are fixed on a plate that rotates centrally around the cam plate, in order to advance and retard the ignition.

The high tension current in this type of magneto is conducted from the secondary windings through a small insulated tube into which is inserted an Ebonite insulator carrying a contact, also bearing on its front end a brass disc which forms an electrode of the safety spark gap. A brass spring contact and high-tension terminal moulded into an insulated cover rests against this disc.

From the small insulated tube, the high-

ABOVE Complete Hispano-Suiza 8a awaiting installation.

tension current is conducted via the brass spring contact to a terminal in the moulded cover of the safety spark gap housing and thence by an external wire to the centre of the terminal of the distributor cover. From this terminal it passes to the distributor rotor via a spring-loaded carbon brush located in the distributor block.

The high-tension voltage is conducted away from the coil of the fixed armature through a rubber-insulated terminal, which has a disk on its end that, with the protection box, forms the safety spark gap. The high-tension voltage is led through a cable to the distributor block.

The cylinders of the Hispano-Suiza are numbered from the front of the engine to the rear. Each cylinder block is numbered left 1 to 4, right 1 to 4, and the firing order as given in the Wolseley Hispano Instruction Manual is 1L-4R-2L-3R-4L-1R-3L-2R. On the original Hispano, the cylinder blocks are numbered 1-4 on the right and 5-8 on the left, with the firing order given as 1-6-3-5-4-7-2-8.

The left magneto operates the outer spark plug bank and the right magneto operates the inner spark plug bank. One of the first Hispano-Suiza engines captured had no variable ignition timing, but the left magneto was set at 4 mm advanced ignition while the right magneto was set to 10 mm advanced ignition. The engine was started off the left magneto and only after the engine was running were both magnetos in operation. In the direct-drive engine the drive to the magnetos is taken directly from the vertical driving shaft of the camshaft, while in the engines fitted with reduction gear it takes place through a special pair of worm gears.

Cooling

Cooling water is circulated through the integral water jacket by means of a centrifugal water pump of normal construction.

In order to measure the temperature a small cylindrical metal container is screwed into the cooling water circuit from the cylinder to the cooler; this metal bulb is connected to the pressure gauge by a very small bore hard copper tube. The bulb contains a liquid of very low boiling point (sulphuric ether, carbon disulphide, etc).

The vapour pressure of this liquid changes during operation, with the increase in temperature. The pressure is indicated on a pressure gauge on the pilot's instrument panel. The dial of this gauge indicates not pressure but temperature as a function of pressure, the instrument being empirically standardised.

The radiator is constructed as a ring-radiator between the foremost cylinders and the plane of rotation of the propeller. The radiator can be partly covered in order to raise the temperature of the cooling water; this is done by means of a hinged flap system operated by hand from the pilot's cockpit.

Lubrication

The construction of the oil pump is extraordinarily simple. The pump is geared with the crankshaft to the ratio of 24/20, and thus rotates at 1,920 rpm when the crankshaft rotates at 1,600 rpm. At this rotation the supply is 17.3 litres per minute. The oil is cooled by a special oil cooler fixed under the fuselage.

The oil pump is of simple rotating vane design. The lubrication system is a forced circulation method with no fresh oil added. The oil pump is a recent design of Hispano-Suiza and is geared to the engine in the ratio of 1:1.5. At 2,100 rpm (corresponding to 1,400 rpm for the engine) the supply of oil is 417 litres/hour or approximately 7 litres/minute.

Engine weight

In conclusion, some data on a recently captured engine may be of interest:

Weight of the engine with reduction gear transmission (without hub)	217 kg
Weight of water content	21.5 kg
Weight of oil content (15 litres)	13.5 kg
Total	252 kg
Weight of radiator (without water) inc casing and cover	33.5 kg
Weight of water content	10.8 kg
Total weight	296.3 kg – about 300 kg
Weight for 1 hp (Ch.V.)	
Engine alone	1.26 kg/hp (Ch.V.)
Engine with radiator	1.5 kg/hp (Ch.V.)

LEFT Early S.E.5a retaining 'car radiator' on direct-drive 150hp Hispano-Suiza 8a. *(Farnborough Air Sciences Trust)*

LEFT Experimental S.E.5a with rounded tail fin, balanced rudder and ailerons and experimental cooling design for 220hp-geared Hispano-Suiza. *(Farnborough Air Sciences Trust)*

Appendix 1

Star performers: the S.E.5 in fiction

If the subject of airmen and the Great War comes up in casual conversation, most people can name the Sopwith Camel, the Fokker Triplane and the Red Baron. Yet the more prosaically named S.E.5 has remained an almost constant presence in recreations of the period on our screens and on our bookshelves for more than 80 years.

In the immediate aftermath of the war there was a great slew of lurid literary fiction that relied heavily upon Lloyd George's image of a 'cavalry of the clouds'. Tales of aerial swashbuckling abounded, torn straight from the pages of wartime propaganda, and even among those who should have known better there was always an element of whimsy.

That is surely the only explanation for 'Taffy' Jones – confidante of 'Mick' Mannock – to attribute the following quote to his lost friend in his book *King of Air Fighters*: 'When you see that tiny spark come out of my S.E. it will kindle the flame which will act as a torch to guide the future air defenders of the Empire along the path of duty.'

Among the penny dreadfuls there were still gems to be found, most notably in the Biggles series by W.E. Johns and *Winged Victory* by V.M. Yeates. Both authors were veterans of the air war – Johns had flown DH4 bombers and Yeates' book is effectively a dramatised diary of his own life in a Camel squadron, written as his last testament while he succumbed to tuberculosis.

In both cases the Camel-flying protagonists of Johns and Yeates look wistfully upward at the formations of S.E.5s cruising hawk-like overhead while they are forced to fight for their lives several thousand feet below. Yeates described S.E.5 pilots as 'these supermen with rows of ribbons', but Johns was a little more charitable, making 'Wilks' Wilkinson and the S.E.5 pilots of 287 Squadron valued, if slightly supercilious, comrades to 'Biggles' Bigglesworth and 266 Squadron.

For many years interest in the war ebbed away but it was revived in the 1960s. There was a shift towards nastiness in Frederick E. Smith's *A Killing For The Hawks* and Jack D. Hunter's *The Blue Max* that can doubtless be attributed to the carnage of Vietnam, the loss of the British Empire, the rise of counter-culture and the overturning of old values.

In 1971 a new novel appeared which rendered virtually all previous works redundant: Derek Robinson's *Goshawk Squadron* (see Appendix 2). For the first – and so far only – time in literary history, the airmen had a laureate who could more than hold his own against the endless literary acreage dedicated to the horrors of trench warfare. Since then the S.E.5 has continued with occasional cameo appearances in other works. Most recent among them has been Louis de Bernières' somewhat tortuous tome *The Dust That Falls From Dreams*, in which his Camel-flying pilot encounters James McCudden and decrees that 'a Camel fights like a cat, an SE5 fights like a shark'.

On film, the S.E.5 has been seen in more than 20 productions to date – although genuine

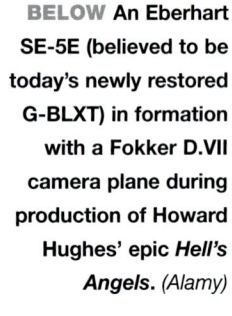

BELOW An Eberhart SE-5E (believed to be today's newly restored G-BLXT) in formation with a Fokker D.VII camera plane during production of Howard Hughes' epic *Hell's Angels*. *(Alamy)*

aircraft have been notoriously thin on the ground. The only motion picture that can lay claim to genuine S.E.5s was Howard Hughes' seminal *Hell's Angels* of 1930. The story was pure hokum but the cinematography was flawless, and featured 137 pilots in the air during the climactic aerial battle scene, contributing to *Hell's Angels* having the highest production costs of any movie at the time it was made.

With the majority of the movie's pilots and aircraft being wartime veterans, and with Hughes pushing them to the limit with his demands for the challenging stunts put together for the set pieces, it was remarkable that the movie's death toll stood at only three airmen and one mechanic. Hughes himself suffered a fractured skull after attempting a stunt that no other pilot would accept. The excesses of *Hell's Angels* would duly be featured as part of the story of *The Great Waldo Pepper* in 1975, when Robert Redford's roguish war veteran finally got to confront the legendary German ace, Ernst Kessler – although Waldo himself flew a Sopwith Camel, rather than an S.E.5.

As with literary fiction, the airmen of World War One suffered terrible typecasting as chivalrous 'knights of the air' for many years. Then, in 1966, came *The Blue Max*, an adaptation of Jack D. Hunter's novel that told a scorching tale of celebrity and excess through the eyes of Bruno Stachel, a German air ace played by George Peppard. The principal foe in *The Blue Max* was a squadron of S.E.5s led by a pair of fairly convincing replicas built by Miles at Shoreham. Pilots on the film recalled that they were extremely pleasant to fly in comparison with the various replica Fokkers and Pfalzes of Stachel's fictitious *Jagdstaffel*.

There were only two S.E.5 replicas made; the rest of the British squadron is represented by Tiger Moths and Stampes in WW1 livery. Both of the Miles S.E.5s would go on to have tragically short careers. After appearing in the WW1 musical *Darling Lili*, one was destroyed during the making of the movie *Zeppelin*, when it crashed into the film unit's Alouette helicopter during one of the flying scenes. The other aircraft was destroyed while filming a low-level sequence for *Richthofen and Brown*. There were no survivors in either accident.

In 1976 the British movie *Aces High* sought to capture the grimness of the air war – and its relentless sacrifice of public schoolboys. The pilots, led by Malcolm McDowell, flew S.E.5s that were in fact a trio of mildly disguised Stampe SV4 aircraft, prepared by Tony Bianchi's Personal Plane Services. Some of the *Aces High* aerial footage was later recycled and used in 1989 for an episode of *Blackadder Goes Forth*, with a broadly similar storyline to the original film that ultimately ended up lost amid the fart gags.

Thanks to the art of CGI a mini-revival of World War One flying on film took place during the 2000s, with the S.E.5 appearing throughout. Hollywood threw a sizeable budget at *Flyboys* as a star vehicle for James Franco, roughly retelling the story of the American volunteers of the Lafayette Escadrille. Precious little of the live action flying made the final cut, with CGI aircraft proving better able to meet the expectations of the PlayStation generation, but a Currie Wot-based S.E.5 is among the props seen in the film.

Another CGI spectacular was the German-led production *Der Rote Baron*, telling the story of Manfred von Richthofen. Spectacular set pieces were delivered with aircraft performing a little closer to their period speeds than had been the case in *Flyboys*, including some expertly modelled digital S.E.5s.

Two films featuring live action from genuine replicas followed. In France *Le Dernier Vol* (*The Last Flight*), starring Marion Cotillard, saw a replica two-seat S.E.5 playing a starring role in this desert epic. Back in Britain, the BBC remade *The 39 Steps* with a whole host of anachronistic vehicles for 1913–14, not the least being a Currie Wot-based S.E.5a replica from the Great War Display Team, used here to chase Rupert Penry-Jones over the Scottish moors.

For now, then, the S.E.5's filming days remain a long and patchy story in motion picture history. But there is still hope that Sir Peter Jackson may yet come to the rescue of the World War One flying movie. Already a short film has been made featuring several of the Vintage Aviator Limited's fleet, entitled *Crossing the Line*, and hopes remain high that a genuine blockbuster might yet be seen from the Hobbit-master – perhaps at long last even a movie of *Goshawk Squadron*?

Time will tell…

Appendix 2

Interview with Derek Robinson

Goshawk Squadron was a novel that changed popular perceptions about World War One in the air for good. Popular images of fluttering silk scarves and gallantry curdled on the pages of a story that turned its author, Derek Robinson, into a literary sensation overnight with its cast-iron research, withering violence and ready wit.

It tells the story of an inexperienced squadron formed largely of public schoolboys as they prepare to fly the S.E.5a into battle. Set on the eve of the German Spring Offensive in 1918, the excitable and idealistic young pilots of Goshawk Squadron prepare for battle under the leadership of foul-mouthed working-class 'temporary gentleman' Major Bernard Woolley, a veteran of 18 months in the front line.

Woolley mocks and bullies his pilots, setting both their nerves and sinews on edge through his relentless training programme. He knows that when the German attack comes the notion of chivalrous jousting between sportsmen that the men under his command anticipate will be proven to be a myth.

'I wrote it not so much in a fit of rage but in a fit of defiance,' Robinson remembered. 'I had already wasted four years writing stuff which nobody wanted to publish, so I said to myself: "Well, I don't give a shit. I'm going to write this and if I like it that's what matters. I'll write it for me and if somebody else wants to publish it then that's good luck."'

The inspiration for Goshawk Squadron came in 1968 from a newspaper article commemorating the 50th anniversary of the Royal Air Force. 'It was a very interesting feature because they had found a World War One pilot who had written a piece about what it was really like to fly planes – fighter planes – in 1918,' recalled Robinson. 'He said it was much more like meeting a guy down a back alley with a sock full of broken glass and cracking him over the head and running like hell. It was just as bad to be shot at 15,000ft as it was in the trenches so let's forget all the chivalry stuff, there was no fair play, there was no duelling in the sky.

'The reason why the newspapers wrote it up in that way was that they were desperate for good copy and there was none to be found in the trenches. The trenches were bad news. Planes in the sky made for good news – so the air war got distorted. Soon I was off and running and so I read everything that I could lay my hands on.'

Living somewhat hand-to-mouth as a copywriter and local journalist, Robinson penned Goshawk Squadron at night. 'I had a lot of energy in those days,' he laughed. 'And a fair bit of anger at the world in general. That seems to have faded a little bit in later years but I was determined that I was going to write this damned book. I used to get an hour's sleep and go off and do three or four hours writing this stuff for about six months. And it really didn't need to be edited by the time that it was finished.'

Part of Robinson's drive for authenticity saw Woolley and co equipped with the S.E.5a rather than the Sopwith Camel, almost a refusal to pander to stereotypes and instead showcase the unsung hero of the air war over the trenches. 'I think the reason for choosing the S.E.5 for Goshawk Squadron was the same reason that Woolley gives in the book: it was a compromise that was most effective in accomplishing the purpose of the pilot being up there, namely to kill the enemy,' Robinson reflected. 'And I also like the look of it. It was a very handsome-looking thing.'

Then there is the magnetic appeal of Woolley, Robinson's uncompromising, Guinness-swilling anti-hero, drawn with significant influence from the two former 'camp rats' who rose to lead S.E.5a squadrons:

Mannock and McCudden. 'Mick Mannock is certainly a large part of Woolley,' he said. 'He was more interesting than Ball – and Ball was an amazing and wonderful character, but Mannock was the interesting one and he was the one I'd like to meet in a bar and have a beer with.'

War stories have seldom attracted the attention of the literary establishment, but *Goshawk Squadron* burst on to the bookshelves as a huge critical success and saw Robinson placed second in the Booker Prize of 1971. It was a hit for his publisher and before long Hollywood came knocking, with Sam Goldwyn Jr personally agreeing the purchase of Robinson's book – although this was something of a non-event for the author: 'I sold the movie rights … didn't make any money on those and that's a long story, but for various reasons I made a couple of thousand pounds on rights that sold for $100,000! But it all bought time. That's what every writer needs – time to write the next book.'

As with any successful story it inspired imitators, among which the movie *Aces High* and the BBC TV drama *Wings* attempted to get closest to the Robinson worldview. 'I think *Goshawk Squadron* is filmable, but the way it's written at the moment there is no happy ending and Hollywood does like a happy ending,' Robinson concluded.

Although his career has spanned a multitude of other genres in fiction and non-fiction in the last 45 years, Robinson's stunning debut novel spawned a series of flying stories that remain his most popular work. *Goshawk Squadron* gained two prequels – *War Story*, set in the skies over the Battle of the Somme in 1916, and *Hornet's Sting*, set in 1917 between 'Bloody April' and Passchendaele, where the reader sees how Bernard Woolley's character was forged. A further four-book series covers World War Two, of which his Battle of Britain story *Piece of Cake* was turned into a brilliant TV mini-series.

In his most recent volume, *A Splendid Little War*, Robinson moved the action to Russia after the Armistice, with a band of airmen – struggling to come to terms with peace – who go out to fight against the Bolsheviks. 'I did finally get round to the Camel in the Russian book,' Robinson grinned. 'That's a sad book in a way and I was surprised that it did as well as it did.'

Sad yet laugh-out-loud funny, angry yet bursting with sympathy … the Robinson canon is the closest that any of us will get to experiencing the perspective of the people and times when aircraft like the S.E.5a were in their prime. You can ask little more of a writer than that.

RIGHT Derek Robinson with some of the books that have changed how we write and read about aerial warfare forever. *(Author)*

Appendix 3

Albert Ball's ripping cake

As part of the Great War centenary commemorations, a combination of the Royal Air Force Museum and students of Barnet and Southgate College got to work on recreating Albert Ball's family plum-cake recipe – the snack of choice for a hungry ace, it would seem.

Ball's mother and his sister Lois both used to regularly send supplies out to him in France, and his requests for fresh supplies were a regular feature of his correspondence. One letter to Lois said: 'I was so pleased to get your ripping cake, but I have nearly finished it. I love to take a huge piece with me when I fly.'

Many years later, after Lois died, the recipe for the cake that Ball so enjoyed passed to his great-niece, who eventually made the RAF Museum aware of this little ray of light from the dark days of 1916 and 1917. Students from the college were tasked with recreating the cake, with the winning baker's methods being used to make the cake now on sale to RAF Museum visitors.

Few among us may have the opportunity to take the controls of an S.E.5 and see the world from three miles high but we can get a flavour of it. Here is the recipe in full:

Ingredients
225g caster sugar
225g softened butter
3 eggs
225g sieved plain flour
225g raisins
110g chopped dates
110g chopped plums

Cooking instructions
Cream together the softened butter and caster sugar, then slowly add the eggs to the mixture. Once mixed, fold in the flour and begin gradually sprinkling the fruit into the mix. Heat the oven to 160°C (gas mark 3) and place a tray of water in the bottom. Pour the cake mixture into a tin and bake for 50–60 minutes until deep brown with a discernable crust. Once cooked, dust with demerara sugar and leave to cool.

RIGHT The perfect accompaniment to an afternoon's reading or model making. *(Author)*

Appendix 4

Surviving S.E.5 aircraft and places of interest

Surviving examples of the Royal Aircraft Factory S.E.5a

Registration/serial	Markings	Condition	Location	Status
F-904/G-EBIA	84 Squadron RAF	Airworthy	Shuttleworth Collection, UK	Available to view in the hangars and takes part in air displays (weather permitting)
G-EBIB	Savage Sky Writing	Static display	Science Museum, London, UK	Available to view in the aviation section
'F-938'/G-EBIC	Generic RFC/RAF	Static display	Grahame-White Factory, RAF Museum, London, UK	Available to view among the WW1 and pioneer aircraft
C8996	TBC	Under restoration	Hawker Restorations, UK	Not available to view
C1916	2 Squadron AFC	Static display	Australian War Memorial, Canberra	Available to view in the aviation section
F7781/F7783	Generic RFC/RAF	Static display	South African National Museum of Military History, Johannesburg	Available to view in the aviation section
E5668	Generic RAF	Under restoration	Currently TVAL	Will be returning to Europe in 2017

Surviving examples of the Eberhart SE-5E

Registration/serial	Markings	Condition	Location	Status
A.S.22-325	18th Headquarters Squadron, USAAS	Static display	National Museum of the US Air Force, Dayton, Ohio	Available to view in the pioneers of flight section
G-BLXT	US Army Air Service	Under restoration to flying condition	Sywell Aerodrome, UK	Not available to view

Places of interest

The Aerodrome
theaerodrome.com.
Forum and reference site for World War One aviation enthusiasts, historians and modellers.

Australian War Memorial
Treloar Crescent, Campbell ACT 2612, Australia.
Extremely emotive museum commemorating the Australian military, with original S.E.5a C1916 in pride of place in the Great War hall.

Bicester Heritage
Bicester Heritage, Buckingham Road, Bicester, Oxfordshire OX27 8AL, UK.
A 348-acre former airfield that was established in 1916 and was used by RAF Bomber Command in WW2. Buildings have been restored, classic aviation and motoring businesses have taken up residency and a variety of aerial and motoring events are held through the year.

Britmodeller.com
britmodeller.com.
Forum and reference site for modellers, with specific sections for World War One aircraft, ships and military vehicles. Ideal to swap tips on the finer points of creating an accurate replica.

Brooklands Museum
Brooklands Road, Weybridge KT13 0QN, UK.
Magnificent and welcoming family-friendly museum at the cradle of British motoring and aviation. Original buildings and race track (opened in 1907) are host to many racing cars, bicycles and motorcycles up to 1939. Aviation museum holds primarily British Aerospace types, but also reflects Brooklands as home of Vickers production of the S.E.5a.

Canadian War Museum
1 Vimy Place, Ottawa, ON K1A 0M8, Canada.
Comprehensive history of Canadian armed forces. Strong content from 1914–18 in all theatres, with several aircraft. Of greatest note to S.E.5 enthusiasts is former 60 Squadron and 85 Squadron ace 'Billy' Bishop's medal collection.

Cross and Cockade
Hamilton House, Wadenhoe, Peterborough, PE8 5ST, UK.
Society for enthusiasts and historians of World War One aviation, publishing many periodicals and books, offering live and online forums for discussion and organising events.

Farnborough Air Sciences Trust
Trenchard House, 85 Farnborough Road, Farnborough GU14 6TF, UK.
Free-to-enter museum based in one of the oldest aviation-related buildings in Britain, built in 1907 by the Royal Engineers to be the headquarters of their Balloon School. Numerous artefacts on display relate to the Royal Aircraft Factory and the S.E.5 and it has a library and archive that is second to none.

Gosport Aviation Society
c/o 5 Martin Close, Lee-on-the-Solent, Hampshire, P013 8LG, UK.
A dedicated group of aviation enthusiasts who perpetuate the importance and significance of Gosport in the history of British aviation. Regular society meetings and talks, publications and activities such as erecting a plaque in honour of Robert Smith-Barry.

BELOW Trenchard House, built in 1907, is the oldest aviation-related building in the country and houses many S.E.5-related artefacts as home to the Farnborough Air Sciences Trust. *(Author)*

Great War Display Team
www.greatwardisplayteam.com.
British-based flying display team of replica World War One types including 7/8-scale S.E.5a aircraft. Regular performers of spirited shows, available for bookings at airshows and other events.

Great War Flying Museum
13961 McLaughlin Road, Caledon, ON L7C 3L7, Canada.
Collection of airworthy reproduction and replica aircraft, including an accurate S.E.5a in the markings of 'Billy' Bishop from 85 Squadron. Open days and air displays are regular summer attractions.

Hawker Restorations
Moat Farm, Church Road, Milden IP7 7AF, Ipswich, UK.
Formerly AJD Engineering, it has created some fine S.E.5a static replicas, including the aircraft on display at the Royal Australian Air Force Museum. Should be the first port of call for anyone with an S.E.5 to restore.

Imperial War Museum
Lambeth Road, London, SE1 6HZ, UK.
Comprehensive museum of British warfare in the 20th and 21st centuries established in the former Royal Bethlem Hospital, London. World War One display is comprehensive, but S.E.5a enthusiasts will gravitate towards the display of James McCudden's tunic, cane, gloves, flying helmet and the windscreen from his last aircraft.

Imperial War Museum Duxford
Duxford, Cambridge CB22 4QR, UK.
Former RAF airfield now home to the IWM's aircraft collection, several private warbird collections and host to several hugely popular air displays each year. As well as the museum's own World War One display, it's a central hub for the warbird industry in Britain and a good spot to find aircraft like the S.E.5 as they move between the UK and USA.

Museum of Army Flying
Middle Wallop SO20 8DY, UK.
Full history of all Army aviation to the present day, with considerable content relating to the Royal Flying Corps on permanent display.

National Museum of the US Air Force
1100 Spaatz Street, Dayton, OH 45431, USA.
Eberhardt SE-5E on permanent display in post-war USAAS colours.

Nottingham Castle
Lenton Road, Nottingham NG1 6EL, UK.
Collection of Albert Ball mementos on permanent display including his medals, pilot's certificate, forage cap, pistols and windscreen from S.E.5 A8898.

Old Rhinebeck Aerodrome
9 Norton Road, Red Hook, NY 12571, USA.
A multitude of static and flying replica/recreation World War One aircraft including a SPAD S.VII and S.E.5a, holding regular flying events through the year.

Omaka Aviation Heritage Centre
79 Aerodrome Road, Omaka, Blenheim 7272,
New Zealand.
Fleet of airworthy and static World War One aircraft built by the Vintage Aviator Limited. Stunning static displays and full-size dioramas as well as regular air display performers and a collection of genuine aviation memorabilia gathered by Oscar-winning movie director Sir Peter Jackson.

Royal Air Force Museum
Grahame Park Way, London NW9 5LL, UK.
Brilliant World War One and pioneers collection housed in the 1911 Grahame-White Factory, moved brick-by-brick from its original location to within the long-term perimeter of the museum. Original S.E.5a F938 resides in the main gallery and displays of weapons, uniforms, medals and factory equipment abound.

Royal Australian Air Force Museum
Point Cook Road, RAAF Base Williams, Melbourne, VIC 3027, Australia.
Full history of the RAAF with recreation S.E.5a featured in a display covering the early years of the service.

Saint Omer Aeroclub
Chemin du Plateau des Bruyères, 62219 Longuenesse, France.
The largest British airfield on the Western Front and the primary administrative and logistics centre for the Royal Flying Corps, Saint Omer is ripe with history. Today it's still a grass airstrip and the British Air Services Memorial acts as a guide to the history made there.

Scarf and Goggles Social Club
scarfandgoggles.wordpress.com.
Stories of adventure on land, sea and air from the first half of the 20th century, with particular prominence being given to the S.E.5a among World War One stories.

Science Museum
Exhibition Road, London SW7 2DD, UK.
S.E.5a G-EBIB hangs from the ceiling and a Wolseley Viper engine is on display among the landmark aero engines.

The Shuttleworth Collection
Old Warden Aerodrome, Nr Biggleswade, Bedfordshire SG18 9EP, UK.
The only genuine S.E.5a flying in the world, G-EBIB/F-904, as part of the largest collection of genuine World War One types in existence. In addition there are artefacts such as Hispano-Suiza engines, propellers and mementos of pilots including uniforms, medals and personal effects. Regular flying events from spring to autumn where these aircraft fly (weather permitting).

South African National Museum of Military History
22 Erlswold Way, Randburg, 2132, South Africa.
Original S.E.5a composed of F7781/F7783 on display in the flight gallery, together with items relating to South African S.E.5a airmen and the foundation of the South African Air Force using 'Imperial Gift' aircraft like the S.E.5a.

Stow Maries Great War Airfield
Hackmans Lane, Purleigh, Chelmsford CM3 6RN, UK.
Magnificent museum contained within the ongoing restoration of the only World War One airfield remaining in existence. Workshops, mess and ready room are all present and correctly restored with significant work to be done on the other buildings. In a sympathetically styled modern hangar, reproduction aircraft operated by the World War One Aviation Heritage Trust can be viewed, including the B.E.2c, Albatros D.V and S.E.5a. Not licensed for air displays, Stow Maries does occasionally hold fly-ins at which these aircraft are seen in action.

The Vintage Aviator Limited Collection
Hood Aerodrome, South Road, Masterton, Wairarapa 5885, New Zealand.
Fleet of airworthy World War One aircraft built by the Vintage Aviator Limited, as well as several airworthy original WW1 aircraft, routinely on display the last weekend of every month from November to April. Check the TVAL website or Facebook page for details.

World War One Aviation Heritage Trust
c/o Dick Forsythe, Chief Trustee, 3 The Willows, North Warnborough, Hook, Hampshire, RG29 1DR, UK.
British affiliate of the Vintage Aviator Limited and Omaka museum, aiming to generate interest in and operation of World War One reproduction aircraft. A good place to go to for support for your own S.E.5a projects.

Appendix 5

Scale models of the S.E.5a

Model kits are a passion for many readers of Haynes books, and the S.E.5 remains a popular choice of Great War subject. Thanks to the arrival of Wingnut Wings the type has enjoyed a model making revival, but kits have been available in almost every scale over the years and can still be found and enjoyed today.

1/144 scale
1979 Mamoli 1/144 'SE.5A'.
2008 Sram 1/144 'SE5a' resin kit.
2013 Valom 1/144 'RAF SE5A' injection moulded kit.

1/72 scale
1964 Revell 1/72 'Royal Aircraft Factory S.E.5a'.
1966 Renwal 1/72 'Capt. Elliot W. Springs S.E.5a' Aero-Skin kit.
1968 Eldon 1/72 'US Air Service S.E.5a'.
1973 Nichimo 1/72 'US Air Service S.E.5a' (reboxed Eldon kit).
1976 Entex 1/72 'S.E.5a' (reboxed Eldon kit).
1979 Sunny 1/72 'S.E.5a' (reboxed Eldon kit).
1980 Takara 1/72 'S.E.5A' (reboxed Revell kit).
1981 Esci 1/72 'S.E.5a' (reboxed Eldon kit).
2003 Roden 1/72 'RAF S.E.5a with Hispano Suiza'.
2004 Roden 1/72 'RAF S.E.5a with Wolseley Viper'.
2010 Encore 1/72 Econo-Kit 'S.E.5a' (reboxed Roden kit).

1/48 scale
1956 Aurora 1/48 'S.E.5 Scout' with geared Hispano.
1958 Lindberg 1/48 'British S.E.5a' with engraved markings and direct drive 150hp Hispano.
1978 Monogram 1/48 'British S.E.5a' kit Wolseley Viper.
1980 Entex 1/48 'Scout S.E.5a' (reboxed Lindberg kit).
1982 Libramodels Scaleplanes 1/48 'S.E.5' (early versions).
1992 Hasegawa/Monogram 1/48 'R.A.F. S.E.5a' (reboxed Monogram kit).
1999 Pegasus 1/72 'R.A.F. S.E.5 (Early)' short-run injection kit.
2002 Revell 1/48 'Royal Aircraft Factory S.E.5a' (reboxed Monogram kit).
2004 Roden 1/48 'RAF S.E.5a with Wolseley Viper'.
2005 Roden 1/48 'RAF S.E.5a with Hispano Suiza'.

1/32 scale
2007 Roden 1/32 'RAF S.E.5a with Wolseley Viper'.
2009 Encore 1/32 'RAF S.E.5a McCudden' (reboxed Roden kit).
2009 Roden 1/32 'RAF S.E.5a with Hispano Suiza'.
2009 Wingnut Wings 1/32 'Royal Aircraft Factory S.E.5a 'Hisso'.

1/24 scale
1993 Sanger 1/24 'S.E.5a' Wolseley Viper vac-form kit.
2015 Merit 1/24 'RAF S.E.5a' Wolseley Viper.

1/19 scale
1964 Aurora 1/19 'SE-5 British Scout' Screwdriver Assembly kit.

1/12 scale
1962 Guillows 1/12 'British S.E.5A' balsa kit.
2002 Guillows 1/12 'British S.E.5A' balsa kit (laser-cut pieces).

1/8 scale
Hasegawa 1/8 'S.E.5a'.

Corgi Aviation Archive 1/48 Royal Aircraft Factory S.E.5a

AA37701 Cecil Lewis, 61 Squadron (Home Defence), 1918.
AA37702 Billy Bishop, 60 Squadron, France, 1917.
AA37703 Francis Magoun, 1 Squadron, France, 1918.
AA37704 Edward Mannock, 74 Squadron, France, 1918.
AA37705 James McCudden, 56 Squadron, France, 1917.
AA37706 USAAS, 25th Aero Squadron, France, 1918.
AA37707 Captain Grinnell-Milne, 56 Squadron, France, 1919.

Radio-control S.E.5a

ECOMRC S.E.5a ARF (71in wingspan kit for 30cc petrol engine).
E-Flite S.E.5a Slow Flyer ARF (30in wingspan – foam airframe/electric motor).
Electrifly S.E.5a (34in wingspan – balsa kit for electric motor).
Flair S.E.5a (51in wingspan – balsa kit for nitro or electric motor).
Flyzone Micro S.E.5a ARF (14in wingspan – foam airframe/electric motor).
Parkzone S.E.5a ARF (37in wingspan – foam airframe/electric motor).

BELOW Roden's 1/32 S.E.5a with the Wolseley Viper engine is a popular build – rigging it can drive modellers to distraction, however. *(Author)*

155
APPENDIX 5

Appendix 6

Glossary of airmen's slang

By modern standards not all of these terms are what would now be considered 'politically correct', but it must be remembered that they were coined a century ago, under very different political circumstances, in a world and environment vastly unlike those in which we live today.

Word	Meaning	Origin	Usage
Abdul	Turkish Army	British Army	'They want me to go and chuck some eggs at Abdul and his chums.'
Ack Emma	Air mechanic	British Army phonetic alphabet	'Your motor sounds out of sorts – send for the Ack Emma.'
Ack Tock	Flipping the aircraft on the ground ('All turtle' or 'Arse over tit')	British Army phonetic alphabet	'There was a damned great hole in the runway and it turned the kite Ack Tock.'
Ak dum	At once	Hindi (*Akh dum*)	'If the Vickers gun jams then get out of there ak dum!'
Albatri	Plural of Albatros (German aircraft)	Airmen's own	'I flew smack into the middle of half a dozen Albatri…'
Archie	Anti-aircraft fire	Music hall song (Archibald! Certainly not!)	'Archie's been barking at me.'
Allay!	Clear off	French (*allez*)	'The CO's a bit savage about you breaking the undercart, I should allay pretty sharpish.'
Aviate	Aerobatics	Airmen's own	'Jenkins aviated a little to buck the troops up.'
Axle grease	Butter	General usage	'Pass the axle grease, this bread's a week old!'
Balloonatics	Balloon observers	Airmen's own	'If I'd wanted to simply get shot at all day, I'd have joined the Balloonatics!'
Beer boy	A poor airman	British Army	'He can't hold formation – he's a regular beer boy.'
Big Ack	Armstrong-Whitworth FK8	Airmen's own	'We saw a Big Ack getting thoroughly Archied.'
Bint	Female	Arabic	'He'll be swanning around Soho with a bint on each arm by now.'
Biff/Brisfit	Bristol F.2B fighter	Airmen's own	'We were outnumbered by those Huns but thankfully some Biffs turned up to shoo them away.'
Binge	Strenuous alcohol intake	Airmen's own	'It really was a topping binge in the mess last night!'
Black	Gaffe (officer's)	British gentlemen's clubs	'He sat in the CO's chair – put up a black there.'
Blighty	Sent home to Britain	Hindi (*Bilayati* – foreign land)	'He got pipped in the arm – it's a Blighty for sure.'
Blimp	Non-rigid airship or balloon	Airmen's own	'Our blimps were out over the Channel this morning.'
Boche	Germans	French (*tête de boche*)	'There were great lines of Boche infantry in the rear.'
Boko	Plenty	French (*beaucoup*)	'*Garçon! Boko vino, s'il vous plait.*'

ABOVE **The pilots of 85 Squadron and their menagerie of mascots, June 1918.** *(Imperial War Museum)*

Word	Meaning	Origin	Usage
Bon	Good	French	'Well that's a bon old mess and no mistake!'
Bought it	Dead	General usage	'His brother bought it at Loos.'
Bradshawing	Navigating by railway lines	Named after the Bradshaw railway timetable	'The compass took a bullet so I had to Bradshaw my way home.'
Brass/Brass hat	Senior staff officer	British Army	'Try not to crash your aeroplane, it's not popular with the brass.'
Breezy	Nervous	General usage	'Old Mellersh is still a bit breezy after this morning's patrol.'
Buckingham	Incendiary ammunition	Airmen's own	'Make sure to get a chit for the Buckingham to say that you're only shooting at their blimps.'
Buckshee	Free of charge	Arabic (*baksheesh*)	'There were Huns everywhere but I got away buckshee.'
Bumf	Paperwork	18th-century English	'With rank and honour comes a disproportionate amount of bumf-shuffling.'
Bung off	Take off on patrol	Airmen's own	'We've got to bung off at 05:00 for early patrol.'
Burgoo	Porridge	Hindi	'Stone cold burgoo this morning.'
Bus	Aircraft	Airmen's own	'The old bus got peppered with Archie but we got home.'
Buzz	Diving on a ground target	Airmen's own	'I spotted the general's motor car from its pennants, so I buzzed it good and proper.'
Caught a packet	Extreme discomfort	General usage	'I caught a packet from the CO yesterday for not checking the aileron cables before take-off.'
Char	Tea	Hindi	'Have a mug of char waiting when we get back.'

Word	Meaning	Origin	Usage
Charpoy	Bed	Hindi	'Dawn patrol for me – early charpoy tonight.'
Cherb	Beer	Hindi	'I'll join you for a cherb later.'
Chipparow	Shut up	Hindi (*chuprao*)	'Calm down, you lot – chipparow!'
Chit	Note or receipt	Hindi	'Sign the chit for this, would you?'
Chokey	Jail	Hindi (*cauki*)	'They'll throw you in chokey.'
Civvy	Civilian	General usage	'What will you do as a civvy?'
Comic Cuts	Intelligence reports	General usage	'I never believe a word of the Comic Cuts – but the cartoons are ripping!'
Compree	Do you understand?	French (*comprenez*)	'From now on you load your own gun belts – compree?'
Comsah	Like that	French (*comme-ça*)	'Opposite rudder and centring the stick will stop a spin comsah.'
Contour chasing	Extreme low flying	Airmen's own	'I was contour chasing and surprised some fellows rigging up telegraph poles.'
Coolie	Chinese labourer	British Empire	'They sent some coolies over to repair bomb craters.'
Crate	Aircraft	Airmen's own	'I think the S.E.5 is a topping old crate.'
Dekko	Observe	Hindi (*dekho*)	'Have a dekko at the Hun lines and come back.'
Devil dodger	Chaplain	General usage	'If the MO can't fix it, call in the devil dodger.'
Dock	Hospital	Royal Navy	'The flight commander's in dock with shrapnel in his arm.'
Donkey Walloper	Cavalryman	British Army	'We found a charming little bar last night – albeit full of half-cut donkey wallopers.'
Doolally	Eccentric	Hindi (*Deolali*, Indian town)	'He's not himself at the moment – a bit doolally.'
Dud/duff	Imperfect	General usage	'I came home early with a duff motor.'
EA	Enemy aircraft	Airmen's own	'The EA came diving out of the sun and we were forced to break off.'
Effel	Windsock	Initials of 'French letter' (*ie* condom)	'Stand down – it's blowing so hard that the effel's standing to attention.'
Eggs	Bombs	Airmen's own	'Camels have a beastly time of it, as they have to strafe the Hun lines and drop a few eggs.'
Erfs	Eggs	French (*oeufs*)	'I could murder some erfs and chips.'
Erks	Air mechanics	Airmen's own	'It's best to try and steer with the rudder on the ground and not rely on the erks.'
Fee	F.E.2b/d aeroplane	Airmen's own	'He used to be an observer on Fees – nerves of pure steel.'
Finny kaput	Broken	French (*finis*) and German (*kaput*)	'I put 50 rounds in him and his wings folded up – finny kaput.'
Fizzer	To be put on charge	British Army	'Dancing in uniform? He'll be on a fizzer.'
Flaming coffin	Airco DH4 bomber	Airmen's own	'I saw a load of flaming coffins heading out behind the lines.'
Flaming onion	Anti-aircraft rounds used to protect balloons	Airmen's own	'Glad we don't fly Camels, they spend half their lives being chased by flaming onions!'
Flying razorblade	Fokker E.V/D.VIII fighter	Airmen's own	'The dastardly Hun has built a flying razorblade and it climbs like billy-ho.'
Fritz	German	Diminutive of 'Friedrich'	'We'll go and have a look at Master Fritz.'
Frog	French	General usage ('frog eaters')	'I can't abide this bloody awful Frog weather – there's been no rain for weeks!'
Funk	Fear or depression	General usage	'Ignore him, he's in a funk about his girl.'
Grid	Aircraft	Airmen's own (originated by Major K. Caldwell)	'He was chucking that grid about like he hated it!'

Word	Meaning	Origin	Usage
HA	Hostile aircraft	Airmen's own	'I spotted a flight of four HA approximately 4,000ft below.'
Harry Tate	Royal Aircraft Factory R.E.8	Music Hall	'That poor Harry Tate caught a packet from Archie.'
Hun(s)	The enemy (be they Germans or simply novice pilots)	General usage	'I was about to dive on a Hun two-seater when I noticed his pals lurking behind the cloud.'
Huntley & Palmer	Twin Vickers machine guns	British biscuit manufacturer	'There's a new SPAD coming with full Huntley & Palmer.'
Immelmann	To roll off the top of a loop	German tactic devised by Max Immelmann	'I overshot on the first pass and did an Immelmann.'
Imshi	Clear off	Arabic	'If there's more than ten of them, imshi!'
Jildi	Hurry up	Hindi	'Stick the nose down and jildi!'
Kibosh	Finish off	London slang	'The Huns will try and get at the Quirks, so we'll have to put the kibosh on that idea.'
Kite	Aircraft	Airmen's own	'I had to put the kite in a spin to get away from those Huns.'
Knut	Vain officer	Music Hall ('Gilbert the Filbert, Colonel of the Knuts')	'He's had his uniform made in Savile Row – a proper knut.'
Land creeper	Tank	British Army	'Look out for our land creepers supporting the PBI.'
Land owner	Dead	British Army	'Alas, he's left us to become a land owner.'
Mafeesh/napoo	Nothing	Arabic	'Couldn't see a thing in that fog – Napoo, old chap.'
Maiden's prayer	Airship	Airmen's own (due to airships' phallic shape)	'It must be terribly queer, floating around in a maiden's prayer all day.'
Matlow	Seaman	French (*matelot*)	'Only matlows fly Sopwiths. Rum, bum and the Camel is their sorry lot in life.'
Mesopolonica	Middle East posting	British Army	'He got himself sent up to Mesopolonica somewhere.'
Nine	Airco D.H.9 bomber	Airmen's own	'Rotten Archie battery at Flesquiers was getting rather big for his boots so they sent some Nines over to drop an egg or two.'
Nix	Nothing	German (*nichts*)	'Flew over the lines but there was nix trade.'
No bon	Not good	French	'I say, Archie was laying it on thick today. No bon.'
Office	Cockpit	Airmen's own	'The Fee 2 is a decent kite, although the office is somewhat draughty.'
PBI	Poor bloody infantry	General usage	'A Hun two-seater was strafing the PBI.'
Penguin	Non-flying officer	Airmen's own (flightless bird)	'Who dreamt this up? Some damnfool penguin at Wing, one assumes.'
Pip	Wounded	General usage	'He got pipped by a bit of shrapnel.'
Plonk	Wine	French (*vin blanc*)	'I'm rather getting a taste for this plonk.'
Plug	Wounded	General usage	'I got plugged by a Hun rear gunner.'
Poilu	French serviceman	French	'Those poilus fly some odd-looking aeroplanes.'
Quirk	Royal Aircraft Factory B.E.2c	Airmen's own	'I hear that they're sending Quirks up against the Zepps these days.'
Ripping	Very good	General usage	'We toddled over to Saint Omer and dropped bags of flour on the Mess. Ripping sport!'
Rooti	Bread	Hindi (*roti*)	'The Frogs know a thing or two about rooti.'
Rot	Rubbish	General usage	'Bishop beat the entire German air service single-handed? What absolute rot.'
Rumpty	Maurice Farman training aircraft	Airmen's own	'I wrote off at least three Rumpties in training. I deserve a medal for services rendered to my fellow aviators.'

Word	Meaning	Origin	Usage
Saida	Greetings	Arabic	'Tell him saida from me.'
Sammy	American soldier	Uncle Sam	'There's a new Sammy in B-Flight.'
San fairy ann	It doesn't matter	French (ça ne fait rien)	'The plane's a bit broken but san fairy ann.'
Sausage	Airship	Airmen's own	'They bombed the sausage sheds in Belgium, didn't they?'
Shooting a line	Boasting	General usage	'He was shooting a line about dogfighting with the Red Baron.'
Shop	Official business	General usage	'Don't talk shop in the mess. Poor form, you see.'
Sidcot	Quilted flying suit	Airmen's own	'It's damned stuffy sitting around in a Sidcot but you'll thank the Lord for it at 10,000ft.'
Sling the bat	Talk in slang	General usage	'He slings the bat so hard that one barely understands him!'
Split-arse	Rapid change of direction	Airmen's own	'There were dozens of Huns firing at me, I was split-arsing all over the place.'
Spree	Strenuous alcohol intake	Airmen's own	'Three days' leave – I shall be on the spree throughout!'
Stick	Control column	Airmen's own	'My belt came loose and I was hanging on to the stick for dear life.'
Stiffs' paddock	Cemetery	British Army	'The MO says poor old Jarvis went west last night. We'll have to put on a show in the stiffs' paddock, I suppose.'
Strafe	Attack a ground target with machine guns	German (attack)	'Strafing a column of troops is satisfying, but God help you if the engine cuts out.'
Stunt	Perform aerobatics	Airmen's own	'I went stunting over the New Forest once.'
Swing the lead	Shirking	General usage	'He says that he's got duff eardrums, but he's swinging the lead.'
Tripe/Tripehound	Triplane	Airmen's own	'I heard that those Tripes can fall to bits in a dive.'
V-strutter	Albatros D.III and D.V	Airmen's own	'I was circling over Douai when a flight of V-strutters arrived looking for some sport.'
Vamoose	Get lost	Spanish	'I had to vamoose, there were too many of them.'
Vin Blanc Anglais	Scotch whisky	French humour	'It'll take a quart of vin blanc anglais to settle the old man after that lot.'
Volplane	A gliding descent	French	'I ran out of petrol but had just enough height to volplane back to the lines.'
Wallah	Person	Hindi	'Some ghastly Frog farm wallah tried to spear me on his pitchfork.'
West	Dead	General usage	'Old Paxton went west yesterday. A decent sort, we'll miss him.'
Windy/wind up	Afraid/nervous	General usage	'He's got the wind up about strafing balloons.'
Wing	Administrative headquarters	Airmen's own	'One of the chaps from Wing came over. Might have been talking about spare parts or the jam ration – never can tell.'
Wipers	Ypres (town)	General usage	'He was in the last show at Wipers.'
Wonky	Poorly made	General usage	'These tracer rounds are wonky.'
Yank	American	General usage	'It's swarming with Yanks in Rouen.'
Zigzag	Stumble	General usage	'I zigzagged back from the bar in reasonably good order.'
Zoom	Fast climb using the momentum of a dive	Airmen's own	'I dived on him, giving him a quick squirt, then zoomed up under him for another go.'

Postscript

Requiem
(Robert Louis Stevenson, 1850–94)

Under the wide and starry sky
Dig the grave and let me lie:
Glad did I live and gladly die,
And I laid me down with a will.

This be the verse you 'grave for me:
Here he lies where he long'd to be;
Home is the sailor, home from the sea,
And the hunter home from the hill.

Index

Admiralty 10, 18-19, 32, 49, 51, 82
Aerial Derby, Hendon, 1921 115-116
Aerial League of the British Empire 9
Aeronautical Inspection Department 130
Aeroplane, The magazine 10
Aeroplane Supply Depots (ASDs) 130
Air Acceptance Park 130
Air Board 50, 132
Aircraft losses 11-12, 37-38, 40, 80, 88, 90, 97, 101, 130
Airfield facilities 130
   automatic refuelling pumps 131-132
   Bessoneau hangars 130
   field canteen 130
   squadron flights 130
Airfields 93-98
   Aux-le-Château 85
   Bekesbourne 49-50
   Biggin Hill 102
   Boffles 85
   Chattis Hill 89
   Douai 38
   Gontrode 48
   Gosport 32, 88-89
   Greenham Common 60
   Hawkinge 36
   Hesdin (RAF HQ) 85
   Hendon 9, 114-116, 118
   Hounslow 85
   Joyce Green 101
   Le Hameau 37-38
   London Colney 31-36, 97, 102
   Manston 48
   Martlesham Heath 44
   Netheravon 104
   Rendcombe 104
   Rochford 48-49, 50-51
   Saint Omer 29, 36, 95-96, 103
   StowMaries 48
   Vert Galant 36-37, 39
   Westgate 48
Air Leasing, Sywell 60
Airmen 94
   alcohol consumption 95-96, 98
   batmen 94-95
   casualties 88-90, 97
   home leave 97-98
   life on the airfield 93-99
   NCOs 94, 130
   officers 94
   pay 94-95
   slang 156-160
   victories in combat 90-91
Air Ministry 33
Air Navigation, Addlestone factory 43-44
Air races 114-116
Albatros 28, 37-39, 55
   D.II 32
   D.III 32
   D.V 121
Alouette helicopter 147
Alphonse, King of Spain 16
Animal mascots 94, 157
Anti-aircraft artillery 11
Armament 24
   changing ammunition drums 91-93, 103
   gun mountings 70-71
   Hotchkiss gun 18
   interrupter 'CC' gear (synchronised) 11, 18, 25, 28, 34, 37, 39, 70-72, 89, 91, 93, 101
   jamming 91-92
   Lewis machine gun 24, 28-29, 34-38, 71, 91-93, 102-103
   Puteaux cannon 25
   Vickers machine gun 18, 24, 29, 34-35, 59, 70-72, 89, 91, 93
Armament School, Uxbridge 100
Armistice 57, 85, 113, 137-138
Armstrong Whitworth, Baginton 57, 118
Arnold, Doug 60, 124
Austin-Ball A.F.B.1 34, 37, 44-45
Austin Motor Co. 27-28, 33-34, 44, 67
   Longbridge factory 28, 42, 44-46, 59, 123
Austin, Sir Herbert 46
Australian Flying Corps 46, 102, 122
   No. 2 Squadron 122
Australian War Memorial, Canberra 122
Aviatik C.II 18
Avro 504J and K 34, 88-89, 127

Balcombe-Brown, Capt R. 88
Ball, Capt Albert 26-29, 31, 33-35, 44, 50, 71, 77, 80, 102, 149
   cake recipe 151
   crash site markers 40
   criticisms of the S.E.5 27, 84
   investiture at Buckingham Palace 27
   last flight (death) 40, 80-81
   meets Gen Trenchard 37
   personal markings 79
   test flight of S.E.5 27
   victories claimed 39
Ball, Albert Sr 27-28, 37, 40
Barlow, Lt 38
Battle of Arras 31-32, 36, 49, 88
Battle of Britain 149
Battle of the Somme 31, 149
Battle of Ypres 50
Beardmore 84
Beauchamp-Proctor, Anthony 123
Bèchereau, Louis 17-18
Béquet Delage car 65
Bianchi, Tony 59, 107, 147
Birkigt, Marc 16-17, 82, 139
Bleriot, Louis 9-10
   Type XI monoplane 9-10
Blomfield, Maj Richard Graham 32-33
Bloody April 37, 88, 90, 101, 149
Boeree, A.R. 115-116
B Icke Oswald 22
Bolsheviks 114
Bomb shelter 48
Brancker, Brig Gen Sefton 19, 84, 99
Brasier factory, France 83
Bristol
   F2/F2B Fighter 13, 19, 31-32, 84, 107, 114, 126-127
   Scout 35, 54
British Aerospace 42
British & Colonial Aeroplane Co. 19
British Army 10-11, 31, 50
British European Airways 118
Brooke-Popham, Brig-Gen/Lt-Col Robert 17, 35, 37, 83-85
Brooklands – see also Vickers 9, 42, 115, 118
Burbidge Committee 12-13, 18-19, 23, 25, 31
Burbidge, Sir Richard 12

Café Royal, London 98
Caldwell, Keith 'Grid' 79, 102
Cambridge, Duke and Duchess of 120
Card, Cpl Bert 80
Cashmore, Don 107
Caudron 89
Chakraborty, Dr Surya Kumar Goodeve 99
Charles, Hubert 34, 36, 85
Chu Chin Chow musical comedy 98

Churchill, Winston 10
Civil Aviation Authority 64
Civil registrations 56, 59, 114-115, 118
Classic Fighters Airshow, New Zealand 126
Clayton & Shuttleworth 84
Cobby, Arthur 102
Cockpit 29-30, 41, 71-73, 81, 89, 91, 93, 105, 108-109, 111, 126
   bomb release 71
   communications 94
   'greenhouse' semi-enclosed canopy 34-36, 41, 71
   heating system trial 139
   instrument panel 71-72
   pilot's seat 71-72
   windscreen 39, 41, 70, 77, 85
Cody, Samuel Franklin 9
   Army Aeroplane No. 1 9
Colour schemes and camouflage 51, 59, 78, 93, 104, 114-115, 118
Commonwealth War Graves 103
Conspiracy theory re WWI 96
Cotillard, Marion 147
Coty, Roland 65
Crowe, Lt 38-39
Croydon Airport 118
Currie Wot 147
Curtiss Aeroplane & Motor Co 48
   Helldiver 120-121
Curzon, Lord 131

Daily Mail newspaper 12, 81, 117
Daimler 21
Dallas, Roderick 79, 93
Davids, Arthur Rhys 33, 40
de Bernières, Louis *The Dust That Falls From Dreams* book 146
de Havilland
   D.H.2 32, 80, 101
   D.H.4 89, 146
   Tiger Moth 104, 107, 147
de Havilland, Geoffrey 10, 20-21, 23
de la Cuadra, Emilio 16
de Marco, Gene 63, 65-67, 79, 105-111, 125-126
Department of Aeronautical Supplies 46
Display flying 66, 125-127
Disposal companies 114
Dolan, Henry 103
Doping 45, 78
Drawings and documents 45-46, 64
   cutaway 74-75
   Hispano-Suiza engine blueprint 143
   Replicraft 63
   Royal Aircraft Factory 63
Eberhart S.E.5E 55, 59-60, 104, 108, 111, 123-124, 146
Egyptian Expeditionary Force 51
Elliott Lynn, Mrs 114-115
Emile Mayen 18
Engine Repair Shops (ERS) 83
Engine (Hispano-Suiza V8)
   camshaft 141-142
   connecting rods 142
   cooling system 106, 137, 144
   crankcase 64
   crankshaft and transmission 142
   cylinder block 64, 140-141
   ignition 143
   knocking 131
   lubrication 145
   magnetos 110
   maintenance and repairs 125-126, 130
   pistons 141
   starting 71, 109

Epsom Derby, 1922 117
Exhaust system 41, 117
   flame-damping mufflers 51
Eyles, Jim 101, 103

Faber, Lt Col Walter 12
Farman 'Rumpty' box kites 88-89
Farman, Maurice 89
Farnborough Air Sciences Trust 9, 152
Festner, Viz Sebastian 38
Films
   Aces High 147, 149
   Crossing the Line 147
   Darling Lili 147
   Der Rote Baron 147
   Flyboys 147
   Hell's Angels 59, 124, 146-147
   King Kong 120
   Le Dernier Vol (The Last Flight) 147
   Richthofen and Brown 147
   The Blue Max 58, 147
   The Great Waldo Pepper 147
   The Hobbit 119-120
   The Lord of the Rings 119-120
   The 39 Steps 147
   Zeppelin 147
Fire extinguisher experiment 138-139
First (maiden) flights 9, 20-21, 25-26, 57-58, 60, 105, 111, 118, 124
Flight magazine 100, 116
Flying surfaces and controls 71, 108, 136
Fokker
   DVII 56, 100, 146
   Dr.I 91, 121
   monoplanes 18, 22
Fokker, Anthony 11
Folland, Henry P. 19, 21-24, 26, 70, 76, 110
   resignation from Royal Aircraft Factory 31
Ford Model T 56
Forrest DFC, Capt H.G. 122
Fowler, Henry 23
Franco, James 147
Fuel tanks and system 70, 77, 89, 105-107, 109, 127, 131
   carburettors 85, 131, 142-143
   refuelling 106-107, 131
Fuels 131-132, 137, 142-143
   aviation spirit 131
   fuel cans 131
   octane 131
Fuselage 23-24, 47, 66-67, 70, 76, 130
   bracing 23, 70, 76
   truing up 133

German Air Service 28
   bombing raids 48-51
   Jagdstaffeln 32, 37, 39, 113
   Jasta 11 32, 38
   Jasta 29 100
   Kagohl 3 48
German Spring Offensive, 1918 97, 148
Gibson MBE, Maj T.A. Edwin 103
Gnome engines 17, 21-22
Goldwyn Jr, Sam 149
Goodden, Maj Frank 19, 23, 25-27, 29-31, 77, 111
   fatal crash 30-31
Goodwood Revival 55
Gotha G.IV 48-51, 80, 121
Gould Lee, Arthur 95
Grace, Carolyn 107
Grace, Nick 60
Grace, Richard 55, 60, 105, 107-108, 110-111, 124, 126
Graham-White, Claude 9, 116, 119
Gray, Alex J. 80
Great War Display Team 147
Green, Maj Frederick 23
Grey, Charles G. 10, 12
Guynemer, Capt Georges 18

Haig, FM Sir Douglas 31, 49

Handling 27, 29, 107-108, 110-111
   landings 105, 107
   take-offs 105-107
Hanna, Mark 59-60, 124
Hanna, Ray 59-60
Hanna, Sarah 59
Hawker
   Hind 107
   Hurricane 55, 61, 67
   Sygnet 107
Hawker Restorations (ex-AJD Engineering) 61, 122
Henderson, Brig Gen Sir David 10-11, 13, 17, 28, 84, 102
Hendon Air Day, 1921 115-116; 1937 118
   Aerial Derby, Hendon, 1921 115-116
   Varsity Air Race, 1921 115
Henkel pharmaceuticals (Persil) 118
Hervey, Tim 6
Hill, Lt Roderick 29, 35, 111
Hiscocks, Stanley 23
Hispano-Suiza automobile company 16
   45CR Voiturette 16
   XIII car 16
   Type 8A/8B V8 engine 16-18 *et seq.*
      150hp direct-drive 25, 41, 82, 145
      200hp direct-drive 8Ab 82-83
      200hp geared 30, 41, 78, 82, 99
      220hp geared 81, 145
      German report 139-145
Home Defence duties 48-51, 80, 93, 97
Hotel Cecil, London 50-51
Hucks, B.C. 116
Hughes, Howard 59, 124, 146-147
Hunter Jack D. *The Blue Max* book 146-147
Hunter, K. 115

Immelmann, Max 22, 80
Imperial Gift programme 61, 114, 122-123
Imperial War Museum, London 85
Industrial action and unrest 13, 42-43, 46
   alcoholism 44
   drugs 44
   strikes 44
Isle of Sheppey 9

Jackson, Sir Peter 119-121, 147
Johns, W.E. Biggles book series 146
Jones, Jim 105
Jones, 'Taffy' *King of Air Fighters* book 103, 146

Kay, Lt Maurice 38
Kennard, John 25
Kenworthy, John 19, 23, 26, 31, 77, 110, 138
Kiger, Jim 63

Labouchere, Henry 59, 104, 107, 124
Lafayette Escadrille 147
Lal Roy DSO, Indra 'Laddie' 99-101
   grave 100
   victories 100
Lal Roy, Piera and Lolita 99
Lambert DFC, Bill 78, 89, 124
Laventie Military Cemetery 103
Leach, 40
Le Clerget engines 84
Le Rhône engines 17
Letcher, Al 60
Lewis, Lt Cecil 35-36, 50-51, 88, 91, 93-95, 97
Lindberg, Charles 59, 123, 125
Lindsay, Hon Patrick 59, 124
Linen covering 57, 66, 76-78
Lloyd George, PM David 8-9, 33, 146
London Heathrow Airport 118
London Southend Airport 50
LVG 81

Maddocks, Lt Gwynne 115
Mannock VC, Edward 'Mick' 80, 100-104, 109, 146, 149
   criticisms of S.E.5 101-102
   shot down and killed 103
   Wellingborough lodgings 100, 103

Mannock, Patrick 101
Markings 79, 118
Material shortages and delays 42-43, 78
Martinsyde factory, Woking 41-42, 44, 78
Maxim, Hiram 8
Maxwell, Gerald 33, 81
Maybery, Capt Richard 99
McCudden, Amelia Byford 80
McCudden, Bill 80
McCudden VC, James T.B. 'Jimmy' 59, 80-81, 85, 91, 101, 137, 149
   fatal crash 85, 103
   medals 80
   victories 81
McCudden, Sgt-Maj William 80
McDowell, Malcolm 147
McElroy, George 100
Meintjes, 40
Middle East Brigade 40
Miles, Shoreham 147
Millinship, Rob 54-55, 105, 107, 109-110, 124-127
Ministry of Defence 119
Morane monoplane 11
Muspratt, Lt K. 49
Musters, Chatworth 40

Nash Collection 118-119
National Archive, Kew 46
National Defence Association 9
National Museum of Military History, Johannesburg 122-123
National Museum of the US Air Force, Dayton, Ohio 123
Nieuport scouts 27-28, 32, 37-38, 101
   17 29
Nivelle, Gen 31
Norman, Maj G.H. 138-139
Northcliffe, Lord 12, 34, 81, 117

O'Gorman, Mervyn 9-10, 12-13, 20, 23, 26
Old Flying Machine Co., Duxford 59
Old Rhinebeck Aerodrome, New York 55, 106
Old Warden – see Shuttleworth Collection
Omaka Aviation Heritage Centre, New Zealand 55, 62, 120-121, 124-127

Palen, Cole 106
Parachute 138
Pasha, Bob 51
Pattishall, Northamptonshire 6-7
Pemberton Billing, Noel (PB) 11-12, 18, 26
Peppard, George 147
Performance 13, 137
   climb 110
Personal Plane Services (PPS), Booker 59-60, 147
Peugeot 16
Pickthorn MC, Maj C.E.M. 56
Pilot training 88-89
   accidents 88, 90
   Gosport System 88-89
   spinning 88-89
Places of interest 151-153
Poland 114
Pre-flight checks 108-109
Production 40-48, 78
   batches 48
   cost 48
   paid for by donations 79
Production figures
   Hispano Suiza engines 18, 54
   S.E5/S.E.5a 30, 33, 41-42, 45-46, 48, 137
      1,000th S.E.5a 40
   S.E5E (licence-built) 59
Propellers and hubs 30, 41, 137, 139
Provenance 55, 67
Pulpit fighters 17, 19

RAF Museum, Hendon 76, 82, 118-119, 133
Redford, Robert 147
Regent Palace Hotel, London 98
Renault 90hp engine 115

Replacement parts (spares) 130
   present-day 54-55, 65, 124-125, 128
   wartime shortages 51
Ricardo, Harry 131
Richthofen's Flying Circus 91
Rickenbacker, Eddie 121
Ridge, Theodore 20
Robinson, Derek 6, 146, 148-149
   Booker Prize runner-up, 1971 149
   Goshawk Squadron book 146-149
   Hornet's Sting book 149
   Piece of Cake book 149
   War Story book 149
Robinson, Capt William Leefe 32
Rogers, Cpl Tom 80
Rolls, Charles 8
Rolls-Royce
   Eagle engine 19
   Falcon III engine 84
Rotary engines 16-17, 19, 21, 107, 110, 120
Royal Aero Club 9, 115
Royal Aeronautical Society 118
Royal Aircraft Establishment (RAE), Farnborough 56-58, 77, 118, 139
Royal Aircraft Factory, Farnborough 9-13 et seq.
   aircraft designations 10
   B.E.2 10-12, 18, 27, 48, 51, 66
   B.E.12 48, 51, 66
   B.E.9 18
   B.S.1/S.E.2 20-22
   F.E.2b 62, 80
   F.E.8 26, 32
   F.E.10 (abandoned) 19, 25
   R.E.7 28
   R.E.8 28, 36, 66
   S.E. series 1911-15 20-22
   S.E.1 10, 12, 20
   S.E.2a 22
   S.E.3 (cancelled) 22
   S.E.4 22-23, 76
   S.E.4A 22
   S.E.5 and S.E.5a – throughout (see also Eberhart S.E.5E)
      construction 69-73, 132-136
      design changes 46, 78
      designing 23-26, 69
      first active patrol 38, 97
      first deliveries to France 32, 89
      first production accepted by RFC 34
      ground attack role 51
      major experiments at Farnborough 138
      modifications by Ball/56 Squadron 31, 34-36, 38, 40-41, 77, 81
      modifications by McCudden
      night flying 51, 79
      pre-production 71
      prototypes 15, 25-26, 28, 30, 40-41, 69-70, 77
      surviving aircraft 114-127, 151
      tool-room copies 54
      two-seat trainers 61, 89-90, 147
   S.E.5b 137
Royal Air Force (RAF) 11, 46, 48-51, 69, 113-114
   50th anniversary 148
   formation 51
   84 Squadron 56, 59
   85 Squadron 157
   111 Squadron 51
   145 Squadron 51
Royal Australian Air Force 61
Royal Australian Air Force Museum, Point Cook 61, 122
Royal Automobile Club, London 98
Royal Flying Corps (RFC) 10, 13 et seq.
   80th anniversary 104
   Central Flying School 89
   No. 1 Reserve Squadron 88
   S.E.5/S.E.5A Squadrons on the Western Front 92
   S.E.5 Squadrons in otter theatres 92
   1 Squadron 94-96
   3 Squadron 22, 80
   4 Squadron 102
   5 Squadron 21

19 Squadron 29, 37-38
24 Squadron 79
32 Squadron 94
40 Squadron 79, 93, 99, 101
48 Squadron 32
56 Squadron 31-46, 49, 58-59, 77, 79, 81, 84-85, 88, 91, 97, 99, 102, 137
   first victory 38
   flew to France 42
60 Squadron 29, 79, 81
61 Squadron 51, 79
66 Squadron 37
72 Squadron 51
74 Squadron 79, 102-103
85 Squadron 79, 81, 103
143 Squadron 51
Royal Flying Corps Club, London 98, 102
Royal Naval Air Service (RNAS) 12, 32, 50, 116
Royal Navy 10-11, 50
Rumpler C.VIII 80-81
Ruston Proctor 84

Salisbury Plain trials, 1912 10
Samson, Cdr Charles Rumney 11
Sanderson, Leslie 6-7
Santos-Dumont, Alberto 10
Savage, Maj John Clifford 'Mad Jack' 57, 116-119
Scale model S.E.5as 154-155
Schäfer, Karl-Emil 37-38
Science Museum 57-58, 118-119
Selous, Lt Frederick 29
Serial numbers 25, 48, 61, 79
Servicing and maintenance 124, 128
   ground crew 130
   mechanics 130
   points to observe 136
Sharman, Paul 60
Shell 116, 131
   Astra subsidiary 131
Shipping losses 42
Short brothers 9
Shuttleworth Collection, Old Warden 5-6, 28, 53-59, 64, 69, 72, 79, 84, 104-105, 107, 109, 113, 118, 124-126
Sidcot flying suit 97
Skywriting 57, 116-118
Smith, Frederick E. *A Killing For The Hawks* book 146
Smith-Barry, Capt Robert 88
Smuts, Gen Jan 50
Sopwith 19
   5.F1 Dolphin 44-45, 82, 84, 111, 113
   F.1 Camel 13, 19, 31-32, 51, 67, 84-85, 90-91, 95, 111, 120-121, 146
   Pup 32, 37, 51, 80
   Snipe 65, 113
   Triplane 19, 32
Sopwith, Thomas 9
South African Air Force 70
SPAD 17-18, 38, 65, 84, 111
   SA series fighters 17-18
   S.VII 18-19, 25, 29, 32-33, 37, 82
   S.XII 24-25
   S.XIII 81-82
Specifications 13, 78
   dimensions 136
   engine weight 145
Spratt, Norman 22
Stampe SV-4 105, 107-108, 147
Standard Oil 131
Stevenson, Robert Louis *Requiem* 161
Stow Maries Great War Aerodrome 54-55, 65, 97, 131
Strand Palace Hotel, London 98
Supermarine 11
   Seafire Mk III 107
   Spitfire Mk IX 60, 107

Tail section and rudder 25, 76-77, 137-138, 145
   bracing 77, 109, 135
   control wires 135
   elevators 76, 137

fixing the empennage 135
   rounded fin 145
   skid 77
   trim mechanism 76
   twin-boom trial 138
Taylor, Edgar 97
Tolkien, J.R.R. 119-120
Townsend, Philip 114-115
Trenchard, Gen Hugh 'Boom' 13, 18-19, 31-32, 36, 38, 49, 84-85, 101
Turkish Army 51
Turner, Cyril 116-117
TVAL – see Vintage Aviator Ltd
TV series
   Blackadder Goes Forth 147
   Piece of Cake 149
   Wings 149

U-boat campaign (naval blockade) 42-43, 4677
Undercarriage 72-73, 78, 137
   legs 72, 77
   truing up 133
   tyres 72
   wheels 35, 72
United States Army Air Service 46, 59-60, 121
University Air Race, 1921 115-116

Verdon-Roe, Alliot 9
Vickers Crayford factory 43-44, 78
Vickers Weybridge factory, Brooklands 40, 42-43, 47, 78
Vimy Ridge 31, 37
Vintage Aviator Ltd, The (TVAL) 54, 62-67, 79, 87, 105-106, 110, 119, 121, 124-125, 147
   Hood Aerodrome, Masterton, New Zealand 55, 63, 121
Vintech 60
von Holtzendorff, Admiral 42
von Richthofen, Lt Lothar 38
von Richthofen, Baron Manfred (Red Baron) 32, 37-38, 91, 120-121
   Great Dane Moritz 38
   victories 91

Waghorn, H. 115
War Office 10-12, 17, 21-22, 28, 32, 81, 84
Watt, Dudley 115
Wells, H.G. *The War in the Air* book 8
Westland Scout 104
Wheeler, Cdre. Allen H. 57-58, 115, 118-119
Whitehead-Read, Dr 115
Wind tunnels 9, 23
Wing and Wheels Museum, USA 59
Wingnut Wings kits 119, 121
Wings 23-24, 30, 34, 41, 57, 66-67, 77-78, 111, 130, 136
   attaching the main planes 134-135
   failures 30, 35, 43, 78, 111
   loading 24
   lower 23, 72-73, 76, 137
   revised 39
   rigging 23, 76, 130, 132, 135
   truing up centre section 134
   upper 23-24, 72-73, 78, 135, 137
   wingtips 23, 30
Wolff, Kurt 37
Wolseley, Adderley Park factory, Birmingham 17-18, 41, 44, 56
   Adder engine 83
   Viper engines 48, 51, 57-58, 61, 64, 83-85, 109, 116
Woolfe, Virginia *Mrs Dalloway* book 117
Wood for airframes 43
Wood, Second Lt F.M. 89
Wortley, Stuart 94
Wright-Hispano F engines 59, 105

Yeager, General Charles 'Chuck' 59, 123
Yeates, Vernon M. 95-96, 146
   Winged Victory autobiographical novel 95

Zeppelin air ships 8, 11